THE CHAIRMAN

THE CHAIRMAN

THE MAN WHO SAVED AFC BOURNEMOUTH

JEFF MOSTYN

First published in 2025 by
Jeff Mostyn, in partnership with Whitefox Publishing Ltd

www.wearewhitefox.com

Copyright © Jeff Mostyn, 2025

EU GPSR Authorised Representative
LOGOS EUROPE, 9 rue Nicolas Poussin,
17000, LA ROCHELLE, France
E-mail: Contact@logoseurope.eu

ISBN 978-1-916797-94-9
Also available as an eBook
ISBN 978-1-916797-95-6

Jeff Mostyn asserts the moral right to be
identified as the author of this work.

All rights reserved. No part of this publication may
be reproduced, stored in a retrieval system or
transmitted in any form or by any means, electronic,
mechanical, photocopying, recording or
otherwise, without prior written permission of the author.

While every effort has been made to trace the owners of
copyright material reproduced herein, the author would like to
apologise for any omissions and will be pleased to incorporate
missing acknowledgements in any future editions.

All photographs and illustrations in this book
© Jeff Mostyn, © AFC Bournemouth, © Bournemouth Daily
Echo and © Sophie Cook (Bournemouth Daily Echo)

Designed and typeset by Euan Monaghan
Cover design by Arneaux
Project management by Whitefox Publishing

This book is dedicated to my beloved wife Rose, known as Rosie, our children, Darren, Janine, Blake and Alexandra, together with our grandchildren, great granddaughter, and my brother Mike.

Together we have shared triumphs, challenges and unforgettable moments. Your unwavering love and support have been the heartbeat of my journey.

To my late parents, Sadie and Ralph, thank you for making me the person I am today. You taught me to always remain humble.

Finally, my extended family, the devoted supporters of AFC Bournemouth – your passion and loyalty has always meant so much to me.

CONTENTS

Foreword by Neville Koopowitz ix
Foreword by Eddie Howe xi

Introduction by Jeff Mostyn xiii

PART I – MY JOURNEY

Chapter 1: Leaving School at 15 Years Old 3
Chapter 2: Discovering My Talent in Sales 13
Chapter 3: How the Armed Forces Changed My Life 17

PART II – AFC BOURNEMOUTH: ONE OF THE GREATEST FOOTBALL STORIES EVER TOLD

Chapter 4: How I Saved AFC Bournemouth 35
Chapter 5: A Football Dream Come True 45
Chapter 6: The Greatest Escape 62
Chapter 7: Enter Maxim Demin 87
Chapter 8: 'Together, Anything is Possible' 95
Chapter 9: 'I Love These F***ing Boys!' 100
Chapter 10: From Catch of the Day to Match of the Day 111
Chapter 11: Tough Times during the Global Pandemic 140
Chapter 12: The Fairy Tale Comes To An End 146
Chapter 13: Getting Back to the Premier League 159

PART III – GIVING BACK

Chapter 14: Time To Step Aside 173

Chapter 15: My Charity Work in the Community 186

Chapter 16: My Role With the FA and Inspirational Managers 206

Chapter 17: Inspiring the Next Generation of Business
and Football Professionals 217

Chapter 18: The Football Family 251

Chapter 19: My Final Gift To You 276

Acknowledgements 279
Index 283

FOREWORD

NEVILLE KOOPOWITZ, CEO, VITALITY

I am honoured to write the foreword for this book about a remarkable person, Jeff Mostyn, his extraordinary journey and enduring relationship with AFC Bournemouth and Vitality.

Jeff's story is one of resilience, vision and unwavering commitment. His leadership has been instrumental in transforming AFC Bournemouth from the brink of collapse to a respected Premier League club. He has been at the heart of that journey bringing people together, building community and inspiring belief. Alongside this, his partnership with Vitality has exemplified the power of ambition. Both organisations have grown from challenger brands into recognised leaders in their respective fields.

What stands out for me, is Jeff's authenticity and his utmost humility. Whether rallying support during difficult times or celebrating the club's greatest achievements, Jeff has always led with his heart. His presence in the stadium, in the boardroom, and in the community leaves a long-lasting impression on everyone he encounters.

This book is more than a history of footballing milestones. It is a tribute to a man whose passion and perseverance have shaped not only a club but also the lives of those around him. Jeff's story reminds us that success is not just measured in trophies or promotions, but in the strength of relationships, the courage to act, and the legacy we leave behind.

I hope readers find this book as inspiring as I have. It's a powerful tribute to an extraordinary individual and a celebration of leadership, loyalty and the beautiful game.

FOREWORD

**EDDIE HOWE, HEAD COACH AT NEWCASTLE UNITED
AND FORMER MANAGER AT AFC BOURNEMOUTH**

I find it difficult to put into words how much Jeff Mostyn means to me and how much he has done for AFC Bournemouth. The very least I can say is that I will always be grateful for the love and kindness he and his wife Rose have shown towards myself and my family. But we owe him so much more than just that.

Without doubt, his diligence, hard work and love for the football club was put to the test on many occasions, and such was his determination not to let down its loyal supporters that he could not let it die. His commitment and contribution must never be underestimated, nor the huge role he played in enabling AFC Bournemouth to enjoy the success it so readily deserves today.

Our journey together for more than a decade was quite simply an incredible one and I feel immense pride when looking back at what we and everyone at the club achieved together in that time. Jeff inspired the culture that we helped to build and create during that time, and it was that culture which ultimately enabled us to enjoy the success that we did.

The club motto became 'Together, Anything is Possible', and that was something that I know Jeff firmly believed in. For my part, I believe that quote is representative of everything we achieved as a club, and it reflects the values that we all shared together. With Jeff's commitment and leadership, a vision and a dream became possible through hard work and an unrelenting desire to continuously improve, and as a result we were able to achieve many of our objectives.

On matchdays, whatever the result, Jeff would come down to the dressing room after the game with messages of encouragement for players and staff. He could easily have shied away and not done so after a disappointing performance or defeat, but such was his wonderful passion and loyalty for the club, he was there to support us when we needed him, and it was a gesture that meant so much to us all.

Aside from his involvement with AFC Bournemouth, Jeff's expertise and comradeship was also used to good effect in roles he has undertaken with the Football Association (FA). Whether it be as an ambassador or in his unstinting support for its international teams or his work in an ambassadorial capacity on the FA Council, he has made a welcome and positive impact in the association's quest to spread accessibility and love for our national game.

But there is far more to Jeff's life and career than just the football side. So, so much in fact, and while reading this book, I have been fascinated to learn more about the man who I will always know as 'The Chairman'. It quickly became very clear just how much his love, generosity and enthusiasm has been shared with and by so many others during his remarkable journey through life.

It is evident that, from an early age, Jeff has been able to adapt to the most testing tasks, often under very difficult conditions yet always with seemingly indefatigable energy. Time and again we see examples of the thought, care and empathy he exudes and the many occasions when he has put the interests of others above those of himself.

A proud Mancunian (of the blue variety), he has been driven throughout by his desire to be successful at whatever he has turned his hand to. His career provides a perfect example of what can be achieved by hard work and determination and tells the fascinating story of how a former bank employee and door-to-door salesman went on to launch his own very successful company that provided financial advice and services to members of the armed forces.

During this period, Jeff's commitment to his customers and personable nature regularly saw him visiting war widows and soldiers who had experienced trauma, and such was the way he carried out these tasks with respect and humility, he received the honour of two awards: a 'Coin of Excellence' and an 'Armada Dish' for his lifetime of exceptional support to the Adjutant General's Corp.

During my time at AFC Bournemouth, he was also awarded an Honorary Doctorate in Business Administration from Bournemouth University, and through his involvement in charitable work, he continues to make a significant impact in the area today. He is a patron or ambassador to a number of local charities, such as Lewis-Manning Hospice Care, Julia's House and Dorset Cancer Care just to name a few.

With the loving support of his wonderful Rose, long may he continue to provide us all with love and inspiration.

From the bottom of my heart, Jeff, I thank you for everything.

INTRODUCTION

JEFF MOSTYN

'Jeff, here's what will happen. I will need a cheque for £100,000, and you'll stand at the back of the room. I'll conduct the press conference as usual. When I ask if you can pay the £100,000, you'll nod if it's a yes and hand me the cheque. If you shake your head, I'll proceed to liquidate the club after the conference.'

* * *

My heart was thumping, my palms were sweating, and I had absolutely no idea how the day would end at AFC Bournemouth on that fateful Friday 27 February 2009.

I had just emerged from a 10 a.m. meeting with Gerald Krasner, the former Leeds chairman and administrator. We were preparing for a crucial 12 p.m. press conference at Dean Court. The future of AFC Bournemouth as a football club hung in the balance and a decision loomed large.

With this clear but daunting plan, I found myself at the back of the room. Even though my lawyers advised me to jump back into my car and drive straight back to Manchester, without giving a second thought to Bournemouth, there I stood.

During the press conference, when Gerald stated, 'Without Jeff's funding this club would not have gone beyond Sunday, and AFC Bournemouth Football Club will face liquidation and extinction' the weight of responsibility hit me.

On the flight home from our holiday to attend the press conference, my wife Rosie and I had agreed that enough was enough. I had funded the club and administration thus far, and there seemed to be no future for the club without a huge injection of capital from a new investor. It was simply throwing good money after bad and prolonging the inevitable. We both felt I had done everything in my power to save the club and agreed I would not write another cheque.

As the moments ticked by, back in the room and faced with over a hundred years of history about to be erased in a matter of seconds, the conversation I'd had with Rosie evaporated. How could I let the club, its history and the entire community end on my watch as chairman? Once again, my heart was ruling my head. I could not let our incredible supporters, staff, players down, and the entire Bournemouth community.

I weighed all the information swirling in my mind and, in a mere millisecond, evaluated the stakes. Gerald asked the question for the second time: 'Jeff, can I have an answer?' I gave him the now famous nod five minutes before the conference ended. This £100,000 cheque was possibly the most significant cheque I have ever written in my life. It was the second time I had saved the club, having bought it in 2006 after acquiring the Community Golden Share of the club, and thus began the most incredible journey in the club's history.

Gerald responded in the live press conference with: 'Once again, Mr Mostyn has stepped forward and provided enough funds to pay all wages as of yesterday. Together with several other bills, he has been the only person to write a cheque to keep the football club alive.'

Reflecting on those words still gives me goosebumps. That decision was a defining moment in my life. That 'nod decision' saved the club. Instead of the club going into administration and coming to an end, it was the start of a bright new beginning. My aim was to guide AFC Bournemouth towards financial stability and sound business practices, and to inspire collaborations within the Bournemouth community.

In my motivational presentations, I often share how, despite my twenty-year tenure as a qualified financial adviser and my work with the armed forces in financial services, that 'nod decision' was paradoxically the worst financial decision of my career.

Yet, I followed my heart and not my head. The thought of letting a football club slip away from inspiring the Bournemouth community was one regret I couldn't face. This journey taught me that anything is possible with the right people around you, a clear vision and a siege mentality.

The key phrase in the last sentence is 'anything is possible'. Though my 'nod' helped save the club in that critical moment, this book will reveal the many people who have worked tirelessly behind the scenes to bring AFC Bournemouth to where it is today.

Over the years, countless friends, mentors and acquaintances have encouraged me to share my story in a book, so here it is! I must say, crafting this has been a labour of love, designed to create a memorable and inspiring reading experience for you.

In these pages, I've included rich perspectives from cherished colleagues, mentors and dear friends who accompanied me throughout this journey, particularly during my seventeen remarkable years as chairman at AFC Bournemouth. Yet the driving force behind this book is to inspire you.

You'll discover how my upbringing and childhood adversities, like being bullied at school, shaped who I am today. I'll reveal how I discovered a natural talent for selling, which led me into the realm of financial services. This path eventually saw me founding my own financial services company and working with the armed forces for two decades.

I also have the privilege of sharing what I believe is one of the greatest sporting stories ever told in football. It's about the Community's Golden Share investment in AFC Bournemouth, my pivotal 'nod decision', and how the club's astonishing ascent from a minus seventeen-point standing led to securing a place in the Premier League in just seven seasons, under the inspiring leadership of Head Coach Eddie Howe and Assistant Coach Jason Tindall. It was the most incredible journey, despite the challenges of death threats, administration issues, point deductions, and even experiencing a heart attack at the Premier League Conference, and I loved nearly every minute of it.

Beyond recounting my life and the AFC Bournemouth football fairy tale, I hope this book will inspire you to try and achieve the seemingly impossible with hard work and enthusiasm.

Let's embark on this journey together...

PART I
MY JOURNEY

'My love for football started at age five... I knew the training schedules of Manchester City and Manchester United better than the players themselves.'

CHAPTER 1
LEAVING SCHOOL AT 15 YEARS OLD

'Nah then, lad, why aren't you at school?' asked Bobby.

'Uhh... it's teachers' training day today, so no school,' I said sheepishly.

We were outside the YMCA in Castlefield, where United had been training for the day. I was 11 years old, and I'd been waiting all morning for the chance to get an autograph or two from my footballing heroes.

As a 19-year-old youth himself, Bobby could smell a rat. 'Listen, lad, I'll sign your book... but only if you promise me you'll get straight back t' school after,' he winked.

Not a bad deal, I thought. It was Bobby Charlton, after all. And not only did he keep his end of the bargain, but he invited me for a visit to The Cliff, United's training ground, so I could add to my prized collection of autographs.

Who says entrepreneurship is dead?

* * *

My family history is both intriguing and fragmented, my roots extending back to Lithuania. A particularly fascinating aspect of our family narrative is my grandfather's emigration from Lithuania, which we believe took place in around 1895. Persecution drove many people, including my grandfather, to seek refuge abroad. Trained as a hat maker, he continued his trade wherever life led him. Legend holds that he was unexpectedly disembarked in Hull en route to the USA. He eventually settled in Manchester. I love embellishing this tale in public speeches, humorously imagining my grandfather wandering Hull for months in search of the Statue of Liberty, not realising he hadn't reached American soil!

The journey from Lithuania to England, from persecution to opportunity, is a narrative that defines my family and continually shapes my identity and aspirations. Reflecting on these experiences fills me with gratitude for my ancestors' resilience, which afforded me opportunities they could scarcely dream of.

My father was born and raised in North Manchester, as one of nine siblings. At the time, industrial Manchester was a hub of diverse cultures where different communities and traditions co-existed, each with their own challenges. I am certain my family faced many of their own. My family history has been a constant presence in my life, instilling a deep sense of strong family values, respect and traditions. I know these continue to be a fundamental part of our wider family today.

My mother was raised in Bolton, Lancashire. She was a ballet dancer, passing her passion on to my daughter Alex, who attended the esteemed Tring Park School for the Performing Arts and aspired to a stage career. This artistic inclination attests to our familial blend of nature and nurture.

My parents balanced the reality of a working-class lifestyle with family values and ambition, demonstrating an incredible work ethic. My father juggled multiple jobs, working in the raincoat manufacturing business and the markets in Sheffield to support our family. This was the backdrop of my upbringing.

My parents also instilled a philosophy in me to always remain humble, irrespective of how successful you may become. That philosophy has been passed onto our children and has remained front and centre of my working life. I was the third of four children, with two older sisters and a younger brother. Although my sister Stella was considerably older and more distant due to her age and life trajectory, my bond with Rosalyn was strong and nurturing.

A defining event during my childhood was when Rosalyn contracted polio. I suspect this was when I began acting out, possibly to grapple with the changes and pressures surrounding me. Navigating home dynamics with a sibling needing attention made me feel overlooked, and school disarray mirrored my internal struggle. Rosalyn's illness was pivotal, not only for her but for our entire family. Her resilience and strength during her health challenges symbolised the love intrinsic to our family. Despite her illness, our bond only strengthened. In hindsight, her role was nearly as influential as my parents' – her endurance inspired respect and admiration that guided many of my life decisions.

BEING BULLIED SHAPED THE PERSON I AM TODAY

My youth was a turbulent journey, heavily influenced by experiences of being bullied. As a small and easy target, being bullied stripped away my love for school and learning, leading to frequent absences and fuelling my rebellious streak. I remember concocting stories to disguise my truancy, painting pictures of productive school days despite struggling with subjects like English and Maths.

In hindsight, it's clear that this painful period of bullying deeply impacted my upbringing and caused significant anguish for my parents. Firstly, I had to understand and compartmentalise why I was being bullied. It wasn't enough to state that I was bullied at school without delving into what that meant. Back then, it was more physical, while today, bullying tends to be emotional, primarily through social media. I'm uncertain of the exact statistics, but it seems more prevalent emotionally now compared to when I was a child in the fifties.

In trying to compartmentalise the background of my bullying, antisemitism seemed to be the overriding factor. Often, the bullies told me to 'go back to where you came from', not realising this was indeed where I came from, confusing identity with religious origin.

Given my physical appearance, notably my size, I became an easy target. Now, at 80 years old, at five foot six, and ten and a half stone, my physique hasn't altered much. At that time, it humorously seemed that my prayers for height were misheard as five foot six instead of six foot five. I felt so slight that even a wind could knock me over.

There was no point in attempting to educate those who bullied me, as they weren't interested in learning. Thus I removed myself from that toxic environment by not attending school. Consequently, I left school at 15 with no qualifications, jokingly claiming a degree in truancy, something that still gets a laugh when I mention it in jest during speeches.

Humour became my tool, like the great athletes who convert nerves into performance. Interestingly, I still use humour today to manage my adrenaline and will imagine speaking to strangers rather than acquaintances in order to keep calm. This is a strategy instilled in me by my mentor, Noel, who explained that caring naturally induces nerves. It was humour though that helped me to navigate school, that and my true passion – football.

My love for football started at age five and was my singular focus. I knew the training schedules of Manchester United and Manchester City better than the players themselves, and I collected their autographs that I later sold at school to fund watching further games. This entrepreneurial streak taught me more about business than I realised then.

Without such compelling motivation, my school path would probably have led to an average career. Despite having no qualifications, however, I reached remarkable heights, and developed a strong work ethic, as taught to me by my parents. My dad's methodology – hard work as the sole path to success – resonates with me, supporting the principle that effort surpasses innate ability.

In life, it's crucial to surround oneself with positivity. Positive individuals align, whereas negativity gravitates towards itself. By embracing positive influences, one can thrive and achieve beyond apparent limitations.

During my school years, when I faced bullying, many people aligned themselves with that negativity. This insight remains with me, fuelling my disdain for bullying and shaping the person I've become. It is also entwined with my passion for football, a refuge and inspiration throughout my life.

WITH LOVE FROM MANCHESTER

As I write this, I reflect on the electric atmosphere of a Manchester City game against AFC Bournemouth that I attended recently. It was Kevin De Bruyne's last home game for the club, and the energy in the stadium was palpable. Fifty thousand fans, each one staying until the very end, celebrated a player who had become a legend in the Premier League. It was a moment that reminded me of the deep connection I have with this city and its footballing history.

During the game, I met Simon and Rob, an unexpected yet thrilling encounter. Simon Heggie, the head of communications at Manchester City Football Club, and Rob Pollard, head of editorial, approached me in the boardroom, camera in tow. They were eager to discuss a project involving Mike Summerbee, my hero and a football legend. Mike, who shares the Holy Trinity statue outside the stadium with Colin Bell and Francis Lee, is an icon in every sense.

When they asked about my first encounter with Manchester City, I was suddenly transported back to my childhood. My admiration for City began when I was just 10 years old, during the 1955 FA Cup Final against Newcastle at Wembley. Although we lost, Bobby Johnson's goal for Manchester City was a highlight. The following year, we returned to Wembley and triumphed over Birmingham, with Bobby scoring again. These memories were etched in my mind and sharing them brought a sense of nostalgia.

Having watched City through one their golden eras of the late 1960s and early 1970s my admiration for Mike and the holy trinity raised my love of football to a new height. Getting to know my hero took this to an entirely new level. I was introduced to Mike by Malcolm Wagner, a dear friend and George Best's hairdresser, and this introduction led me to a world of glamour and style. Malcolm's father had cut my hair as a child, sitting me on a plank on the barber's chair to raise me up to a sensible level. Years later, Malcolm opened a salon next to the George Best Boutique. George and Mike Summerbee launched Edwardia in Manchester, which I often frequented, emerging each time looking like a dandy, ready to take on the world.

These experiences, intertwined with the vibrant culture of Manchester, shaped my journey. The city's energy was palpable, and being a part of its history was an honour. As I sat with Simon and Rob, recounting these stories, I realised how each connection, each moment, contributed to the tapestry of my life.

The project with Mike Summerbee was more than just a recounting of events; it was a celebration of the friendships and memories that defined us. As Simon and Rob captured my stories, I felt a renewed sense of appreciation for the path I'd travelled. From the bustling streets of Manchester to the hallowed grounds of its football clubs, my journey was a testament to the power of connection and the enduring spirit of a city that never sleeps.

After leaving school, I found myself diving into various trades, from selling electrical goods in Jersey to running a boutique in Manchester. I saw myself as a Jack the Lad, a competent trader, though not quite as flamboyant as Del Boy. Despite yearning for respectability, I lacked a definitive career path or formal qualifications, relying instead on my street-smart skills in selling and communication. Manchester in the 1960s and '70s was a city alive with an incredible energy that was impossible to ignore. The air was electric, and the club scene was the heartbeat of it all. Places like Slack Alice's were the epicentre, drawing in crowds and creating unforgettable nights. It was here that I found myself mingling with legends, rubbing shoulders with icons like George Best. The music scene was just as thrilling, with bands like 10CC (Kevin Godley was a neighbour of mine and Graham Gouldman was a friend of Malcolm's), Herman's Hermits, Wayne Fontana and The Mindbenders and, later, The Stone Roses, setting the rhythm for the city's vibrant pulse. It was in this dynamic atmosphere that I met my beautiful wife, Rosie, in 1977. Our first date was nothing short of spectacular. I invited her to an engagement party hosted by David Davies and Miss Great Britain, Susan Cuff. I wanted to make a great first impression, and as I often say in my motivational speeches, 'you only get one chance at a first impression'. It must have worked, because I am grateful to have Rosie by my side to this day.

These experiences are more than just memories; they are woven into the very fabric of Manchester's vibrant culture. They stand as a testament to the city's enduring energy and the incredible journey I've had within it. The spirit of Manchester in those days was not just about the music or the nightlife; it was about the connections, the passion and the life-changing moments that defined an era and continue to inspire me.

Incredibly, I reconnected with Mike many years later through my friendship with Kevin Reeves (nickname 'Revo'), who joined the football club as the second million-pound player to join City (after Steve Daley), and the fourth player to move at this figure overall. Kevin and I became close, and I drove him to all the home matches, enjoying the camaraderie of the players' lounge. The simplicity of those times, with tea and toast before games, contrasts sharply with today's scientifically optimised pre-match routines. It was actually in the players' lounge after a training session that I once again met Mike, who was making shirts for the players at the time. Revo introduced me and Mike said, 'OMG, we don't need any introduction I've known Jeff for years.' After reminiscing, Mike proceeded to measure me up for half a dozen tailored shirts. I thought I had the gift of the gab, but Mike could certainly teach me a thing or two about closing a sale.

Kevin Bond had originally introduced me to Kevin Reeves. Kevin Bond's family, including his dad, John, the Manchester City Manager, coincidentally lived next door to my best friend in Manchester. It was through Kevin Bond that I became involved with AFC Bournemouth, where he was the manager.

Fast forward many years and our promotion to the Premier League in 2014/15. Another sliding door moment as Mike Summerbee and I were reunited when we made our first trip to the Etihad Stadium. I will never forget 17 October 2015, taking my team as chairman to play Manchester City in my hometown. The entire board of directors made me feel like the messiah, knowing my boyhood allegiance to the club. Despite the 5-1 defeat, the day was memorable in so many ways for me and my entire family who all joined me at the match. From that day forward Mike and his gorgeous wife Tina have been close friends to me and Rosie, continuing the friendship formed almost four decades earlier.

> **Jeff may be an adopted son of Bournemouth**, but his heart has always had room for Manchester City. His deep affection for both clubs is evident to all who know him. Above all, he should be remembered as a distinguished Premier League chairman, respected across the football world.
>
> **MIKE SUMMERBEE OBE #THECHAIRMAN**

IN THEIR OWN WORDS ON JEFF

Mike Summerbee OBE
Former Football Player

It is rare in football to meet someone as thoroughly decent as Jeff Mostyn.

I remember Jeff from as far back as the late 1960s and early 1970s. He was someone who would frequent the shop I owned with George Best called Edwardia. He was always so polite and kind, and he was really interested in what George and I were doing with the shop.

But it was only years later when he became the chairman of AFC Bournemouth that our friendship really flourished.

He really is a top person who I admire and respect greatly. Whenever I see Jeff, he lights up my day. Every single time I see him in a boardroom or bump into him at an event, we share a warm, genuine embrace and some kind words. It isn't often you find this kind of connection with someone in modern football.

I value our friendship so much, and his wife Rosie and my wife Tina are also very close, which is really lovely to see. He is a very special man, one who has always made me feel appreciated and welcome.

He has also made a really sizeable impact on football in this country. Jeff did a wonderful job at AFC Bournemouth. Few people could have had the impact he had at the football club. He did it because of his ideas, vision, passion, wonderful personality and his love of the game. And to achieve all of that while being such a nice person says everything you need to know about him.

To spend seventeen years at AFC Bournemouth and establish them as a regular Premier League side and, by the way, make them one of the best-run clubs in England, is incredibly impressive. I'm not sure he gets the credit he deserves, but I can assure him everyone at Manchester City respects him, both personally and professionally.

The fact he is a lifelong City fan and Manchester lad makes it even better! It's funny because City brought us together, and Jeff's time in AFC Bournemouth, a place that my family hold dear as we have in-laws who live not too from there, has helped deepen our bond.

Jeff may be an adopted son of Bournemouth, but his heart has

> always had room for Manchester City. His deep affection for both clubs is evident to all who know him. Above all, he should be remembered as a distinguished Premier League chairman, respected across the football world.
>
> Football needs characters like Jeff. He is totally humble, down to earth, hardworking and kind.

TAKING RESPONSIBILITY FOR MY CAREER

As much as I loved the entrepreneurial spirit of Manchester, at 31 I realised it was time to take my career more seriously, especially as I was married with two children. One day, I came across an advertisement in the *Manchester Evening News* for the TSB Trust Company, seeking recruits ideally with financial backgrounds. At that time, soaring mortgage rates above 15 per cent were a concern, so I consulted my accountant, John Cottrell, about the opportunity. as I was living hand to mouth and frequently remortgaging to avoid debt, the perks advertised – including a mortgage subsidy and a company car – were appealing, even though I didn't fully understand the role.

Given my lack of qualifications, I asked John about my chances. He suggested using my selling skills to convince them of my ability to help transform the company's fortunes through creativity, objectivity and teamwork. Encouraged by having nothing to lose, I proceeded to the interview.

After multiple interviews, I was hired by the TSB Trust Company. Out of about twenty participants, I was the only one without a financial background. Fortunately, formal qualifications weren't mandatory during that era as they are now. I leveraged my sales experience instead of financial expertise. The turning point came when I met Noel Audley, the sales and marketing director. He became my first mentor and enrolled me in a three-month training course at the company's headquarters in Andover that shaped the next chapter of my life.

The course focused on products aimed at encouraging regular savings, from as little as a pound a day. The government offered incentives to save through life insurance premium relief, which at the time was 17.5 per cent, making it attractive to TSB's clientele.

I transformed my lack of financial education into an advantage by simplifying explanations during client interactions in Chester, prioritising clarity over technical complexities. My approach was 'keep it simple', contrary to typical advisers who delved into intricate details of funds, often to impress clients.

This training period emphasised the value of self-education and adaptability. Embracing a straightforward communication approach enabled me to excel, even without financial qualifications. My success in sales reflected my focus on grasping essential product details, building sufficient confidence in what I sold, and tailoring my style to resonate with the audience.

These lessons solidified my conviction that confidence and adaptability were vital, proving that sometimes unlearning existing paradigms to embrace new methodologies was crucial for growth and success.

In August 1995, Alan Hansen said on Match of the Day of the Manchester United team: 'You can't win anything with kids.' Yet, Manchester United's class of '92 proved otherwise by being unbeaten for years. Their success stemmed from their fearlessness and lack of experience, enabling them to play freely and set their own standards. While experienced players benefit from their background, they lack youthful exuberance and must continue learning.

Over the years, I've noticed that coaches often rely on past habits rather than new techniques, especially in football. I've frequently highlighted Eddie Howe's greatest strength as his relentless pursuit of personal development, earning him player respect. Unlike many coaches who use familiar methods, he continuously learns, setting a different example. Applying this to my life, I realised that my peers at the training course shared old habits, whereas I had none.

This period marked a wake-up call to embrace responsibility. Married at 22, I experienced a significant transition with the birth of my first children, Darren in 1968 and Janine in 1971. This experience taught me the importance of responsibility, mentorship and continuous learning, driving the next chapter of my life.

CHAPTER 2
DISCOVERING MY TALENT IN SALES

That Halloween day of 31 October 1978 starts triumphantly. I have just wrapped up the largest sale the bank has ever recorded. I was eager to add this milestone to my sales record-breaking statistics and headed to Andover to deliver the documentation personally.

Despite the offer to stay for dinner, my determination has me insist on the nearly 500-mile round-trip back. That ill-fated night, as fatigue gnaws at my focus, I swerve to avoid a stray vehicle, resulting in a calamitous accident. My car careers into a garden, and I am left with a knee so mangled it's still held together by wire today.

Lying in the hospital, the police officers visiting my room tell me, 'Jeff, you're the luckiest person we've ever met.' They describe how my car somehow navigated between two metal posts, so narrowly spaced they couldn't retrieve the vehicle without incurring damage. They solemnly add that if I had hit a post, this conversation wouldn't be happening.

The accident, born from sheer exhaustion and relentless driving, was a stark reminder of my father's motto that is etched in my mind: 'The first way to succeed is to work hard, the second is to work hard, and the third is to work hard.' It's a philosophy that has guided me, but that night also taught me the importance of knowing when to rest and recalibrate – the balance between ambition and well-being.

* * *

After completing the three-month training course, I was ready to manage my seven branches. As a TSB Trust Company representative, I was responsible for covering multiple branches in my region, including locations in the Wales and border area, such as Ellesmere Port and Chester.

I'd meet the bank managers of each branch, who would draft letters to three high-net-worth clients. These clients were significant for a savings bank as they had substantial deposits and could benefit from financial advice. My job was to follow up the letter with the client and arrange an appointment at their convenience to meet them personally, often in their own home. This process was repeated on a daily basis.

I quickly realised that my activity was being constrained to a maximum of fifteen interviews per week, as a consequence of this sales system. I was determined to step back and endeavour to redefine the current sales system to enable me to interview potential clients in a free flow situation in the bank branch itself – as opposed a limited number of clients in their own home each week.

With support from my sales managers, Noel Audley and Frank Struggles, I decided to ingratiate myself with the bank staff to gain their support. My unique approach involved visiting the branch daily – something no one else did. I built rapport by making tea for staff, placing stamps on letters and serving as an all-round helper, understanding the future benefits of these relationships. I was now being accepted as part of the team.

After three months of such dedication, I met with Frank and Noel at Château Impney in Droitwich, a beautiful French-style château. I suggested dedicating a full day a week to using the bank manager's office, as it could also positively reflect on the manager's performance. Cashiers could direct clients to meet me, granting me the moral high ground of being seen behind the manager's desk. This strategy soon began generating double-figure sales daily, and I broke numerous records, becoming Salesman of the Year my first year and retaining the title the following year. The chairman promised me a trophy if I won a third time. In those three years, my success seemed endless, even leading to a speech at the Heathrow Hotel before four hundred individuals. On that day, Noel found me overcome with nerves in the bathroom. He reassured me, saying, 'There's only one person out there, not four hundred: that's me. Just focus on me', which I embraced wholeheartedly.

I was driven by my work ethic, striving to instil this mindset in my children and others I had the privilege to work with. With a solid work ethic, anyone can learn the skills needed to succeed in any area, for even prodigies require hard work to triumph.

Reflecting on this life phase, my hard work was yielding success. I felt accomplished in two ways: first, as a winner who outperformed veteran colleagues through sheer dedication and innovation that benefitted everyone, quadrupling incomes and boosting the bank's profits.

Secondly, I discovered previously unknown leadership traits, such as daring to discuss strategy with superiors to revolutionise the bank's methodology.

As if I were standing atop an Olympic podium with the audience in awe, they sought to hear every detail of my success story.

Noel assured me that no nerves or script were necessary as everyone was eager to hear my journey. At that moment, I realised my evolution into a leader and teacher.

TAKING THE LEAP AND STARTING MY OWN BUSINESS

In my fourth year at TSB, I realised I was exhausted, teetering on the brink of burnout. Like a top football team such as Manchester City winning a title, the real challenge lay in retaining it amid relentless competition. With four hundred people pursuing me instead of only nineteen, the pressure was intense, and it nearly cost me my life.

Having just married Rosie in 1981, I approached Frank Struggles and Noel Audley about ascending the management ladder to a more relaxed training role, driven by my interest in inspiring others. They were candid, explaining that advancement was unlikely in a 'dead men's shoes' scenario, where managerial positions were vacated only through retirement or death.

As the bank's top revenue generator, promoting me wasn't financially feasible without straining their budget, considering my earnings were higher than even the chief executive's (CEO's). . Realising my options were limited, my thoughts turned to America, a place I had always admired for its embracing of success. Inspired by Noel's stories from earlier in his career, my aspirations veered towards working in Florida.

Exploring opportunities, I connected with Jeff Moss, who owned Caribbean Connection, which later became ITC Travel. Jeff inquired if I'd considered joining him since I was familiar with Wirral area in my TSB days and my wife Rosie had recently joined his travel team. Jeff proposed offering package holidays to the Caribbean or Florida, securing accommodations for hotels seeking to sell their apartments.

Intrigued, I joined Jeff and spent three years thriving in Florida, excelling in selling property across the region. Through my networks, I facilitated property sales to familiar faces. I even considered permanent relocation to Florida.

On Florida's west coast, I negotiated a monumental sale akin to my achievements at the bank. I was offered a four-bedroom repossessed house on Sarasota's Intracoastal Waterway in place of my commission, but I chose the commission instead. I was drawn back to Chester for family reasons.

I had also asked Noel to join me in Florida on this business venture, nearly securing his involvement until a last-minute change. He had reconnected with John Brown, whom he had mentored at Barclays, sparking a new opportunity with John Brown International, a firm providing financial services to military personnel. John enlisted Noel as sales and marketing director, tasked with creating a team to serve military establishments by offering insurance, particularly Barclays products.

I'd spent three successful years marketing real estate, but I knew my wife Rose's heart was still in the UK. Having received a call from Noel Audley to discuss joining him at his new venture at John Brown International (JBI), I found the prospect of working alongside him once again very appealing. This call proved to be a sliding door moment in my life and my career. Noel's persuasive encouragement led me to accept, marking the start of a transformative chapter within the armed forces sector.

CHAPTER 3
HOW THE ARMED FORCES CHANGED MY LIFE

Here they are lying in a bed, having lost an arm, a leg, and they're at the most vulnerable time of their life. But never once did I hear a single amputee – soldier or officer – complain that they had lost something; the strength they had was with what remained. If they had lost two arms, they had legs to stand on. If they were unfortunate enough to lose their legs, they were holding their hands up, and they reflected on the colleagues that had lost their lives. In the face of huge adversity, they gained strength from the fact that they were alive and with their families.

* * *

So I met John Brown, Tony Richards and Noel at Shillingford Bridge Hotel. After a fruitful discussion, John asked to speak privately, and at that time Tony and Noel left the room. Upon returning, they extended a job offer. Noel was to become the chief executive and they wanted me as the sales and marketing director.

Initially, I hesitated, saying, 'I have my own business.' John eagerly interrupted, saying, 'Jeff, we've been briefed by Noel. We're impressed and want you on board. We will cover your office expenses in Chester, allowing you to continue your business while integrating with ours. It's a trial phase. If it suits you, we hope you transition fully to us.'

From 1983 to spring 1984, I explored this opportunity. On 1 May 1984, I officially joined John, relocating from Chester to Kintbury in Berkshire due to the office being in Kingsclere.

Reflecting on this opportunity, I saw it as remarkably fair. Why should I give up everything I'd developed over three years, especially considering the embryonic state of their business? They were investing in me joining them. Their proposition seemed risk-free, only offering rewards.

Opportunities are rare, like luck or being in the right place at the right time. A bit of good fortune is always needed, like the opposition's ball hitting the post and landing safely rather than leading to a goal.

Gary Player once said, 'The harder I work, the luckier I get', but opportunities and courage significantly define life's course. This opportunity was life-altering, like accepting the TSB job with few qualifications yet full conviction. Training provided basic knowledge, but I seized opportunities wholeheartedly, leading to success.

With each change, I committed fully. I always embraced opportunities as a path to success.

Moving forward with this opportunity felt right. I took on roles including being the face of JBI at Army camps, and managing recruitment, training and motivation of salespeople providing financial advice within the armed forces.

STARTING ABACUS FINANCIAL MANAGEMENT LIMITED

By early 1988, I was thinking about leaving the company. I had the support of the partners, and careful discussions took place about initiating a new business founded on integrity and solid relationships with Commanding Officers. In October 1988 Abacus Financial Management Limited was born. I leveraged my work ethic and my rapport with the military community. Joined by partners with elite education, I became the face of Abacus.

Over two decades, we built a premier independent brokerage, advising Her Majesty's Forces, especially the Army. Operating within military settings presented an intriguing challenge. I viewed these environments using fundamental principles rather than overcomplicating business approaches.

"

Jeff never sells anything. Instead, his success is based entirely upon his engaging personality. If you want to feel good about yourself, go and have a chat with Jeff Mostyn who will always put a smile on your face.

TONY RICHARDS #THECHAIRMAN

"

IN THEIR OWN WORDS ON JEFF

Tony Richards
Business Partner at Abacus

Since being asked by Jeff to write a few words to be included in his book, I have taken the opportunity, perhaps for the first time, to sit down to consider my feelings towards him as a very dear friend and a hugely important work colleague. This is my history with Jeff and does not therefore include the success he has enjoyed within football. I am not therefore really able to comment on the whys and wherefores of his undoubted success other than to say that, at least to me, he has always taken pains to refer to himself as very much the new boy who was pleased to follow behind those he recognised as having greater knowledge and experience. However, if I were to guess as to the reason for his success I would put it down to his quick thinking and empathy with others, talents that I experienced in abundance during our successful business relationship.

Early on Jeff said to me, 'If you can sell, you will always be able to put a crust on the table.' Undoubtedly, Jeff is the consummate salesman and it always gave me huge confidence whenever we were involved together in making a 'pitch'. Interestingly enough, his success as a salesman has not been based upon the 'hard' sell. Instead it was because of his ability to win over others with his warm and endearing personality, something that can only really be appreciated upon the occasion of your first meeting with him. I can think of no better way to illustrate what I mean by his selling technique then to relate what my wife Sandra said to me after visiting our office one day to pick up some papers for me. She told me, 'I overheard Jeff talking to some trainee salesmen. I don't know what he was talking about but I came away convinced that whatever it was, I wanted one!'

Although, as I say, Jeff is the consummate salesman, I think it is also fair to say that that makes him a little susceptible himself to a good sales pitch, even if it comes from somebody as leaden and dour as myself. This brings me to the day when I was first introduced to Jeff at what was in effect an ambush that we had set for him at the

Shillingford Bridge Hotel, overlooking the River Thames outside Wallingford.

Jeff had been recommended to my then boss for the role of sales manager and latterly director of a planned new venture. My boss, and shortly to become Jeff's new boss, was also the consummate salesman. However his success was based upon being rather loud and extremely assertive, somewhat different to Jeff's gentle, easy-going style.

To give some credibility to our recruitment efforts, it was decided that I should give the presentation of what Jeff's future earnings might be if he enjoyed a modicum of success. Jeff and I still laugh and joke about the now famous 'pyramid' which demonstrated that he would shortly be earning an untold level of income. At the time, I think I may well have had some belief in what I was telling him and that scintilla of sincerity clearly won him over. We both acknowledge that his apparent gullibility led us into a long-term friendship and business relationship which proved life changing for both of us. Later, if I ever suggested to him that my salesmanship skills were not up to his standard he would always jokingly say, 'Remember Shillingford Bridge.'

At that time I was working with the armed forces whereas Jeff was working in the civilian market. We would nevertheless pass the time of day together and we got to know each other reasonably well. After a few months, and in passing, I asked Jeff what he would be doing during the coming weekend. He told me that he would be travelling back to his family in Chester, where he still lived, to attend his son's bar mitzvah. I was somewhat taken aback and without thinking blurted out, 'You're not Jewish, are you?' His response was 'Of course I'm f* * *ing Jewish. What did you think I was?' This exchange was of course a long, long time ago and I have to admit that his use of an expletive may well be incorrect if only because, on reflection, Jeff's use of crude language was a rarity except when he was telling one of his wonderfully colourful Jewish jokes.

Apart from the jokes, I think it would be fair to say that Jeff wore his Jewishness lightly. He was of course very proud of his heritage and would always speak very warmly and emotionally about his family and particularly Friday nights with his mum and dad. He took great delight in introducing me to traditional Jewish food, the highlight of which to my mind was chopped herring. Even to this day I can always expect a tub of this wondrous delight as a leaving present when I visit him.

Of course, this cultural culinary education was not entirely one way. For my part, I introduced him to the salty delights of 'fried brown chicken' in French baguettes during our breakfast meetings. I cannot go into any more detail about brown chicken as Jeff and I may well be struck by lightning.

Nothing said about Jeff can ignore the presence beside him of his beautiful wife Rose. If for no other reason, my relationship with Jeff was forever cemented by Rose and I becoming aware that we had attended the same school, albeit some fifteen years apart. I would like to think that I have played an important part in Jeff's life but my presence pales into insignificance when compared to her role in supporting him throughout the most important period of his business life. He would not be the man he is without his best friend and, on the rare occasions when he could become a little intense, Rose would always be there to provide some calming words to put the smile back on his face.

Only very recently has Jeff spoken to me of some of the unhappiness in his childhood caused by antisemitism at school. I think therefore that Jeff would have been absolutely delighted when he started working with the armed forces and found that he deservedly received the most wonderful welcome, and I sense that this has been equally so within the world of football where he has enjoyed so much success.

In saying that Jeff is the consummate salesman, which is of course a compliment, it also does him a disservice. In truth Jeff never sells anything. Instead, his success is based entirely upon his engaging personality. If you want to feel good about yourself, go and have a chat with Jeff Mostyn who will always put a smile on your face.

WORKING WITH THE ARMY

Army camps mirrored bank branches, just with soldiers as clients. My task involved adapting to needs while maintaining service, work ethic and trust – the cornerstones of success.

Winning favour with military leaders required more significant effort than banking. I needed to gain entry by winning hearts and minds, beginning with the Commanding Officer, senior officers and new Sandhurst graduates. It quickly became apparent that the Regimental Sergeant Major, alongside the Commanding Officer and senior officers had crucial influence.

This understanding led to a foundational development strategy resembling a pyramid structure. Upon establishing initial rapport with leadership, I respected the military hierarchy, fostering connections at every level, from Sergeants to Corporals to Privates.

The military's disciplined structure contributes to its organisational prowess, showcasing leadership unparalleled by any business I've encountered. This structured integrity and communication fosters profound insights into serving a complex marketplace with respect and effectiveness.

Reflecting on my experiences, I've understood that effective leaders lead through positive example – a revelation because such leadership wasn't prevalent in my civilian life. While inspirational sales managers like Noel existed, their influence was often limited to specific work areas. In contrast, I observed officers who led effectively through their actions. In that environment, I learned that teamwork surpasses individual achievements and relies heavily on clear communication, a vital aspect of military life.

My role included ensuring soldiers could afford homes and secure savings upon leaving the Army. Soldiers live in a cocoon, provided with clothes, food and shelter. Due to such subsidies, they seldom require mortgages, often resulting in a lack of personal home ownership.

Establishing a facility for savings, potentially through mortgage products, became crucial to offering soldiers financial stability for the future. There is a perception that young soldiers spend more than they earn, so my mission extended beyond offering products to providing future hope and security.

One significant challenge was the lack of financial literacy among some soldiers, which we addressed by introducing military kit insurance. Soldiers and officers must ensure they have personal and military kit cover, including for items signed out on loan. While products existed, they were limited, offering basic military kit insurance for a fixed price.

In 1990 my partners and the product providers designed a bespoke military kit insurance called Abacus multi-choice, offering soldiers and officers options to insure what they needed, making insurance economically viable. Though not compulsory, we emphasised that it was a safeguard against potential losses. By the end of our tenure, two-thirds of British Army soldiers had held one of our policies. We developed presentations showing financial security, appealing to Commanding Officers to reduce Army debt and prevent risk.

Young soldiers in debt posed risks to themselves and their regiments, potentially leading to fatalities. We got permission to begin working with young soldiers entering the Army at 16. Without selling, we aimed to plant seeds of financial responsibility for the future through a presentation titled 'The Cost of Credit'.

This groundbreaking advice explained the pitfalls of debt, emphasising the reliance on credit cards. Presentations asked soldiers if they knew their credit balances; most did not, and the answer was: it's a debt, not credit. Expletives were used humorously to connect with the soldiers, illustrating that they were paying only interest, not capital, on their debts.

Our advice led to consultations for financial management, including comprehensive group kit insurance. We prioritised genuine no-cost guidance over sales pitches, winning endorsements from Commanding Officers. Meetings for singles occurred in barracks, while we met with married personnel at home to discuss insurance, savings and endowments, and provide debt-free advice and reputable service via Abacus.

Three years in, we aligned with the Adjutant General's Corps paymasters, who were responsible for all the financial matters, in the regiment and battalions. This proved to be a strategic part of our working relationship with the Armed Forces. At this time we were also granted approval to present at the AGC Paymasters induction course at Worthy Down. As part of their training, we accompanied them to London, visiting the Bank of England and Lloyd's of London, which left a lasting impression consistent with Abacus's reputation for excellence.

I'll never forget the experience of ringing the Lloyd's of London bell and learning the rich history of insurance started in Docklands coffee houses, where handshakes and 'my word is my bond' sealed deals – the ethos continuing to inspire and guide the insurance world today.

"

Jeff is a great person to bounce ideas off or share a problem with. His advice was always considered and valued.

LT COLONEL JED MCINALLY #THECHAIRMAN

IN THEIR OWN WORDS ON JEFF

Jed McInally
Lt Colonel British Army

I first met Jeff in the late 1980s when he came into the barracks to sell insurance to the soldiers. Not one for salespeople in shiny suits, I was immediately taken by how humble and sincere Jeff was. As I spent more time with Jeff and his team I came to realise just how good they were – they clearly understood their customers and genuinely cared about their wider welfare and financial well-being.

Over the years of knowing Jeff I would marvel at how he could control a room with his radiant personality – something I was fortunate to witness on a few occasions in the boardroom at the Vitality Stadium some years later!

Jeff was someone you always looked forward to seeing, along with his team, who all espoused similar values, not too dissimilar to that of the military, specifically loyalty, respect and integrity. Jeff's contribution to sports and adventure training in the Army was outstanding – be it providing prizes for golf and football competitions or very generous contributions for skiing exercises. On a personal level, Jeff is a great person to bounce ideas off or share a problem with. His advice was always considered and valued.

To this day, despite being 7,000 miles apart, I still enjoy Jeff's company, be it over WhatsApp or whenever I'm back in UK. He and Rosie are the most incredible couple and we're proud to call them friends.

THE IRAQ WAR CHANGED MY LIFE

Working with the armed forces changed my life and business. As we gained momentum, the Iraq War began, and we were among the first called to help. This demand underscored a crucial gap – no insurance coverage existed for many troops on short notice. The soldiers often pleaded for assistance, saying, 'Jeff, we are leaving in ten minutes. Please help protect my family.'

Countless lives were impacted, especially those of spouses who lost loved ones. One poignant memory remains with me to this day – of a family in Paderborn, Germany. I accompanied the families officer to visit a young lady who had just lost her husband in Afghanistan. The connection formed through shared sorrow, as she grieved with her family and two children, was profound. Her husband's thoughtful video of himself reading a bedtime story for their children before deployment, just in case, was incredibly moving, highlighting the emotional weight of our work.

This experience taught me about genuinely impacting lives. The young widow smiled for the first time when I, overwhelmed with emotion, couldn't hold back the tears. Her sister remarked on the smile I had brought to her face, and the experience reinforced for me the importance of managing the financial implications of loss wisely. I reassured them that I was there to protect and guide them, ensuring they wouldn't fall prey to any potential unscrupulous advisers.

I also recall visits to Headley Court and Queen Elizabeth Hospital, where I met multiple amputees. The company had designed critical illness insurance to provide financial support for any injury, including loss of limbs. These brave soldiers motivated me profoundly and the impact of my work, comforting families during hardship, was deeply moving.

Taking responsibility, I provided unapologetic and candid advice to soldiers, urging them to consider the broader implications of not protecting their families financially. Some accused me of hard selling, but I intended to ensure soldiers realised the gravity of the choice between financial security and neglect.

The twenty-five years of success were rewarding, building a business that provided me with experiences and an education I would never have enjoyed outside of a military environment.

Enduring relationships were formed throughout this journey, notably with Brigadier Andrew (Andy) Griffiths OBE. I committed to meeting these officers promptly when required, embodying support from Hong Kong to Cyprus. Collaborating with local advisers, I ensured a comprehensive service, furthering these bonds through regular visits and gratitude-affirming gestures.

My relationship with Andy flourished post-service, especially during my tenure as chairman at AFC Bournemouth – he has been a steadfast supporter. A cherished memory was a dinner arranged at Worthy Down's officers' mess in my honour. I believe I was one of the first civilians honoured in this way, cementing our bond and respect.

I have also enjoyed events such as dining with the Gurkhas in Aldershot, where playful traditions and respectful interactions deepened my understanding of military culture. These experiences laid the foundation for my next chapter – how I helped save AFC Bournemouth, a remarkable football story.

Jeff's selfless commitment is mirrored by his amazing wife and soul mate Rosie, who has 'shared' Jeff for so many years, and it is fair to say that she is the foundation upon which his values are built. Rosie is absolutely the battery that powers this diminutive, five-foot something whirlwind of dynamism and enthusiasm!

BRIGADIER ANDREW GRIFFITHS OBE #THECHAIRMAN

IN THEIR OWN WORDS ON JEFF

Brigadier Andrew Griffiths OBE
British Army

Throughout my career I've been asked on countless occasions for advice and top tips. While that advice has invariably been tailored to the situation, one tenet has endured – always strive to be in the position to say I did, as opposed to I wish I had. I can think of no better living embodiment of this than Jeff.

As a young Army officer, I remember attending a course during which various financial companies visited to explain who they were and what they offered to members of the armed forces. While all were informative, they seemed to be largely transactional and bland – if you pay this, we'll do this, if you pay even more, you get better cover and so on. With one presentation left, cynicism had infected us, and our thoughts shifted to anything other than the next hour and the final speaker that stood between us and our weekend. And then in walked this diminutive, five-foot something absolute whirlwind of dynamism and enthusiasm, someone who really knew their stuff, someone who understood the military, someone who clearly cared more for their clients than the transaction or the money, and somebody that blew us away with their passion for our country's armed forces. It was here that our twenty-plus-year journey together began – a journey that quickly transformed into a deep friendship that has bound our two families together.

As anyone who has met Jeff will testify, it is almost impossible not to instantly warm to him, but for me, there was something else that drew us together, something that drew him to the military and the military, regardless of rank, to him. The realisation of why 'we' were drawn to each took another few years to dawn, and that 'Eureka Moment' came as we met on the eve of one of my deployments to Afghanistan. We were discussing how we as soldiers deploy on such operations, to live and fight as a team, and to potentially make the ultimate sacrifice, and that regardless of who you are or what rank you hold, we are all bound by the Army's Values – six values that we hold dear and seek to live our daily lives by. And there it was… the instant recognition that Jeff, unknowingly, also subscribed to these values in thought and deed and that we were inextricably bound together in our team of teams.

Our first shared value is Courage – doing and saying the right thing, not the easy thing. Jeff exemplifies this value. Be it taking the morally (and financially) courageous act of saving AFC Bournemouth from extinction and giving continued hope and joy to thousands of Cherries fans and the wider Bournemouth community as a whole, lending his support and unwavering backing to a charity or academic institution, or championing women's football long before it enjoyed the stage it does today, he has consistently done what is right regardless of the impact upon him or his family.

Second is Discipline – doing things properly and setting the right example. As a company director, chairman, patron or ambassador, Jeff has consistently set the example that others aspire to emulate. Be it an opposing fan, a fellow chairman or member of the FA, I have seen first-hand the high regard Jeff, is held in throughout the footballing world. Doing things properly, and in the right detail, is especially important to Jeff and when he says 'it's sorted' you know it is – he will never let you down.

The third value is Respect for Others – treat and trust others as you expect to be treated and trusted. In Jeff's case, when I say others, I mean everyone. It does not matter who or what you are, Jeff will have the same amount of time, generosity and warmth for you – a real stand-out trait that comes as naturally to him as breathing does to others. His links with the military remaining as strong as ever, Jeff was my guest several years ago at a Regimental Dinner – an occasion during which we 'Dine Out' officers as they become Veterans and celebrate those that have made an outstanding contribution to Service life. The near two-minute standing ovation from some two hundred officers for his contribution to the military was just another example of the unstinting respect he holds across our fold.

Fourth is Integrity – being honest with yourself and your team. When the going has got tough and the pressure has been on, I've seen people crumble and say what they think people want to hear as opposed to the truth. Jeff has no issues with speaking truth to power, regardless of how unpalatable it may be. In all of his roles and appointments, his integrity has been rock-solid, and it's one of the reasons that he is held in such high regard by the military. It's also a reason why he is in demand to speak at high-profile international events such as a delegation from the UN General Assembly in New York. – when he speaks, everyone listens.

The fifth value is Loyalty – supporting your teammates, looking after and helping them, putting their needs before your own, not letting them down, even when the going gets tough. At the height of concurrent and bloody operations in Iraq and Afghanistan, Jeff made numerous visits to both the Queen Elizabeth Hospital and Headley Court to visit our most seriously injured teammates. He didn't have to, but his loyalty to them, and his desire to ensure that he could meet their needs in any way he could, proved to be truly inspiring and way above that which could have reasonably been expected. Ignoring the emotional toll these visits took on him, such unswerving loyalty to the military underscores just how special Jeff is.

Our final value is Selfless Commitment – mates, team and mission first, me second. In Jeff's case, I think it's often him ninth or tenth, such is his commitment to the military, to AFC Bournemouth, to the wider Bournemouth community, to the FA and to his countless charities. I am acutely conscious though that his selfless commitment is mirrored by his amazing wife and soulmate Rosie, who has 'shared' Jeff for so many years, and it is fair to say that she is the foundation upon which his values are built. Rosie is absolutely the battery that powers this diminutive, five-foot something whirlwind of dynamism and enthusiasm!

It has been my utter honour to have joined Jeff for the odd leg or two on his truly inspiring journey, and I am privileged to call him both a friend and brother. He is an extraordinary servant leader, role model, husband and father, and has given hope, comfort, joy and pride to many across the world, such is his reach. Above all, Jeff can confidently and proudly say 'I did!'

PART II
AFC BOURNEMOUTH: ONE OF THE GREATEST FOOTBALL STORIES EVER TOLD

'How a boy who left school at 15 with no qualifications bought a football club'

CHAPTER 4
HOW I SAVED AFC BOURNEMOUTH

'There's no such thing as a free lunch.'

I'm not sure I'd ever heard that saying before I arrived at AFC Bournemouth for the first time on what some could perceive as that ill-fated day in October 2006 and strode through the doors of Dean Court.

The lunchtime meal that I enjoyed that day with Abdul Jaffer, the chairman of AFC Bournemouth, probably cost me over a million pounds before I realised that my trousers were around my ankles... Never mind a free lunch, it turned out to be the most expensive lunch I ever had!

* * *

My involvement with AFC Bournemouth began when Kevin Bond called me in October 2006. Kevin was at that time manager of the League One club. He invited me to meet Abdul Jaffer, who had recently taken over as chairman but was looking for people to join a consortium to take over the club. There was no pre-planned agenda on my part; it wasn't as if I decided, after twenty-five years in the military, that it was time for a new venture like buying a football club. Financially, the club was looking for new backers though, and Abdul was there basically doing exactly that. He was never a long-term option in the future of the football club.

Little did I know that the meeting would become the most expensive lunch I've ever been to, after I decided to invest in the club! At the time, it was simply another opportunity that I seized with both hands and with excitement.

Historically, although AFC Bournemouth was admitted to the EFL as far back as 1923, it had never ventured beyond the Championship. Even then, it had experienced only three seasons in the old Division Two under the management of Harry Redknapp during the late 1980s. As a result, the club had once again become accustomed to competing in the lower divisions, where it had spent all but three seasons of its tenure in the EFL since being elected in 1923, and continued to strive for a return to the familiar, modest successes of its past.

The history of AFC Bournemouth is marked by an incredible journey that many would never have expected. Periodic difficulties both on and off the pitch had blighted the club throughout its modest history, particularly when the club found itself in the fourth tier, when the primary goal was simply to maintain the existence of the football club and achieving this target was considered a significant accomplishment.

In more recent times, supporters still spoke of the 'Great Escape', a term referring primarily to the team's on-pitch activities during the 1994/95 season. At that time, ownership struggles were apparent, with the dismissal of manager Tony Pulis on the eve of the new campaign, which led to the team being briefly managed by a committee of senior players and coaching staff.

It was no surprise that the season began poorly. Mel Machin was appointed manager during the autumn, but with the team accruing just nine points by Christmas, relegation back to the League's basement division seemed inevitable. However, Machin was gradually turning the side's fortunes around by acquiring loan players and young talents from Premier League clubs, and by the new year, they were beginning to display promotion-winning form. Defying the odds, AFC Bournemouth managed to escape relegation, despite facing the challenge of the League's need to balance numbers, which saw five teams relegated that season. This miraculous turnaround led to the season being referred to as the 'Great Escape', and another landmark moment was created in the club's history. Needless to say, it did not prove to be the last formidable challenge that had to be overcome before AFC Bournemouth could reach the new millennium.

In January 1997, with the club £4.5 million in debt, the receivers had been called into Dean Court, and it seemed the club may have already played its last game. Despite being warned that they were unlikely to be paid, the team had won 1-0 against Bristol City the previous weekend. Supporters were called to attend an emergency meeting at the town's Winter Gardens theatre a couple of days later and the auditorium was packed out. Perhaps the bravest man there was the receiver, Alan Lewis. Over £30,000 was collected in buckets passed around that evening to aid a trust fund set up by supporters to try and save the club. The fund would be independent of the club's existing debts and the Trust, led by solicitor Trevor Watkins, eventually kept the club afloat for the rest of the season. In fact, the Trust did more than just that, lobbying local businesses for further support that enabled the club to satisfy the needs of the receiver and the Inland Revenue before a Company Voluntary Arrangement was finally accepted by other creditors.

Off the hook for the time being, AFC Bournemouth became Europe's first community-run football club when the Football League sanctioned the Trust's takeover in the summer, with Watkins as chairman. Remarkably, less than a year after it had been on the brink of extinction, the club went on to make its first appearance at Wembley Stadium in the Auto Windscreens Shield Final.

In March 2001 Watkins stood down, and with the club effectively forced to say goodbye to its old and dilapidated Dean Court ground for safety reasons, everything from turf to t-shirts was either auctioned off or sold by its Independent Supporters Association. The ground was demolished the following summer, and a ground-sharing agreement was arranged with Dorchester Town until the first League game at the new stadium could take place in November.

The funding for the new stadium once again put considerable strain on the club's finances, and the team was relegated to the fourth tier at the end of the 2001/02 season. It immediately bounced back the following year under manager Sean O'Driscoll despite increasing financial difficulties, which saw the new ground sold to property developers and leased back to the club to raise some immediate capital. This helped to fend off the visits from bailiffs, which had become increasingly regular.

When I accepted the challenge, the club was still in the third tier, known then as League One. Kevin had taken over from Sean and was doing his best, but we weren't brilliant. We were struggling. We would go on runs that saw us win a few games and then go backwards again.

I was first introduced to lifetime Bournemouth supporter and local businessman Steve Sly by Abdul Jaffer in the chairman's sponsored box at the stadium. From the moment I met Steve, I realised the importance of not judging by appearances. A much larger figure than he is now, he was wearing shorts, was covered in tattoos and had a massive gold chain around his neck. Initially, I had reservations, thinking I was getting into business with a character reminiscent of the Kray twins! Yet, I quickly learned in life never to judge a book by its cover or a man by his clothes. Steve epitomised these sayings.

I could not have met a more sincere and committed supporter of the club. Steve was well respected by his fellow supporters, and his presence at the table carried great weight for reasons other than just his size. It was to prove an iconic introduction and marked the beginning of a superb working relationship, between the two of us and a respect and friendship that I cherish to this day.

Abdul explained that previous chairman Trevor Watkins had set up this Community Mutual scheme to enable supporters to create a Fans Club. Together with his fellow trustee, a gentleman named Ken Dando, who had since passed away, the scheme was set up to ensure that 51 per cent of the shares (the Golden Share) were dedicated to the Ken Dando Stadium Appeal fund.

As we discussed this further, I realised that putting in £25,000 merely gave me a token gesture membership with a share of those 2,500 shares. It didn't mean much. As a member I might have got the rights to a ticket for each match; I might even have been first in the queue. If ever there was a situation where we needed 18,000 through the gate and could only get 9,000, being a member might have put me first in line, but it meant nothing substantial. However, the agreement did give the Community Mutual ownership of the club with a 51 per cent voting right, which was significant in its own way.

It struck me that the other members of the scheme should have been the ones on their knees, pleading with Steve and I to buy the club. Instead, we found ourselves, metaphorically, on our knees before those blocking the sale of the club, begging them to sell it. They should have been eager for us to take over.

Without securing this Golden Share, buying the club just didn't make sense. That's why all other previous consortiums had lost interest; they wondered why they should buy a club they wouldn't even be in control of.

One by one, potential investors walked away, despite one or two of them already having paid a £25,000 deposit. And there was no point in asking for a refund as the money had already been spent on running the club.

> **Jeff displayed unwavering determination.** When told he couldn't participate in the EFL Conference, he remained, showing remarkable fortitude and optimism. It's these qualities that have earned him admiration and respect, turning adversity into an opportunity to showcase his resilience and commitment to the club and its community.
>
> **KEVIN BOND #THECHAIRMAN**

IN THEIR OWN WORDS ON JEFF

Kevin Bond
Former AFC Bournemouth Manager

I first met Jeff, and Rose, at a party, through a mutual friend who remains close to this day. Jeff always had a presence at Portsmouth when I was assistant manager there, before his involvement with AFC Bournemouth. If there was ever a chance to get into the boardroom or its equivalent with Jeff, you took it, because those were wonderful times. There was a genuine love for him to be present at those gatherings and Jeff relished such moments, long before Bournemouth became a focal point for him. As soon as I took the job as manager at Bournemouth, I invited him to come along to our first match. True to form, he said yes and attended the game together with Rose.

He sat next to Abdul Jaffer, who was fantastic with me. Abdul, curious about Jeff, struck up a conversation, eager to know about his interests and ventures. Naturally, we all have our egos, and Jeff's involvement piqued Abdul's interest. Surprisingly, on that very first day, Abdul persuaded Jeff to invest in the club.

That act, initially perceived as naive, wasn't foolish at all, as it marked the beginning of Jeff's deeper involvement with the club. There seemed to be no one else stepping up, and as various potential buyers came and went, Jeff remained steadfast, essentially becoming the last man standing.

The club faced administration, which naturally brought criticism and challenges. Jeff worked tirelessly with the administrator to find someone to take over, yet many were unsuitable, leaving him still holding the fort. Despite numerous trials, Jeff ultimately struck a deal that maintained his presence at the club. Thankfully, things eventually turned out positively for him. His reputation grew stronger, and, financially, the outcome wasn't detrimental. However, there were times when the future seemed bleak and disaster loomed over his decisions.

After the club and I had parted ways, Eddie Howe made some wise manoeuvres in the market to keep the club advancing, showing great skill and resilience. Ultimately the club required significant financial input in order to remain competitive, and having the right people at the club was of the utmost importance. Jeff's background in sales, selling everything from vacuum cleaners to insurance, had honed his resilience, and taught him to face rejections and setbacks without faltering. This strength of character was evident throughout his journey with the club.

Even in challenging moments, like attending an end-of-season EFL Conference in Portugal despite the club being in administration, Jeff displayed unwavering determination. When told he couldn't participate in the meetings, he remained, showing remarkable fortitude and optimism. These qualities, the ability to turn adversity into opportunity and his unfailing commitment to the club and its community have earned him enormous admiration and respect.

MY FIRST SIX MONTHS AT AFC BOURNEMOUTH

For the first six months of our involvement at the club, Steve and I were constantly firefighting. It felt like that period added six years to our lives. The football club was on the verge of going out of business. We didn't have the luxury of a plan, so we had to navigate on a daily basis, scrambling to find capital to save the club, and make critical decisions. Although we had not known each other for long, there was a strong trust between Steve and I as we embarked on this journey together, and we just kept going, despite all the let-downs.

Our main job was to try and find the right investor to join us, and to commit to the club, but it felt like trying to climb a mountain. Steve and I were ready to travel anywhere to find someone with the right ethics and a strong desire to move the club forward. Equally important was securing the right level of funding.

Between meeting Abdul and Steve for the first time and finalising the takeover, six months had elapsed, and we were no nearer to finding anyone else to join a consortium. Having made the mistake of buying the football club – which I readily admit was unquestionably the worst mistake of my life – it was imperative to avoid repeating it. That decision had to remain isolated. No rational person, let alone more embarrassingly a qualified financial adviser, should have made such a mistake. But I quickly became emotionally involved with AFC Bournemouth, the history and supporters, and without that I would never have carried on. Would I have invested in a shop with that level of debt? Certainly not.

Our takeover was ultimately ratified by about 93 per cent of those who voted, which was in effect the Community Mutual. They were primarily concerned about the Golden Share that had been held in trust in memory of the late Ken Dando, which was a sensitive issue as he had been a lifelong fan, as were his family. However, it had reached a point where this was now preventing the club from making decisions or opening the door to investors.

During those six months and throughout the administration period, Steve and I focused on finding the right investors. These investors were meant to come in and purchase the club from us, leaving us as part of the board. We had numerous, very amicable meetings with potential investors, often over lunch at hotels. We always aimed to meet away from the club to avoid prying eyes, including press. We held meetings as far apart as Manchester Airport and Kings Park Café opposite the stadium. Despite the promising discussions, the investor could never quite deliver the final cheque or reach the contract stage. We even progressed to solicitors' contract stage at one point, but ultimately that also turned out to be another fantasy.

THE CLUB'S FINANCIAL POSITION

From a financial standpoint, the extent of the club's debt was quite a revelation. We uncovered a total debt of circa £6 million, although about £3 million of this was contentious, taking the form of loan notes from previous directors and other secured loans.

A substantial loan was secured against the stadium land, and our understanding was that Richard Kingham, of Parkcrest Construction, had no intention of calling that in. As a developer he was confident his investment would generate income as a result of building behind the east stand at some future date. From a cash flow perspective, with an average crowd of 5,000 attending each home game, we benefitted from separate and significant sponsorships. Money came in annually from shirt sponsors and ground boards. As we didn't have a commercial department at the time both Steve and I took responsibility for reviewing all our contracts. For example, why were we paying £4,500 for 3,000 programmes a week when we could only sell them for £3,000? Who signed off on such a deal?

Steve stepped in and negotiated for a meeting with senior supporters of the club. He openly questioned the logic behind the existing commercial arrangements. I had already gone out for other quotes, finding a company in Portsmouth that printed match programmes for big Premier League clubs that was eager to do business with us in order to enhance their brand.

We managed to reduce costs by more than 50 per cent. We could then sell programmes containing sponsorship at a profit. This was just one example of many. Steve and I often worked out deals on the back of a cigarette packet, plugging leaks that were affecting the cash flow and turning the club into a viable business. Commercial contracts typically run for a predetermined time and aren't often reviewed. But because we had to identify where money was haemorrhaging, we gained a clear focus on the bad practices we had inherited. Together, we swiftly corrected them using fair market rates.

I have to say, Steve Sly has never received the recognition he deserves for the incredible support he afforded me in helping save AFC Bournemouth at its most vulnerable time. His outstanding business and communication skills rival those of anyone I've met. And we shared a profound passion for the football club. Just as Eddie Howe and Jason Tindall would later excel with the team on the pitch, Steve and I worked wonders off it. If anyone else without Steve's dedication had been involved, keeping the club alive would have been out of the question.

There were many times when supporters questioned why I was involved, wondering why a guy from Manchester would buy a football club he didn't even support. They assumed it must have been to make money. But Steve was known by the 5,000 hardcore fans, and having him on board was crucial in reassuring the fans that our decisions were always taken to benefit the club. While the fans judged me for my motives, they trusted that Steve would do nothing to harm the club. I can't emphasise enough how vital this was.

During this critical and emotional time, contrary to popular belief, we did not take a single pound of income from the club, and paid all our own expenses. Indeed money only flowed in one direction and that was into the club's account in an effort to keep it alive, to reduce the debt, and to ensure staff and players alike received their salaries on time. Without financial support, I knew the club could not survive.

We were constantly let down by people who promised to pay outstanding accounts, or promised investment – it became so commonplace, we were getting immune to it. Having fought so hard to keep the club afloat, giving up was not an option. We just focused on the future and what this club meant to so many people.

I made a commitment to fund the club and I wanted to prove to everyone I am a man of my word. The club wasn't balancing the books on a monthly basis; there was always a shortfall. We needed around £100,000 each month to survive, including the salaries, and we often had to make cuts. It was an absurd amount of money, and the original consortium members had moved on, leaving just the two of us to take over the club's shares and ownership.

Steve and I weren't interested in investing in worthless shares, but we needed them because if we could acquire the Golden Share from the Community Mutual, it would enable us to make the decisions this wonderful football club required to stabilise its future once and for all. The shares were valued at minus £6 million. At this point I was putting in my own money but had no voice in the boardroom. It was sheer lunacy – I was funding the club, paying its staff and players, and I didn't own it.

Given the above I would have had no answer to being accused of financial insanity. Finally, after six months of funding the club and demonstrating a level of integrity above and beyond anything expected from an investor, we faced a vote of confidence at an emergency meeting of the Board of Directors to approve our ownership of the club.

At that meeting we were given a mandate of 93 per cent which gave us outright ownership of the club and possession of the Golden Share. At this point I became chairman and Steve, vice chairman. We were under no illusions, however; this was not the end of our difficulties, it was just the beginning!

CHAPTER 5
A FOOTBALL DREAM COME TRUE

I'm standing in the boardroom beside Steve, both of us brimming with a mix of nerves and excitement. We then make our way down the tunnel together, feeling a bit like gladiators ready to enter an arena.

The chief executive approaches us with a microphone, ready to let the new owners say a few words. Before I can utter anything, Steve, ever the gentleman, turns and says something that stays with me forever. With a cheeky grin, he turns off the microphone, places his arm around my shoulder, and whispers, 'The last time I was on this pitch, I was chased off by the old bill!'

* * *

Dreams really can come true, and I swear our first official game as co-owners of AFC Bournemouth against Millwall on 17 March 2007, still feels like a vivid dream.

For Steve, walking onto that pitch held a special significance. He was a local boy from a council house just a couple of miles down the road. Though he joked about feeling like a fish out of water, there was comfort in knowing we had achieved this incredible feat together. It was more than a dream, it was history in the making.

The day was capped off perfectly when the team clinched a 1-0 victory, a promising start to this new chapter. We celebrated in the boardroom afterwards, surrounded by Rosie and our families, toasting to the team's success and the journey we had embarked on. The day felt monumental, a testament to dreams realised and a future filled with promise.

Despite all the hard work Steve and I had put in and the miles we had travelled up and down the country seeking support in the face of adversity, no one had believed it was possible to save the football club, because of its structure and the challenge of acquiring the Golden Share.

However, Steve and I had shown that it was, and getting the Golden Share was just as critical as my iconic nod to save the club would prove to be two years later. It was significant because it meant two things: one, it gave us the authority to make decisions that would bring investment and capital to the club, and secondly, it meant that we could speak to investors with a voice of some value as they considered putting money into the club.

Reflecting on that day, it is a cherished memory, an escape from reality. We didn't dwell on the enormity of the task ahead, although we were aware from six months of funding the club of the challenges that lay in store. While ownership brought additional legal and moral responsibilities, that day was about embracing the moment. I never imagined, as a young boy collecting autographs in Manchester, that I would own a football club, let alone beside someone as remarkable as Steve.

"

Together with Jeff, navigating death threats and managing financial pressures to keep the club afloat, as well as attracting new investors with his charismatic charm, was crucial. Without his involvement, the club wouldn't be what it is today.

STEVE SLY #THECHAIRMAN

"

IN THEIR OWN WORDS ON JEFF

Steve Sly
Former Vice-Chairman at AFC Bournemouth

The first day I met Jeff Mostyn, I was in my box at AFC Bournemouth, and in comes this little fella to be introduced to me by Abdul Jaffer. And the memory will remain vivid for me till the day I die: I shook hands with Jeff, he checked to see if I'd stolen his ring! With a great big smile on his face, Jeff made an opening remark in front of my guests, 'From that handshake I still got my ring!' and then off he went. We didn't have any business dealings then; it was just a social hello. This was the start of an exciting journey together at AFC Bournemouth.

I'm still not sure how we navigated that first meeting without any incident, but Jeff has a certain charm that helps him glide through any moment unscathed. Fast forward to walking out on the pitch to face Millwall FC, as a co-owner of the club with Jeff, received the club's Gold Community Share. It was surreal. Imagine this: a boy from a council house just two miles away, making a business success and then standing on the pitch next to Dapper Dan, looking like someone who just walked out of Savile Row, while I felt like a complete fish out of water in every way. Yet, standing alongside Jeff, I was comfortable knowing we had made it work. The rest, as they say, is history. We did make it work.

Was it a fluke? No, had fought with all our energy to keep the club alive. It was a journey we embarked on together; we became inseparable and created a long-lasting friendship and memories. There I was, standing on the pitch as a co-owner of a football club. I have never felt so proud – as a Bournemouth fan and businessman. I still recall that day's one-nil victory against Millwall: good vibes in the boardroom, a broad moment for me.

As we went on to navigate death threats, financial pressures to keep the club afloat, as well as attracting new investors, Jeff's charismatic charm was crucial. Without his involvement, the club wouldn't be what it is today.

EDDIE HOWE ENDS HIS PLAYING CAREER

Alongside our traumatic six months off the pitch, Kevin Bond's team encountered plenty of difficulties on it during the 2006/07 season. Kevin had had to wait until his eighth game in charge before getting his first win as manager and, given the financial situation, he could do little more than bring in a series of loan players as he tried to find consistent levels of performance.

To his credit, safety was secured on the pitch, at least in the penultimate game of the season. The team had taken time to adjust to the more physical and direct style of play that Kevin favoured, but as the season progressed he became more comfortable in his new surroundings and was rewarded with an extension to his contract in the summer. At the same time, Eddie Howe was forced to end his playing career prematurely as a result of injury and joined Kevin's backroom team as reserve team coach, alongside assistant manager Rob Newman.

Together, they set about making further changes to the playing squad, and after a hectic close season, the first game of the following season saw seven players make their Bournemouth debuts. Just one victory in our first eight games left the team struggling near the bottom of the table. Our first home win did not materialise until mid-December and, to be honest, at that stage we looked like we were going to go down.

Off the pitch Steve and I continued to seek new investors in a desperate attempt to keep the club afloat, but any joy surrounding our 1-0 success against Gillingham on 15 December was tempered by the increasingly difficult financial issues that were arising. I would like to think that we kept things relatively balanced, but the challenges were relentless. You would arrive at the club in the morning, park your car, and find the bailiffs trying to seize assets from the club shop. Situations like that were all too common.

What we did achieve was to maintain the loyalty of the few staff that we had. There was Laurence Jones, our chief executive, Elizabeth Finney as general manager, and our accounts were handled by Mark Luther. Looking after the regulatory matters were long-serving club secretary Keith MacAlister and football administrator Neil Vacher. At the time, we had no commercial team. Steve Sly essentially took on that role until Rob Mitchell joined us later from Southampton.

The team's support throughout was absolutely pivotal. There were occasions when I had to admit to them that wages wouldn't be paid on payday but would be covered after a matchday, highlighting just how tightly we were managing the finances. Sometimes, the Professional Footballers' Association

(PFA) had to step in and make contributions, which we topped up, and were expected to repay later. People often assumed the PFA's contributions came with high interest, and I can confirm that their assumptions were absolutely correct.

Match tickets were effectively our currency to manage cost, and we worked hard to reduce spending, for example by using minibuses rather than coaches whenever possible. As I mentioned previously, we inherited poor commercial deals that we tried to renegotiate one by one, conscious of the pressure to generate more income. If we needed £100,0000 and could only bring in £50,000, we had to find ways to make up the difference. By the end of the year though, I had become desperate. It was crucial to maximise revenue to alleviate stress and reduce the need for personal financial input.

Wins against Luton, Port Vale and Nottingham Forest in the new year lifted the team to within one point of safety, but by February the club had almost gone out of business. We had debts of around £6 million, but instead of walking away, Steve and I believed that if the club went into administration, this would potentially allow us to find a buyer who could help take the club forward.

BOURNEMOUTH GOES INTO ADMINISTRATION

If AFC Bournemouth had gone into liquidation, it might have been reborn under a different name. However, the challenge would have been to find a place to play. The football constitution prohibits a team from playing outside its local area. The situation with Wimbledon becoming Milton Keynes Dons was a rare exception, where they were granted a Golden Share. Each club in the EFL and Premier League possesses a Golden Share, awarded under specific legal agreements. If a club enters administration, it loses this share, which then reverts to the Football League. When we went into administration, we lost our Golden Share and the EFL could then dictate the terms for any takeover and also insist that all club directors met with the conditions of the recently introduced fit and proper persons test. This new rule required a certain offer to be made to creditors and prevented the same directors from restarting the club under a different name the next day.

From a business perspective, the situation didn't make logical sense, but my heart was involved. If this were a traditional business, you would shut it down and start a new one elsewhere. But the football business is different. Without a Golden Share or regulator, entering administration could have been seen as an opportunity, closing the shop for a few years and writing off a £2-million loss as experience. Then, you might go and buy another business, or not. But with a football club, you can't do that. You have 400,000 people in the community relying on you. Emotion is the driving force in football; it dictates your decisions. It's not about logic or business acumen, it's about heart overruling the head, leading to decisions you'd never consider in any other business context.

Working in football and running a football club involves managing emotions day in and day out. For instance, when I sat in the boardroom making decisions, a fog would often cloud my mind and affect my judgment. There were 5,000 hardcore supporters in our area, and we were financially tethered to a point where we wanted to maintain and control our finances to avoid massive losses, especially for me. It was somewhat like gambling, chasing another hand in blackjack or betting on a roulette spin, hoping to get it right. We dreamt of drawing Manchester United away in the FA Cup to bring in half a million pounds of revenue, which would have made a significant difference to little old Bournemouth at the time. Unfortunately, we never had that luck.

By entering into administration, the club suffered a ten-point deduction, and that put us in serious danger of being relegated at the end of the season. We were not alone in suffering this fate, however, as Luton Town had also recently entered administration and had suffered the same penalty. Ironically, the Hatters were our next opponents in what was dubbed the 'Administration Derby'. Typically, the team responded positively with two goals from Jo Kuffour and one each from Sam Vokes and Max Gradel helping us to a 4-1 win at Kenilworth Road.

I continued to finance the club during the period of administration, although Kevin could not strengthen the side in any way as we had been placed under a transfer embargo by the EFL. This was put to the test, however, in March, when both of our goalkeepers, Neil Moss and Gareth Stewart, sustained injuries and we were eventually given special dispensation to bring in another keeper, Millwall's David Forde, on a short-term emergency loan.

The financial pressure continued to intensify, and things were close to reaching breaking point. The administrator, Gerald Krasner, was all set to close down the club unless further financial guarantees came forward. Desperate for some time to gather my thoughts on what would be my next step, I spent a few days away with Rose.

Upon our return, I was in the boardroom with Steve and there were about five minutes to go before a press conference at which we knew Krasner was prepared to liquidate the club live on television. Never mind the pressure to score a winning goal, this was about the club's survival. Serious pressure. On the way home from holiday with Rose, I had promised her, 'I'm not putting any more money into this football club.' But now I was in the boardroom and I was in an emotional state.

Tears were dripping down onto my suit. I said to Steve, 'Mate, I can't let it go!'

'I've now accepted it, Jeff,' replied Steve. 'You've got to. We're going to have to, mate, we've done our bit. We can hold our heads up high.' We walked out though the boardroom door and up into the top floor restaurant to attend the conference.

We stood at the back of the room and Krasner looked up. He's ready to go live now on the radio. In about one minute's time he is going to go on to the news channel. All the press corps and the other usual suspects are looking around, cameras everywhere. At this point I look at Krasner and nod my head to agree to save the club. In doing so, I was giving him another £100,000 but it meant that the football club had another stay of execution.

I cannot adequately put those five minutes into words. It was a roller coaster, an emotional roller coaster, and particularly so for me. Once again, I had gone completely against any sensible business acumen, completely against my wife's wishes and what she believed was going to happen, but I couldn't let it go. I was so determined not to be beaten.

I was acutely aware that over 100 years of club history could be ended on our watch, not to mention the hopes and dreams of a local conurbation that, at the time, had a population of a quarter of a million. The effect that would have on so many people in the town, not to mention the loyal staff and players. The loss of the club would have had a massive impact in the community, because a football club is the centre of influence in any town or city. It doesn't matter whether it's Real Madrid or AFC Bournemouth, or Eastleigh down the road. And at that moment, I just could not allow the club to be liquidated live on air.

I was touched when Gerald Krasner said on air, 'Without the funding, this club would not have gone beyond Sunday in my opinion, and next week you could have seen the liquidation and extinction of Bournemouth Football Club.'

What he added afterwards was less reassuring, however. 'You know, you're not just writing a cheque for £100,000 though, Jeff. That's today. I'm going to need another one next month!'

The off-field uncertainty continued throughout the remainder of the season, with only one bid for the club being accepted in principle, but ultimately proving unsuccessful. However, on the pitch, we achieved an incredible run of six straight wins, which meant we travelled to Carlisle on the final day of the campaign, still with hope of staying up. We needed to win and for our nearest rivals, Cheltenham or Crewe, to lose. Unfortunately, our wonderful efforts to try and recover from the ten-point deduction ended in heartbreak.

I was forced to miss this match because it was my daughter Janine's wedding day. Sixteen hundred supporters saw Carlisle lead at Brunton Park until Brett Pitman's goal levelled things. As you can imagine, my emotions were once again a mess as I desperately tried to support Janine on her big day as a father should, while also trying to keep up with events in Cumbria.

Elsewhere, although Crewe lost, Cheltenham caused an upset by beating promotion-chasing Doncaster (ironically managed by our former manager Sean O'Driscoll) to save themselves. All our hard work came to nothing. Without the ten-point deduction, we would have finished comfortably in mid-table, but if supporters thought things couldn't get any worse, I'm afraid there would be more trauma to follow in the months ahead.

> **To save the club**, it was vital to have legitimate prospects and a diligent process to ensure the investor's commitment. We received over 1,000 requests, but at the end of the day, Jeff was the one paying the bills.
>
> **DAVID HINCHCLIFFE #THECHAIRMAN**

IN THEIR OWN WORDS ON JEFF

David Hinchliffe
Football Administration Lawyer

Jeff's passion is unparalleled. He has devoted his time and resources to AFC Bournemouth, always working in the club's best interests. To this day, people in the world of football hold him in high regard not just for his contributions to the club, but for his character and personality.

Without a doubt, Rosie's role was crucial in supporting Jeff during the emotionally taxing administration period – something very few will experience or understand. Rosie was an integral support system, especially when it came to covering the administration costs and finding a legitimate investor for the club. Together, Rosie and Jeff made the boardroom a warm and welcoming place during matches.

I had the opportunity to work closely with Gerald Krasner, who served as the administrator when AFC Bournemouth went into administration. People often do not realise the points deduction process and the costs involved. Jeff paid £500,000 in club costs and administration fees over a six-month period while managing to find an investor. This was during a time when AFC Bournemouth was in League One, and buying a football club in the mid-2000s wasn't sexy. In fact, a global financial crash, which had been looming upon the horizon for some time, would eventually bring such things to a head only a few months later and continue into 2008. Unlike today, there were no international investors – local business professionals with a love for football were the ones investing in clubs.

When Jeff chose to go into administration, it was a matter of buying time to find another investor. The football business differs significantly from most other businesses. If a regular business fails, you shut it down and start another. In football, however, going into administration means facing two choices: either stop paying the large overhead costs and close down the club, forcing the team to reapply and start from the bottom of the league system, or enter administration and pay an additional fee to bring in another investor. From a financial standpoint, Jeff was covering the bills with no guarantee of getting his money back, all to keep the club alive. From a fan perspective, football is deeply meaningful and brings communities together.

Jeff, Gerald and I had a crucial meeting where Jeff faced the tough decision of saving the club. Gerald suggested that at the next AFC Bournemouth press conference, he would publicly ask Jeff if he would continue funding the club – Jeff's nod or lack of response would determine the club's fate. It was a highly emotional meeting, and Jeff's nod saved the club, despite the financial burden. This decision aligned with the CVA agreement, with a seventeen-point deduction and approval from the Football League. Six months later, investors came in, ending the administration period.

To save the club, it was vital to have legitimate prospects and a diligent process to ensure the investor's commitment. We received over 1,000 requests, but at the end of the day, Jeff was the one paying the bills. While many potential investors had bank cheques that bounced, Jeff's cheques never did.

I continue to admire Jeff's courage and cherish the long-lasting friendship forged during the administration period. Reflecting now, I am inspired by Jeff's refusal to quit under immense pressure.

As a result, Jeff was a fantastic chairman who saved the club, secured the Golden Share with Steve Sly, and ultimately brought back Eddie Howe and Jason Tindall, which welcomed new investor Maxim Demin. This combination led to success both on and off the pitch. Jeff's style of communication with the boardroom, players and coaching staff was inspirational, always characterised by his humility.

> A glance from Krasner to Mostyn was going to determine **the outcome of this press conference and the future of the club**.
>
> Jeff leaned at the bar. This wasn't a Del-Boy moment; the hatch was down, and this certainly wasn't a moment for comedy gold. The press settled and Krasner looked up.
>
> I had fixed my eyes on Jeff for some movement. I stood at the back of the press pack, he waited, I waited, and every second seemed like an eternity. A silence swept across the room and then it came. Jeff nodded.

MARK MCADAM #THECHAIRMAN

IN THEIR OWN WORDS ON JEFF

Mark McAdam
Sports Reporter, Sky Sports

I'll never forget the first time I met Jeff. Well, actually I heard him before I saw him, but I remember it well. Who wouldn't! There was a noise, an energy, a personality in the room adjacent to mine and I had to find out who it was.

As I walked into the office, there stood, all five foot and a quarter inch of him, a man that could have been my grandad, my dad, my boss, my best friend, my long-lost uncle and anything in between. He was a stranger, but it didn't feel like that. A warm friendly handshake greeted me. Months later it became a hug and a kiss such is the affection he shows me now.

In football you don't find many people like this, not in this macho heterosexual world that generates billions of pounds, but Jeff didn't care about that, he was just his honest authentic self from the very first moment I met him.

Jeff was introduced to me as the new chairman. I didn't know whether to get down on one knee or kiss his rings, but he commanded respect and always made you feel special. I could fill a library with stories about Jeff and his times as custodian of my club. Yet there are two that stand out most when I think about his place in the upper echelons of AFC Bournemouth history and my dealings with him.

Jeff had been at the helm for eighteen months or so. Despite his best efforts, he made the difficult but right choice to bring the administrators in.

The only issue was someone had to agree to fund the club while the administrator, Gerald Krasner, would re-shape the business and find a new owner. At this time things still looked bleak. The club didn't have an asset to its name, no stadium, no training ground, nothing worth anything. Just a badge, a team and some history. As time wore on, it became obvious things weren't looking good.

I spoke to the administrator one afternoon, and he said he was calling a press conference to tell everyone he was liquidating the club.

The process to find a new owner was coming to an end and there was no one in town willing to take the club on. Jeff had paid for the process, but it couldn't go on indefinitely.

The date was set, and the press were alerted. I was half working for the club and freelancing in the local media at this point. The club had made me redundant (for the second time) so I had a foot in both camps.

While the waiting press were in the top floor restaurant, we had a conversation ahead of the press conference. Krasner made it clear he was winding the club up unless Jeff continued to fund it, which Jeff seemed torn about doing. Imagine being asked to fund something, knowing you were just delaying the inevitable? Black holes for money exist a lot in football.

Krasner blurted in his thick northern accent, 'I can't wait any longer, I'll have to go upstairs. The media are waiting, and time is money.'

He added, 'Jeff, when I sit down to speak to the media, I'll look at you. We need money to carry on. You nod to say you'll fund the club moving forward or shake your head and it's over. And I'll tell everyone the club is being wound up immediately.'

I walked up to the restaurant, knowing we could be minutes away from the end of AFC Bournemouth as we knew it.

We walked into the room and Krasner sat down. The clicking of the photographers' cameras seemed louder than normal, there were more journalists than I had ever seen. But I knew something they didn't; a glance from Krasner to Mostyn was going to determine the outcome of this press conference and the future of the club.

Jeff leaned at the bar. This wasn't a Del-Boy moment; the hatch was down, and this certainly wasn't a moment for comedy gold. The press settled and Krasner looked up.

I had fixed my eyes on Jeff for some movement. I stood at the back of the press pack, he waited, I waited, and every second seemed like an eternity. A silence swept across the room and then it came. Jeff nodded. And Krasner got on with the press conference.

In that moment, Jeff had kept the club alive. He paid for the ongoing search to find a new owner and continued to lose yet more money in what became the most expensive meal he ever had. But I'm sure he'll tell you all about that at some stage in the book!

The press conference continued, and Krasner explained this was the last chance saloon. The end was near, and they needed investment quickly. Luckily the end never came, just the end of a chapter in the most glorious football story to ever be told.

My second memory is a mistake that still haunts me to this day. It was a cold winter's day and Jeff rushed into my office in a state of bother.

'I've not done my programme notes and I'm being scolded and pressurised to get them done. Can you help?'

'Of course, Jeff,' came my reply. 'You dictate, I'll type.'

We set off on our mission to produce the best programme notes the world had ever seen. There we were, working on an antiquated computer, slower than time eternal but pumping out word after word, like Lennon and McCartney in their prime. Well, that's what we thought we were; the reality was probably more like the Two Ronnies.

Anyway, the notes were finalised, a quick proofread and we hit send. Phew. We made it.

It was only on the matchday, forty-eight hours later, I realised we had dropped the ball.

Jeff had told the world 'It's so important that our expenditure exceeds our income.'

It clearly should have read 'It's so important our expenditure DOESN'T exceed our income.'

A sentence missing a very crucial word.

How could the chairman, the boss, the owner, the man everyone trusted to steer the ship in the right direction get something so basic so wrong. And there it was in black and white. I still shudder at the thought of it. Terrible mistake, yes, but it still makes me laugh now. It's funny how the small things stay with you.

It's also ironic given I'm now a paid journalist. I'm supposed to be good with words! But in all honesty my writing skills have always left a lot to be desired, much like my maths. I'll happily take 50 per cent of the blame, though Jeff can have the burden of the other 60 per cent.

Yet even after that moment of fine failure on my part, Jeff has asked me to contribute to his book! He must have forgotten about that story and my inability to write...

In all seriousness, it's difficult to sum up my affection, respect and appreciation for this man. But one thing I do know: he's kissed my cheek more than any other man on this planet. So, for that he'll forever be important to me.

He may not be the Chairman anymore, but he'll always be my chairman.

CHAPTER 6
THE GREATEST ESCAPE

We are at Dagenham and Redbridge in 2009 on a cold night, the kind of chill that goes straight to the bone. I find myself nestled among our supporters, trying my best to stay warm and enjoy the match from the stands rather than the confines of the boardroom.

AFC Bournemouth is in dire straits, scraping together a team amid injuries and setbacks. Fast forward to about twenty minutes before the end of this tense League Two game, and the scoreline is frozen at 0-0. Every second feels like an eternity as we cling to hope, desperate for those three points to help us hold onto our place in the Football League. Enter our assistant manager, Jason Tindall, a true legend in his own right, subbed onto the field.

In a twist that could only happen in the most improbable of football fairy tales, Jason conjures up a kick – a toe punt that seems destined for nowhere. But then, aided by the wind, the ball soars downfield. Remarkably, it finds its way to Mark Molesley, who, seizing the moment, scores an exceptional individual goal.

Of course, Jason isn't about to let the opportunity slip by without staking his claim to manager Eddie Howe, cheekily dubbing it an 'assist', as if the whole play has been orchestrated with pinpoint precision.

* * *

When the stories of AFC Bournemouth are told, this is the kind of tale that epitomises the magic and unpredictability of football – the night when the assistant manager became a surprise hero from the bench, solidifying his place in our club's folklore.

Ahead of the 2008/09 season, our future in the Football League was put into doubt when the Football League threatened to block our participation in League Two due to ongoing problems with our administration and ownership changes. They ordered us, along with Luton Town and Rotherham United, to demonstrate that we could fulfil all our fixtures and find a way out of administration. Two days before the season was due to commence, all three clubs were allowed to compete but only if each one accepted their respective sanctions without protest.

We and Rotherham each received a seventeen-point penalty for failing to adhere to the Football League insolvency rules. We were also required to pay unsecured creditors the amount offered at the time of the original CVA (around ten pence in the pound) within two years. At the same time, Luton Town were handed a further twenty-point penalty on top of the ten points that had been carried over from the previous season.

Our exciting young striker Sam Vokes had been sold to Wolves for £300,000, and honestly, that sale gave us a stay of execution for three months. It got us through those summer months, which were critical, because without games on the weekend, there was no income. We needed to pay the full-time staff and players to get us through that period. It felt like a fire sale, since he was worth a lot more, but most of the money went straight to the administrator.

Gerald Krasner was instrumental during this time, supporting us in our efforts to bring in investment when it was most needed. To clarify, when a club goes into administration, it is essentially being put on the map to attract investment at a lower cost, purely to keep it alive. This situation attracted all sorts of investors, including some shady individuals, which heaped more pressure on Steve and myself. I don't like bringing this up, but it even led to some death threats. One moment I was the man who saved the club, and the next moment, I was receiving threats to myself and my family, all while scrambling to pay club costs and administration fees. I'm giving you a taste here of what my situation was like at that time.

From a player development standpoint, I made a conscious decision – one that Steve Cuss, our Head of Community, still compliments me on. If we had considered purely financial logic, we would have shut down the Academy and the Community Sports Trust, which cost the club half a million pounds a year. But we decided that a community sports trust was essential to maintain our commitment to grassroots football for the first team and to develop assets to sell to other clubs. This decision highlighted the commitment Steve and I had. However, none of the players at that time had made any significant money for us.

From day one, **Jeff wanted a family community club**. This is an easy thing to say but a big challenge and takes time as partnerships and plans are developed. Jeff's outstanding attribute is his time for everyone.

STEVE CUSS #THECHAIRMAN

IN THEIR OWN WORDS ON JEFF

Steve Cuss
Head of Community at AFC Bournemouth

It is a pleasure and honour to be able to write this perspective for 'Mr AFC Bournemouth' Jeff Mostyn

My introduction to Jeff came shortly after his takeover of AFC Bournemouth, where as Head of Community I was asked to present to Jeff and the new board the work of AFC Bournemouth Community Sports Trust. As I often do, I spoke passionately about the impact of football community work and how this benefits the club and engages the local community. To my absolute delight, Jeff was instantly engaged and as passionate as myself, intrigued and keen to see the work in action. From that day forward a great bond was formed and the community had their biggest advocate with Jeff always promoting the community alongside the club when talking, presenting or being interviewed.

As passionate as Jeff was for community work, there is no doubt his vision for the future could have been blurred with business decisions that needed to be made instantly. The easy financial decision would have been to shut the Academy and the Community Sports Trust, but Jeff's decision at this time, to keep all in place at some financial loss, has no doubt put the club in the position it is today with youth players progressing to have good careers and a community department with 50 staff and an engagement level of over 150 sessions a week, engaging with over 4,000 people.

From day one, Jeff wanted a family community club. This is an easy thing to say but a big challenge and takes time as partnerships and plans are developed. Jeff's outstanding attribute is his time for everyone and he would always been seen engaging and talking with supporters.

I have learned a lot from Jeff about leadership skills and he has a unique ability to make all staff feel valued and that their role forms an important part in the success of the team and the business. I use these skills in how I manage my staff in the Community Trust and the women's team. To Jeff it didn't matter if you were the team's leading scorer or an apprentice joining the business, all were treated with equal value. And when we achieved the impossible dream of reaching the Premier League, it felt to all staff like we had all scored the winning goal in this achievement and shared the moment together. What's more, as the ultra-sportsman, Jeff always hosts the away team with the ultimate respect and friendship.

Sport is unlike any business and of course results on the pitch dictate so much. Jeff's relationship with manager Eddie Howe, however, was instrumental in the rise of the club: the 'Great Escape' from relegation from League Two to the Premier League. Every season following promotion, the challenge would be greater, the demands more and expectations higher. Jeff bridged these challenges with a strong show of teamwork. Players wanted to play for AFC Bournemouth with Jeff as their chairman, staff wanted to work for the club with Jeff as their leader.

Supporters quite rightly will always talk of Jeff Mostyn and AFC Bournemouth and the incredible journey. Supporters, players and staff who saw their dreams come true have the greatest memories of achievements which no one thought possible. Jeff as chairman, owner, leader and figurehead will always be held in high esteem as we all owe so much to his vision, passion and achievements.

It has been my great pleasure to be close to all of Jeff's great achievements but a greater pleasure to call Jeff a friend, somebody who has supported me professionally and personally, and I will always be thankful for Jeff's unwavering support.

A NEW INVESTOR AND WE FELT LIKE WE HAD WON THE LOTTERY!

The reality was that, at this point in time, we were not in a position to enable Kevin Bond to bring in new players. In fact, Kevin had found it difficult to attract players to the club since he became manager and with just a few exceptions, he had been forced to bring in a mixture of loan players, free agents and trialists. So, he had had to rely on some of these youth players, like Brett Pitman and Danny Ings, who cost us nothing beyond our investment in the youth team all those years ago. That investment turned out to be a very, very good decision, as many players were later sold on, earning good money for the club.

As the new season approached, a significant breakthrough appeared to emerge when Paul Baker and Alastair Saverimutto, the latter representing a Cheshire-based company called Sport-6, expressed an interest in taking control of the club. Discussions were very positive, and they became the first parties to come in with a cheque that didn't bounce! They gave us £50,000, and it felt like we had won the lottery!

With Paul and Alastair, or 'Savvy' as he was popularly known, onboard alongside me and Steve, the whole club was briefly energised. There was new money coming in, and we were thrilled not to have to cover expenses for the current month. In return, we agreed on a payment plan for Sport-6 to purchase 100 per cent of the football club shares.

Although the payment structure still caused us some concerns as they didn't have the funds upfront, receiving the initial £50,000 was at least reassuring.

We had been let down previously by potential investors more times than I could recount, with handshakes followed by excuses like, 'I left my chequebook at home.' Whenever we were close to securing proper investment, they would seek independent advice and back out. But Paul and Savvy came on board as co-owners. Savvy became chief executive while Steve and I remained as chairman and vice chairman, at least for the time being. As a result, this meant the club was out of administration.

Eventually, Steve and I resigned. Although the football club was strictly no longer our direct problem, indirectly it was, because unless Paul and Savvy paid us for the club shares, we still owned the shares by default. Paul took over as chairman and Sport-6 set about making their mark, revealing ambitious plans for the football club. Sadly, their involvement proved to be short-lived due to the global recession, which forced them to retract their investment, leaving Steve and me to seek another investor. Looking back on Sport-6's time at the club, it may have been brief, but some significant changes were made, not all of which proved to be of great benefit.

I now realise how unpredictable running a football club can be. Dealing with pressure and stress was a major part of the experience – and there was an enormous amount of stress. The focus for me, having invested so much, was figuring out the possibilities for recovering that money. I constantly tried to approach this with a business mindset, contemplating the options for recouping the funds without harming the club. That was always foremost in my mind.

Everyone was still reeling at the severity of our seventeen-point penalty when Gillingham arrived for the first game of the season. We led for much of the game through a goal from former England international Darren Anderton, only for us to concede a late equaliser to deny us a winning start.

After we had exited the Carling Cup, our most valuable player, Jo Kuffour, was sold to Bristol Rovers, which enabled Kevin to bring back our former striker Alan Connell from Brentford. It just about summed up the club's lack of good fortune when poor Alan then suffered an injury in his first training session back at Bournemouth and was sidelined for several months.

Failure to win any of our first five games resulted in the dismissal of Kevin and both his assistants, Rob Newman and Eddie Howe, on 1 September. At a press conference the following day, the club's former striker Jimmy Quinn was unveiled as the new manager with another ex-Cherry, Jason Tindall, as his assistant.

More players began to arrive, mostly on loan, as Quinn looked to reshape the side, but five home games produced just one League win before an appearance on live TV at least brought a small cash windfall and a point at fellow-strugglers Grimsby. The next game saw the lowest attendance for a League match at the stadium, with just 3,068 being present to witness a goalless draw with Morecambe. With Rotherham having already shrugged off their points deduction, concern was growing that the club was not strengthening adequately or quickly enough to be able to preserve its League status.

More welcome television money arrived when the team were drawn against Blyth Spartans in the FA Cup, with the prospect of even more to come for the winners in the next round at home to Blackburn. But the nation would only witness two poor Bournemouth performances against the Conference North side, a goalless draw at home being followed by a 1-0 defeat in the replay.

After a 3-3 draw at Luton in early December, Darren Anderton announced his impending retirement, having been left on the bench that evening. In his final game against Chester a few days later, he provided what would become an iconic moment of the season when he came off the bench in the 88th minute to score the only goal, a wonderful strike from outside the penalty area, to clinch the win. The victory was a huge moment for him and for the club as we reached positive points, with us sitting 23rd in the table and Grimsby and Rotherham immediately above us on ten points.

However, a poor Christmas period brought defeat at Brentford and another loss at home to a very ordinary Barnet side two days later. It meant that we were still seven points away from safety at the halfway stage of the season and supporters were wasting no time in venting their dissatisfaction.

Things came to a head on New Year's Eve, when Quinn was placed on gardening leave and Eddie Howe, who had recently returned to the club in a youth team coaching role, took over as caretaker manager. By this time, it had been announced that local businessman Adam Murry had completed the purchase of Sport-6's shareholding, which I believe amounted to 50 per cent of the club's total shares, the other 50 per cent belonging to Paul Baker. However, in January 2009, Murry missed the deadline to buy these shares, and the uncertainty continued as Baker explained that the recession was hitting his business interests hard and this was having a knock-on effect on the finances he was able to provide to the club.

A NEW ERA AS EDDIE HOWE IS APPOINTED MANAGER

By this point, Murry, as Director of Operations, had already confirmed Eddie's appointment on a permanent basis, despite the caretaker manager suffering defeats in his first two games in temporary charge. At 31, Eddie became the youngest manager in the Football League and took over a club almost at the bottom of the League and, by then, ten points adrift of safety.

The club couldn't have hired a manager with conventional managerial skills due to budget constraints anyway, but in Eddie Howe, they had someone who embodied AFC Bournemouth through and through.

As a player, he had been a graduate of our Academy before becoming a linchpin of Mel Machin's side that narrowly missed the Second Division play-offs in successive seasons during the late 1990s. Capped at England Under 21 level, his chances of further honours as a player were effectively ended when he suffered a serious knee injury in his first game for Portsmouth, after a £400,000 transfer in 2002.

Initially Eddie returned to Dean Court on loan early in the 2004/05 season, before around 5,000 loyal supporters, including Steve Sly in a key role, brought him back to the club on a permanent basis. The story deserves a place in the book of fans' folklore and the spirit of football. The fans rallied together, collecting money in buckets to fund Eddie's return from Portsmouth and, thanks to their contributions, they successfully brought him back to the club!

By the time he was forced to hang up his boots in 2007, he had made a further forty League appearances. His return was to prove crucial in his journey from player to coach but already his influence had been woven into the very fabric of the football club's DNA.

Eddie's appointment as manager was, of course, to prove monumental. The fans adored him, he could do little wrong and was truly one of us. He retained the services of Jason Tindall as his assistant, and his first transfer action was to sign midfielder Mark Molesley on a long-term contract, something Mark has regularly reminded him of ever since! Eddie pulled off another masterstroke when he re-signed club legend, 36-year-old Steve Fletcher from Crawley. Steve, also known as Fletch, a veteran of over 500 appearances for the club before being released in 2007, had become the talisman of the club after arriving from Hartlepool in 1992.

Liam Feeney was signed from Salisbury and Anton Robinson from Weymouth, while a number of other players arrived on loan from Football League clubs. A 3-1 victory over Wycombe on 24 January proved to be just the catalyst Howe needed and was the start of a five-game unbeaten run that brought the gap to safety down to five points.

However, when we tried to extend the loan of Jake Thomson from Southampton, the ongoing financial problems reared their head again and the Football League refused to sanction the move, instead placing another transfer embargo on the club. If anything, this made everyone's determination to reach safety even stronger. Eddie and I did our best to bring the club, its players and supporters together as one and soon there was a belief that another 'Great Escape' might be achievable.

A 90th-minute goal from Molesley brought a vital win at Dagenham and Redbridge and a moment that would go down in folk history. It happened when Eddie had to bring on his assistant manager, Jason Tindall, as a substitute for the last twenty minutes of the game because Ryan Garry was suffering from extreme cramp. Jason duly made his bow and 'provided a pivotal assist' for the goal. Some say it was a 'big punt up the line' which Mark got on the end of before gliding past two defenders and scoring with a low strike into the bottom left-hand corner of the net. The win was crucial though. It was Eddie Howe's first away win in management and something Jason never lets Eddie forget!

Fletch then netted his first goal since returning to the club, in a victory against Aldershot on 3 March, and suddenly we found ourselves out of the bottom two. This took place while Paul Baker was still desperately trying to sell the club, as finances got tighter and tighter. In fact, they got so bad that the players were left unpaid before a visit to Exeter City the following week.

The players had every reason to be upset but instead displayed the extent of their integrity and professionalism by producing a wonderful performance on the pitch. After giving away a cheap goal in the first half, in the second half the team showed massive character to come back and win 3-1. Brett Pitman scored an individual goal that I will never forget: running the length of the pitch from outside our own box, he 'nutmegged' two players as he went past a total of seven defenders, before shooting low into the net. It was a magical goal and secured another vital three points.

By mid-April, with Luton doomed, having never looked likely to overcome their thirty-point penalty, it was a battle between us, Chester and Grimsby Town to avoid the remaining ticket to the Conference. Eventually it came down to needing one win from our last two games. In the first of these, our last fixture at home, we faced Grimsby, who also required a win to secure their own destiny.

As I write this, I have goosebumps thinking about the magnitude of that game. We had to win to guarantee survival and achieve the impossible. Grimsby took a first half lead, but a red card soon afterwards saw them reduced to ten men. Eddie regrouped the players during the interval, and they responded brilliantly. Liam Feeney scored in the 47th minute and had a fantastic game, his speed and deftness of touch constantly giving the visiting defenders a problem.

Then, in the 79th minute, Mark Molesley started a move by gliding through the midfield before making a great pass to Brett Pitman, who threaded a through ball to Rhoys Wiggins. He put a great cross into the box, and when Mark was pushed in the back, the ball landed on Steve Fletcher's chest. He controlled it with a half-volley, then connected cleanly and with power to crash the ball into the net.

It proved to be the goal that kept us in the League. An iconic moment in AFC Bournemouth's history, it was richly deserved by Fletch, who had been a leader since his return. Upon the final whistle, the stadium erupted with emotion from the fans, the players and the staff. We had all sacrificed so much.

The celebrations continued the following week with a 4-0 success at Morecambe, the club's best away win in thirty years in what was truly a fairy-tale ending to our troubled season. We had seen three different managers in one season, entered administration, dealt with a transfer embargo, and even our assistant manager had been required to play! It will forever be remembered in Bournemouth's football history books as the year we started with minus seventeen points and still managed to stay up.

All we needed now was a new investor.

"

It may have been cold outside, but the moment we arrived in the boardroom at AFC Bournemouth the warmth was immediately there to be felt. No, the heating wasn't ramped up; it was the sheer warmth and hospitality that Jeff and Rosie showed to us from the moment we arrived.

DAVID BALDWIN #THECHAIRMAN

"

> **IN THEIR OWN WORDS ON JEFF**
>
> David Baldwin
> Former CEO of Bradford City and the EFL in 2020,
> currently Managing Director of Huddersfield Town
>
> My wife Ash and I first met Rosie and Jeff on 17 March 2009. It was a cold Tuesday evening after a long drive from Bradford down to AFC Bournemouth for the midweek fixture.
>
> It may have been cold outside, but the moment we arrived in the boardroom at AFC Bournemouth the warmth was immediately there to be felt. No, the heating wasn't ramped up; it was the sheer warmth and hospitality that Jeff and Rosie showed to us from the moment we arrived.
>
> I have probably been attending club boardrooms on a matchday for the last twenty years, however, I have never felt before or have ever felt since the sheer love and warmth of a welcome that we felt that night.
>
> We spent the time before the game, at half-time and after the game laughing, comparing football notes and family experiences and it was like we had been invited into the Mostyns' home and they wanted to make sure we had a good time.
>
> Bradford got battered on the pitch that night 4-1, but the disappointment would soon pass as we had made precious friends for life as history can testify to.

THE MURRY GROUP

In June 2009, a consortium led by Adam Murry finally took over AFC Bournemouth after the departure of both Paul Baker and Sport-6. The Murry Group actually comprised of only Adam, Steve Sly and me.

We had also approached Eddie Mitchell, a 55-year-old Sandbanks-based property developer and former director of non-League Dorchester Town. Eddie had initially declined to become involved as he could see no benefit in putting money into the club with its level of debt at that time. He did, however, give the impression that he would be interested in investing if the club was put into administration, which would give any investment a chance of success.

On this basis, I approached Eddie for a second time with a view to reaching an agreement for him to purchase half of the club's total number of shares for a much-reduced price, based on him funding the club going forward. This time, an agreement was reached between Steve and myself on one side and Eddie and his wife Brenda Mitchell on the other, to effectively own 50 per cent of the shares each, with Eddie and Brenda having an option to purchase 1 per cent of my shares at some stage in the future.

Eddie became chairman and I took over as vice chairman, but the club continued to live from hand to mouth, though on a larger scale due to having more employees. Eddie was interested in enhancing the stadium's appearance, which required funding. Money was raised from schemes like selling bricks for a walkway outside the stadium, and as a board, we worked incredibly hard. Eddie's approach of leveraging sponsorship for commercial funds was effective, yet the club needed more investment than he was willing to provide.

The extent of the debt that the club had built up since exiting administration had resulted in the Football League placing a further transfer embargo at the start of the 2009/10 season. With just twenty players to choose from and no scope to bring others in, we were understandably not among the bookmakers' pre-season favourites for promotion from League Two.

But a brilliant start to the campaign brought eight wins from our first nine games and we quickly found ourselves at the top of the League. In Brett Pitman, Eddie Howe knew he had one of the best strikers in the League but by the end of September, as injuries began to mount up, the transfer embargo started to impact upon the strength of the playing squad. On one occasion, Howe could only name three substitutes for a match instead of the permitted five, and, once again, assistant manager Jason Tindall was among them.

Schoolboy Jayden Stockley was taken out of the classroom to sit on the bench and youth team striker Danny Ings made his first senior appearance before, after numerous pleas on our club secretary's hotline to the Football League, we were eventually given permission for midfielder Anthony Edgar to come in on loan from West Ham. An injury to goalkeeper Shwan Jalal saw young Dan Thomas, another youth team product, take over briefly before he then suffered an injury on the eve of a trip to Morecambe in mid-December. With Jalal still unfit, only after several more phone calls to the Football League were we granted permission to bring in another keeper on a seven-day loan. Unfortunately though, West Ham's Marek Štěch's one and only appearance for AFC Bournemouth was not one to remember and ended in a 5-0 defeat.

Although results became inconsistent, the team continued to hover around the promotion places and Eddie Howe could do little wrong in the eyes of the supporters, even if his side were showing signs of strain. Howe and his players were never down for long, nor did they complain about their difficulties. Instead, they displayed a togetherness and determination that encouraged the supporters to once again rally around the club and display the sense of togetherness that had brought salvation the previous season. It all led to something of a siege mentality that could be felt throughout the club.

The best crowd of the season so far, 7,626, turned out to witness a 2-1 win against Torquay on Boxing Day which saw the team end the year in second place behind leaders, Rochdale. Off the pitch, the club continued to make progress in addressing its financial obligations. Naming rights to the stadium had been sold and, by March, after an early season-ticket sales drive which raised almost £300,000, the club's remaining legacy debt, which stood at £846,000, had at least been halved since the takeover by the new ownership the previous June.

The financial progress was recognised by the Football League, who gave permission for us to sign another player on loan, and Wiggins rejoined on loan from Norwich City in late January came after the team had suffered a run of three successive defeats.

A victory at Crewe was followed by a midweek trip to a freezing cold Don Valley Stadium, which had become the temporary home of fellow promotion chasers Rotherham United. The Yorkshire club was just below us in the table but had several games in hand, so the match was of particular significance. While I and our hardy band of travelling supporters did our best to ward off hypothermia in the stand, we watched the boys totally dominate the game from the start. Somehow though, we came in at half-time a goal down, but despite the pitch freezing as the game went on, the second half saw Brett Pitman equalise and then two goals from Danny Hollands secured a memorable victory.

My friendship with Rotherham's owner and chairman Tony Stewart is as strong today as was the bond between us then. We often reflect on the hardship we had suffered and the perilous position we found our respective clubs in. Ironically, I met Tony in the Algarve last summer, where we once again reminisced about the days we spent in administration and the parts we had played in saving our football clubs.

Another promotion-chasing side with financial problems were Notts County, where reports of a massive investment earlier in the season were proving to be without foundation. Their expensively assembled team had an abundance of games in hand when they visited what was now known as the Classic Eyes Stadium at Dean Court in February. Once again Eddie Howe's team stepped up to the plate with Hollands grabbing another brace in a 2-1 win.

Just over one month later, in mid-March, came the return fixture against Notts County at Meadow Lane, together with a welcome financial bonus when the match was selected for live television coverage by Sky Sports. We were grateful to a late goal for rescuing a point, but maximum reward was gained in subsequent home games against Accrington Stanley and Bradford City as the season moved into April, by which time Notts County had climbed to the top with Rochdale occupying second place.

On Easter Monday, we made the trip to our Lancashire rivals, but this time lady luck appeared to desert us, the game ending goalless after Pitman had what later proved to be a perfectly good goal ruled out for offside. By now though, promotion was almost within reach and after two home wins inside a week, we had a chance to achieve it with two games to spare if we could win at Burton Albion.

I looked forward to renewing my acquaintance with Albion's chairman Ben Robinson as Steve and I made our way past a fleet of supporters' cars and coaches on our way up to the game. Around 1,800 of our supporters made the trip up to Staffordshire and we shared their excitement and anticipation for the afternoon ahead.

In the boardroom and in the stands, the directors, staff and officials of Burton Albion made every effort to ensure that we were all comfortably accommodated. In fact, I do not believe they could have been more accommodating, except perhaps if they had just given us the three points there and then!

Burton were not planning on being quite so obliging on the pitch, however, but we need not have worried as, roared on by the supporters, Eddie Howe and the players remained cool and calm and gradually took a hold on the game. After a goalless first half, Pitman opened the scoring in the 66th minute to spark wild celebrations before Alan Connell turned the ball home in added time to seal the deal!

The scenes in the dressing room after the game were unforgettable and, on reflection, the players had obviously wanted to set a precedent that afternoon which they might be able to follow up on later. Little did I know as we celebrated then, that five years down the line they would get the opportunity to do just that and produce the now infamous scenes when I was held aloft and given the most embarrassing spanking of my life by Callum Wilson!

Of equal importance that day was the start of a hugely mutually respectful friendship between myself and Ben Robinson. When the final whistle blew, Ben took me aside briefly and told me that he had arranged for a room to be reserved for us to continue our celebrations and that inside the room was a case of champagne. It was the sign of a true gentleman who seemed almost as proud of our achievement as he would have been if it had been accomplished by his own club.

It would also be remiss of me not to mention the incredible stewards at Burton Albion who, with the support of the head groundsman, allowed our supporters to celebrate on the pitch on the same afternoon that he had received the award for the 'Best Pitch in League Two'! Huge respect to everyone for allowing us all to enjoy our moment of glory.

I couldn't help but take a moment though, to think back to the financial problems the club had been through, the points deductions and transfer embargoes. To achieve promotion after all this was an unbelievable achievement that everyone at the club could be proud of – players, officials, staff and supporters.

The celebrations continued on home soil the following Saturday with a 4-0 win against Port Vale which turned out to be enough for us to finish as runners-up to Notts County. There was also another chance for supporters to give Eddie Howe and the players a wonderful reception a few days later, as they arrived at Bournemouth Pier on Sunseeker yachts before transferring to an open-top bus for a tour around the town.

Promotion had been achieved against all the odds but to take full advantage of the wave of support that came with it, I knew a busy summer lay ahead if we were to ensure that the manager could build a capable squad of players to compete at the higher level.

Looking back, the summer of 2010 was remarkable because with the embargo lifted, we were finally able to sign players again! On 4 June, forward Marc Pugh signed a three-year contract with us, which required a compensation fee of £100,000 to be paid to his former club Hereford United. The fee was decided by an FA tribunal, and I thought it was quite excessive at the time, but reflecting on the contributions Marc would go on to make at AFC Bournemouth in the years that followed, he turned out to be a bargain. Marc wasn't going to win the Ballon d'Or, but he won many people's hearts with his dedication and community engagement. He left everything on the pitch and set an exemplary standard for young players, the management team and supporters. He became a true ambassador for the club.

> **There is no doubt in my mind that Jeff is a hero.** He saved AFC Bournemouth from going into administration and out of the Football League. I will be forever grateful for his kindness, generosity and willingness to always put others first before himself.

MARC PUGH #THECHAIRMAN

IN THEIR OWN WORDS ON JEFF

Marc Pugh
Former AFC Bournemouth Player

The moment I met Jeff, I was instantly captivated by his warm smile, infectious personality and genuine enthusiasm for life. I found it so uplifting. His dedication to excellence is evident in everything he does, and he inspires others around him to dream big and strive for greatness.

In 2010, I signed for AFC Bournemouth and the fee was to be determined by a tribunal. Jeff and I both had to attend, so I had the pleasure of spending a full day in London with him. Let's put it this way, I enjoyed it most as Jeff had to fork out £100,000 to sign me! To this day, he still tells me the fee was excessive, and that he was robbed!

After paying the money, Jeff decided to drown his sorrows and treat me to lunch in Selfridges. He ordered a bottle of champagne, and the conversation and laughter flowed. Jeff's charisma filled the room, and I could tell instantly that we were going to have a wonderful relationship that would last a lifetime. After seeing how much the football club meant to Jeff, it was important to me that I repaid his belief in me in some way. The only way I was going to do that was to work tirelessly every day and bring success to AFC Bournemouth.

The start of every season is always filled with anticipation and excitement, both for players and fans alike. I had a fantastic first pre-season at Bournemouth and was ready to hit the ground running. Within the first three months, I won the man of the match award on countless occasions so would make regular appearances in the boardroom afterwards. Jeff and Rosie would always be the first to come over and greet me with a big warm kiss and cuddle.

Rosie and Jeff share a bond that transcends words, a connection like no other, and their mutual respect, unwavering support and unconditional love is there for all to see. Their journey together is a testament to the power of companionship, as they navigate life's highs and lows hand in hand. Rosie's kind and infectious personality compliments Jeff's vibrant energy, creating a bond that is very special.

Together, they inspire one another to dream boldly, to laugh freely and to cherish every moment shared.

There is no doubt in my mind that Jeff is a hero. He saved AFC Bournemouth from being wound up and out of the Football League. I will be forever grateful for his kindness, generosity and willingness to always put others first before himself.

Jeff's business life summed him up; he was always looking to help others. He provided financial advice and services to members of the armed forces. His passion always shone through whenever he spoke about his business, and he deserves every bit of success he has achieved.

My admiration for Jeff is too strong to put into words, especially when it comes to his unwavering love for AFC Bournemouth. His passion and loyalty for the club is infectious. Win, lose or draw, Jeff was always in the changing room after games, supporting, encouraging and showing his love and admiration for every player and staff member. His knowledge of the club's history, players and matches is truly impressive, reflecting a genuine love for football and the community. Jeff's devotion to AFC Bournemouth is so inspiring and the faith he showed in me as a player will never leave my side.

Over the course of my career with AFC Bournemouth, I learned so much from Jeff. His work ethic and love for life is there for all to see. Whenever you are in Jeff's presence, he always finds a way to make you feel special and put a smile on your face. Without realising it, Jeff made a huge impact on me as a person with the way he lived his life and ran his business. He made me appreciate the profound importance of having a strong work ethic, and the importance of showing dedication and perseverance. He also leads by example and treats everybody around him with the same level of respect, no matter who he is interacting with. All these attributes are essential if you want to bring success into your life.

One of my favourite quotes in life is: 'Hard work beats talent, when talent doesn't work hard.' Jeff epitomises this quote. He put in hard work, and he has talent – there is no better combination, and he deserves every success in the world.

One of my fondest moments with Jeff occurred on 27 April 2015. We beat Bolton 3-0 and got promotion to the Premier League. It was

1. The famous 'nod' to Gerald Krasner, together with another £100,000 cheque

2. My vice-chair Steve Sly, who played a huge part in saving the club

3. With Kevin Bond, who introduced me to the club

4. Another league promotion with the boys

5. The film premiere of AFC Bournemouth documentary *Minus 17*, which highlighted our incredible achievement in the EFL

6. The Cherries' tunnel

7. Sorry for the now famous expletive live on Sky TV. Somehow we made the seemingly impossible possible by reaching the Premier League.

8. Matt Ritchie providing me with a free champagne hydration on the pitch during the promotion celebrations

9. Brothers in arms. So proud to have my brother Mike by my side as we celebrated promotion

10. The now legendary 'Premier League Sombrero' enjoying the moment with the fans who inspire me to this day

11. Eddie Howe and Jason Tindall – the two alongside me on the pitch who made our journey to the Premier League possible

12. Victory at the Bridge! Celebrating with (from left to right) Neill Blake, Matt Ritchie and Maxim Demin

13. A special moment with Neville Koopowitz, CEO of Vitality, the club's key partner, a personal friend, and someone for whom I have huge respect

14. Alongside the team that made the Premier League dream come true at the club's end of season awards

15. Alongside my gorgeous bride, Rosie, at the start of a marriage made in heaven

16. With my sister Rosalyn, who inspired me so much as a child, and my brother Mike

17. With our beloved parents, Reg, Sadie, Ralph and Joan on our wedding day

18. With TSB colleagues John Shepherd and Trevor Skelton

19. My treasured family whom I adore

20. The man in black at Club Dinner with my wife Rosie and daughter Alex

21. A special father-and-son moment at the club with Darren

22. Lt Colonel Jed McInally and Brigadier Andy Griffiths OBE, who taught me true leadership values

23. Pitch invasion at AFC Bournemouth with daughter Alex by my side

an incredible night and to share it with Jeff made it extra special. We were both very emotional in the changing rooms after the game and champagne was being squirted everywhere but mainly on Jeff! I was one of several players who picked Jeff up and threw him in the air as we celebrated. I found out the next day that the Sky Sports cameras had caught this moment, and it was on the circular reel on their sports news programmes. Seeing what this promotion meant to the fans, players and staff was truly remarkable. None of this would have been possible without Jeff and his willingness to put the club before himself.

It is so hard to sum Jeff up in one word because he has so many amazing characteristics. However, if I had to choose one, it would be resilient. Through adversity and staring down the barrel of defeat on many occasions, Jeff kept the faith and showed incredible resilience in his pursuit of success.

It is very rare that you get to meet someone as humble and charismatic as Jeff and I feel truly blessed to know him. I am proud to call him my friend and I will cherish the special times we shared together forever. Thank you from the bottom of my heart for everything you have done for me over the years. You have a wonderful family, and they also have a special place in my heart. Keep smiling and enjoying life, mate.

"

That 'Great Escape' paved the way for the club's fairy-tale journey to the Premier League in 2015; a wonderful achievement that epitomised both the beauty and strength of the EFL.

TREVOR BIRCH #THECHAIRMAN

"

IN THEIR OWN WORDS ON JEFF

Trevor Birch
Chief Executive of the EFL

Jeff Mostyn is one of those rare breeds in football. He is universally liked and respected! I first met Jeff during my time as an administrator back in 2012 while attempting to secure the future of Portsmouth Football Club and we have remained friends ever since. After taking up the role as CEO of the EFL in 2021 it was great to have Jeff's wise counsel as Chair of one of our Member Clubs, not to mention his unbridled optimism, particularly as we were all dealing with some very difficult financial problems caused by the Covid-19 pandemic.

By the time I met him, while at Portsmouth, he had performed his own rescue act at Bournemouth after the club suffered financial difficulties in 2007. Jeff funded the subsequent administration, providing the administrator with time to finalise the sale of the club to a consortium put together by Jeff. It was a precarious time for the club, and after suffering a 10-point deduction resulting in relegation from League One they started the 2008/09 season in League Two on minus 17 points. The very existence of AFC Bournemouth was in jeopardy, with safety only guaranteed at the final home game of the season.

That 'Great Escape' paved the way for the club's fairy-tale journey to the Premier League in 2015; a wonderful achievement that epitomised both the beauty and strength of the EFL, illustrating the sheer excitement and despair experienced due to the fluidity of movement through the divisions. That is what defines Jeff. Despite the club's success, he remains first and foremost a football man and has never forgotten the importance of the role the EFL plays in the success of the football pyramid in this country. During his and the club's time in the EFL, Jeff was fully immersed in playing an active role in promoting the League. He has acted as an Alternate Director and then a full Board Member of the League, as well as being an elected Council member of the FA.

Ultimately, the story of AFC Bournemouth is one that provides hope and optimism for all those EFL clubs falling on hard times. It proves that fortunes can change quickly. Jeff played an instrumental role in that change process and is rightly lauded for his efforts!

CONSOLIDATING IN LEAGUE ONE, 2010/11

The summer of 2010 proved to be a busy one, with Stephen Purches returning after three years away, the arrival of 20-year-old midfield livewire Harry Arter from Woking, Rhoys Wiggins returning to the club again, this time on a permanent basis, and Danny Ings receiving his first professional contract.

The downside came soon after the 2010/11 season got underway, when after scoring a hat-trick in a 5-1 win against promotion-favourites Peterborough United, Brett Pitman was sold to Bristol City for £800,000, which was disappointing as he had been a prolific goalscorer for us. However, we needed the cash. Fortunately, Academy graduate Josh McQuoid soon stepped up to fill Brett's shoes. In fact, it was uncanny how he seamlessly took over and made a considerable impact.

For the first time since the early 1960s, our supporters could now enjoy equal divisional status with our traditional rivals from just up the road, Southampton, who had been relegated from the Championship the previous season. In early August, the Saints had beaten us in the Carling Cup but by the time the League fixture at St Mary's came around in October, three wins in our previous four games had lifted us up to second in the table and we had also been able to bring in an exceptional loan signing from Tottenham in defender Adam Smith.

However, it was to be a highly frustrating game at our Hampshire neighbours, during which, after hitting the post in the first minute, we were denied a blatant penalty kick and instead saw two controversial penalties given against us. To add to our woes, Smith was shown a red card after receiving two bookings.

The following month, we enjoyed some amazing games, always on the attack, and playing with a determined unity that overwhelmed the opposition despite limited resources. Josh McQuoid, in particular, enjoyed a wonderful week which began with an amazing FA Cup tie at home to Tranmere. Three up in eight minutes we were cruising, but Rovers hit back to draw level before we eventually won 5-3 with Josh scoring a hat-trick. A week later, the Irish Under 21 International struck another hat-trick in a 3-0 win against Walsall.

By the end of the year, there were plenty of positives to take forward into 2011. Despite three successive home defeats, we were in the top six and our average home gate was around 6,000. Delighted as I was that we were back in League One and doing well, inevitably the achievements of Eddie Howe and his assistant Jason Tindall had not gone unnoticed by other clubs. By now, there was interest from several clubs in higher divisions and even

Peterborough United from our own league. Somehow, we had to face up to the fact that sooner rather than later, we were going to lose Eddie and Jason.

LIFE WITHOUT EDDIE AND JASON

Speculation regarding Eddie Howe's future intensified early in January, with Crystal Palace and Charlton the latest clubs to come in for him and Jason. As the team prepared for an away fixture against Colchester United on Friday evening, 14 January, rumours were swirling around about his departure.

The game had been moved forward from the following Saturday as it had been selected for live TV. The previous Saturday had seen the team put in a brilliant performance to win 3-0 at home to Plymouth Argyle. During the game, banners were held up pleading for Eddie to remain with the club, and his name was chanted continuously throughout. A few days later, Eddie announced that he was staying with us but then came news that Championship side Burnley had made an approach for him.

Although no official announcement had been made before kick-off at Colchester, it had become common knowledge that Eddie had agreed to take charge at Turf Moor, with Jason accompanying him as assistant. Unfortunately, after conceding two late goals, we lost the game, before Eddie broke the news of their departure afterwards.

The next day, Lee Bradbury and Steve Fletcher took temporary charge, and they oversaw a goalless draw at Rochdale three days later. Their first home game in charge saw a brilliant win over League One leaders Brighton, and their permanent appointments as manager and assistant were confirmed.

Thirty-five-year-old Bradbury immediately announced his retirement as a player upon being given a two-and-a-half-year deal to become manager. In 1997 he had been the subject of a £3.5 million transfer from Portsmouth to Manchester City and the former Army serviceman had gone on to complete more than 500 Football League games during a career that had also included spells at Crystal Palace, Walsall, Oxford United and Southend. Since joining Bournemouth in August 2007, his flexibility, professional approach and wealth of experience had been of great benefit to Eddie. So much so that the former striker had played many times as a full-back when no other cover was available.

Lee and Steve did remarkably well, despite all the upheaval. They enjoyed an early run of success which saw the team remain unbeaten for ten games and maintain the challenge for a second successive promotion.

Steve continued to feature in the side on occasions and snatched a late equaliser in a top of the table clash at Peterborough in early April. Although we eventually dropped out of the automatic promotion places, we just needed a win in our last away game of the season at Hartlepool to secure a play-off place. We went two goals ahead, but in typical Bournemouth fashion we then made it hard for ourselves and allowed the home side to equalise in the last minute through a header by their goalkeeper! As it turned out, the point proved enough to set up a semi-final clash with Huddersfield Town.

The two matches against Huddersfield were both thrilling encounters. For the first leg, we set up a temporary stand at the south end of our stadium to accommodate the extra support from a town that was buzzing with excitement. They scored first but a brilliant strike from Donal McDermott ensured that we headed north on level terms despite Danny Ings missing a penalty.

Another electric atmosphere awaited us for the second leg at the John Smith Stadium and an unforgettable game was eventually decided in the Yorkshire club's favour on penalties. Down to ten men and exhausted after the unfortunate dismissal of our captain Jason Pearce, the team had bravely held on in extra-time for the game to finish 3-3. Huddersfield's success in the shoot-out saw three quarters of the stadium erupt in huge celebration, while the other quarter, the one containing around 1,000 of our supporters, suffered heartbreak.

Getting that far in our first season back in League One was impressive. In fact, the end of the 2010/11 season was to mark a significant change in terms of the club's playing personnel, but despite their disappointment, everyone involved could take so much pride in their efforts.

We lost Jason Pearce to Portsmouth for £350,000 during the summer and Danny Ings, who had played so well in the latter stages of the season, made a big money move to Burnley. But better news was just around the corner and it would prove to be the beginning of another exciting new chapter for AFC Bournemouth.

CHAPTER 7
ENTER MAXIM DEMIN

It's 17 September 2013 and my phone rings with Maxim Demin on the other end, calling from Moscow. There is an air of excitement and urgency in his voice, which piques my curiosity.

He begins by mentioning a board meeting they have just concluded. He is puzzled, he says, about why, as vice chairman of the club, I am sitting in Bournemouth while decisions of such magnitude are happening across the globe. 'I'm here with Neill Blake, Eddie Howe and Jason Tindall,' he says. Maxim then shares with a slight chuckle that he has just learned two new English words from Eddie Howe – 'shoe in'. At that point, I still have no idea what story is unfolding.

'Maxim,' I ask, curiosity bubbling over, 'what exactly are you hinting at?'

There is a pause, and then he delivers the news with warmth and a hint of mischief: 'Congratulations. You are once again the chairman of the football club.'

The phrase 'shoe in' suddenly makes perfect sense. In a decisive move, Maxim has secured full control of AFC Bournemouth by acquiring Eddie Mitchell's shares, becoming the sole owner. His first act as owner is to re-instate me as chairman.

It's a staggering vote of confidence, not only validating my past efforts but also entrusting me with the future course of the club under his ownership. This call, above all others, is a testament to our mutual respect and my profound alignment with the club's vision. In all my career, this moment of recognition stands as a powerful symbol of trust and belief, both transformative and deeply affirming.

* * *

Our strong showing in League One during the 2010/11 season meant AFC Bournemouth was still attracting attention, but this time for the right reasons. Eddie Mitchell introduced Steve and me to Maxim Demin, a 41-year-old Russian-born petrochemicals trader. Maxim was having a home built in nearby

Sandbanks, and Eddie invited him to watch a game at the club. He loved the AFC Bournemouth experience and wanted to get involved in the club.

At this stage we were relying solely on commercial sponsorship, and other initiatives, to keep the club above water. However, it was still proving difficult to attract, fund and sustain any form of forward momentum.

During the season, I had a number of personal engagements with Maxim and his family on matchdays and we had established a mutually respectful relationship. Eddie Mitchell approached me and asked whether I would consider selling my shares to Maxim in order for him to propel the club forward with his substantial investment potential. Given my previous experience with Paul Baker and Alastair Saverimutto, I had to ensure that I fully understood Maxim's commitment to the club before giving consideration to negotiations.

We had private meetings and heartfelt discussions with Maxim and Eddie Mitchell, during which Steve and I acknowledged that financially, and emotionally, after nearly five years of stress and pressure, we were not equipped to take the club further. We recognised that Maxim, being a multimillionaire, could elevate the club to a new level. Once I had concluded the discussions, I had no hesitation in agreeing to discuss terms for Maxim to take over our 50 per cent shareholding in the club.

Maxim was the investor we had been seeking for almost five years and he was the right person to propel the club forward. We made the decision without any hesitation. I truly believe that our choice that day epitomised our selfless efforts, knowing that Maxim was in a position to transform the club's fortunes forever.

During my tenure as chairman and vice chairman, I only ever wanted success for the club. Having endured all the trials and tribulations of saving the club, stepping aside as a shareholder was going to demonstrate to everyone that my love and commitment for this football club should always be respected.

I had learned something about loyalty many years earlier from James Beattie, a young England International footballer who was also a neighbour of mine, whose loyalty was questioned ahead of him making a move to a big Premier League club. He told me that owners come and go, chairmen come and go, and players come and go, but when you talk about loyalty you have to look at supporters. The club is their lifeblood. Those words of wisdom came flooding back, and I knew that the decision we made that day was in the best interests of our wonderful supporters, young and old, and that the bond I have with them would last forever.

Selling the benefits of a League One or Two football club to a prospective client remains a challenging endeavour. There are no television rights, and convincing someone to pay £1,500 for a board around the pitch that's only seen twenty-six times a year by a small local audience is tough. You need equally passionate people who believe in your vision and support the club. Back in our day, the ground boards at the stadium were filled by local, long-standing supporters. Attracting major sponsors like Heineken or Carlsberg was beyond our reach. I believe people were drawn to our passion and vision, and I found sponsors would buy into what we aimed to achieve, even though we had little of tangible value to sell.

Returning to preparations for the 2011/12 season, Eddie Mitchell remained as chairman while I continued to serve as vice chairman. However, changes could immediately be seen on the pitch. It's fair to say Eddie Howe's team had been broken up after the play-off defeat, and Lee Bradbury was tasked with its rebuilding. Rhoys Wiggins, Liam Feeney and Anton Robinson all left for pastures new, but for once the club was able to demand fees which represented the players' capabilities rather than whatever we could get for them in a fire sale. Ryan Garry was forced to retire through injury and became reserve team manager, and injury was to soon see Steve Lovell calling it a day.

Another former player, Shaun Brooks, took over from Joe Roach as Head of Youth, with ex-Portsmouth and West Ham coach Paul Groves becoming youth team manager. Lee Bradbury started the rebuilding process by signing experienced goalkeeper Darryl Flahavan from Southend and former Crystal Palace defender Adam Barrett. Steve Cook arrived from Brighton on loan and by the end of the year, he would be joined by Simon Francis and Charlie Daniels from Charlton and Leyton Orient respectively, before all three made their moves permanent when the transfer window opened again in January. They would each go on to play a prominent part in the club's history but at that time were in the early stages of their careers.

Stadium naming rights were transferred to Seward, and Maxim's increasing involvement in all areas of the club became evident with the staging of the EC Group Cup competition in July. Lokomotiv Moscow, 1.FC Saarbrücken and the Glenn Hoddle Academy joined us for the pre-season tournament at the Seward Stadium, which saw Bradbury's side beaten by Saarbrücken in the final.

Worryingly though, our League One campaign began with a disappointing 3-0 defeat at Charlton. Later in August, concern deepened after only one win came in our first seven League games and the side languished very close to the bottom of the table. The arrival of striker Wes Thomas, initially on loan from Crawley, in September finally coincided with a brief upturn in results and more loanees arrived soon afterwards.

Guadeloupe international Stéphane Zubar added to Bradbury's defensive options, but results continued to be frustrating, with good performances away from home often being followed by disappointing defeats on home soil. Eventually, the tide turned and our first home League win in almost three months came against Scunthorpe in early November, but was then followed by a 6-0 defeat in the Johnstone's Paint Trophy at Brentford. Steve Fletcher passed another milestone, making a club record 600th League appearance for the Cherries, but Bradbury felt he wasn't providing the support needed off the pitch, and Russ Wilcox, who had more experience, came in to take over as assistant manager, having previously performed similar roles at Burnley and Scunthorpe United.

We ended the year in 13th place, showing improvement, and three wins in January saw us rise to eighth in the table, but just two wins followed from our next eleven games and both Bradbury and Wilcox were relieved of their positions after a 1-0 defeat at Oldham Athletic on 24 March. Our spending in the January transfer window had included several permanent deals, including the £800,000 re-signing of striker Matt Tubbs from Crawley Town, a player who had initially started his career with us. It was a deal that reflected Maxim's influence but, unfortunately, Lee Bradbury was unable to maintain the level of performance expected from the team.

He was replaced by the youth team manager Paul Groves and Head of Youth Shaun Brooks, and from then until the season's end, Paul and Shaun handled first-team affairs. We finished the season in 11th place, with a record of two wins, four draws and two defeats during their temporary period in charge.

Nevertheless, Eddie appointed Groves and Brooks permanently and allowed them to shape the team for the following season. Over the summer, new players like Lewis Grabban and Tommy Elphick joined, and Richard Hughes and Josh McQuoid returned after a spell at Millwall. We also signed two Dutch players, Frank Demouge and Lorenzo Davids, and the well-known former England international goalkeeper David James, which helped put AFC Bournemouth on the map.

Miles Addison was another significant signing, having been on loan the previous season. He was signed permanently and took over from Adam Barrett as captain, aligning with Paul Groves' leadership style.

Forty-six-year-old Groves was not short of experience. He had previously enjoyed a lengthy playing career which spanned over 600 League appearances at six different clubs and he had then managed one of these, Grimsby Town, before being dismissed in 2004. Before coming to Bournemouth as youth team manager, he had been a senior coach alongside manager Avram Grant at Portsmouth and West Ham United.

As the 2012/13 season began, with such a strong group of players having been assembled, we had high expectations for promotion. But the team didn't start well. Disappointing draws and cup exits were finally followed by our first victory in the seventh game, when a goal from Hughes brought a 1-0 success at Yeovil on 8 September.

Although technically a good coach, by now there were increasing doubts about Groves' style of management, and Eddie Mitchell decided to bring in one of the club's former managers in an advisory role. That was the cue for Harry Redknapp to offer the benefit of his experience on a voluntary basis.

However, as the month progressed, the side continued to struggle in the bottom half of the table and after a heavy defeat at Swindon, Groves described the players' performance as 'unacceptable'. Things came to a head after a 3-1 reverse at newly promoted Crawley at the beginning of October, after which Groves and Brooks were re-appointed to their previous roles in the youth set-up and the search for a new manager began.

RETURN OF THE 'FEEL-GOOD FACTOR'

By now, rumours had reached us that Eddie Howe and Jason Tindall were unsettled at Burnley after spending two full seasons in charge at Turf Moor. They had finished 8th in the Championship in 2010/11 and 13th the following season but the move north had proved to be difficult for them and their families.

While first team coach Dennis Rofe held the fort for a couple of games, Maxim asked me to arrange a meeting with Eddie and Jason with a view to bringing them back to Bournemouth.

They were keen to be closer to their families who had remained in the Bournemouth area, and with Maxim's backing, reaching out to them seemed like a strong proposition to bolster the club once again. The club was no longer one founded upon insecurity and operating against unfavourable odds, but a club that had money to spend and a heightened expectation among its supporters.

Both welcomed the opportunity to return, terms were agreed, and everyone was happy. They received a rapturous welcome when re-introduced to supporters on the pitch ahead of Rofe's second game in temporary charge, which they then proceeded to watch from the stands. Goals from Grabban and Marc Pugh ensured that Rofe marked his brief stay with a win.

Eddie Howe resumed control, with us four places off the bottom of League One. I hoped he would turn things around and maybe get us into the play-offs, but I never expected the dramatic turnaround that happened so quickly. The change was remarkable. I believe the players had been suffering from a lack of direction; they had the ability, evidenced by many going on to play in the Premier League.

Eddie ditched the diamond formation that Paul Groves favoured and encouraged the team to play out from the back and to be more expansive. The players bought into it wholeheartedly, clearly enjoying themselves, and they were good players. Under the previous management, they seemed confused about what was expected of them. Eddie recognised their potential and allowed them to express themselves, which was transformative. Players like Marc Pugh and Harry Arter flourished, given the freedom to showcase their playmaking skills.

Just as he had done when he re-signed Steve Fletcher in 2009, Eddie pulled off another masterstroke when he appointed Tommy Elphick as captain and brought back the popular Brett Pitman from Bristol City. Elphick had made over 150 appearances for Brighton before he joined us at the start of the season and the former Brighton defender proved to be an inspirational leader for him on the pitch. Meanwhile, Pitman's return significantly increased the team's goalscoring power.

We remained undefeated for the rest of the calendar year, going on a thirteen-game unbeaten run, in League and cup matches. This propelled us into the League's top six, and the feel-good factor returned after staleness had prevailed the previous season. It felt like the players had been let loose and given the freedom to play their natural game.

Pitman's move was made permanent in the January transfer window, and he celebrated his permanent return by scoring a hat-trick in a 3-1 win against Crewe. Other arrivals in the window included Swindon Town winger Matt Ritchie, Leyton Orient goalkeeper Ryan Allsop and teenage Aberdeen winger Ryan Fraser.

By the time Eddie suffered his first defeat since his return to Bournemouth in mid-January, his team had matched a thirty-year-old club record of fifteen League and cup games without defeat

After suffering a couple of defeats, the team's response remained positive and they soon set off on a run of five successive wins. By mid-February though, the injuries had begun to mount up and after a defeat at Leyton Orient the side dropped down to seventh and, for the first time since Eddie's return, doubts began to surface about his side's ability to maintain its promotion challenge.

If ever there was a good opportunity to test the resolve of our team and its management, then this was it. Eddie remained calm and focused while the concern among our supporters continued to grow. Significantly, important players like Elphick and Charlie Daniels were able to recover and return to the side. Spearheaded by Pitman and Lewis Grabban, they snatched wins at Stevenage and Oldham to launch a blistering finish to the season that would eventually result in the team achieving a club record: eight successive victories.

PROMOTION TO THE CHAMPIONSHIP: A NEW DAWN

Driving into the stadium prior to our last home game of the season against Carlisle United, I took a moment to reflect upon on just how far we had come and how close we were to achieving what was almost the holy grail to many of our supporters – promotion to the Championship. We sat in second place, two points behind League-leaders Doncaster Rovers. Effectively, with Rovers facing third-placed Brentford in their final fixture the following week, it meant that a win against Carlisle would be enough for us to seal promotion – provided of course we could go on to avoid a 7-0 defeat in our final game at Tranmere!

A crowd packed into Dean Court, or the Goldsands Stadium, as it had become known through sponsorship at the time. In a hugely charged atmosphere, goals from Arter and Steve Cook were followed by another from Pitman to complete a 3-1 victory and launch more euphoric scenes among supporters and players at the end of the game.

I have been asked numerous times how I celebrated our second promotion as I was not such a visible presence on the pitch afterwards. I can recall only a complete state of emotional exhaustion. I think my mind was transported back to the start of our long journey and it was difficult to comprehend what had happened in such a short space of time. I definitely recall having more shots on target in the bar afterwards than our forwards had managed during the game though!

Achieving promotion meant fulfilling a long-standing dream. Reaching the Championship was such a significant achievement for everyone. Up to that point, the club had only spent three seasons at that level since joining the League in 1923. For so long, there was this idea that the board couldn't afford promotion. There had been a series of false dawns and near misses, often with strong performances on the pitch before Christmas and then slip-ups afterwards, which often gave the impression the club was trying to avoid it.

Given that we had been on the brink of going out of business just a couple of decades earlier and how close we had come to that again in 2009, reaching the Championship now was miraculous. It had been incredible to keep winning games as we had done. I wondered when it would all end and if the bubble would burst.

Upon arriving for the final game at Tranmere the following Saturday, I remember driving into the car park at Prenton Park and seeing the pub on the corner heaving with Bournemouth supporters. It was thrilling to see such passion from the fans, and I couldn't wait to join them! Not only had Eddie instilled an excellent team spirit among what become a tightly knit group of players, he had also brought a sense of marvellous togetherness to the club and its supporters.

To share the passion shown by our supporters while accompanied by cries of, 'Jeff, how incredible to see you – thank you for everything you have done for the football club – and now the drinks are on you!' was quite amazing. But I truly believe that, as a result, I bought the most expensive round of drinks ever seen in a supporters' bar anywhere in the world! As the orders were coming in, the till roll was turning over so quickly that it had to be replaced halfway through! I can say without any reservation though, that every supporter who managed to get their hands on a drink that day, deserved not only that one but many more to come.

We did all eventually make it to the ground, but the game itself never really got going and ended in a goalless draw. Unfortunately, it meant that Eddie's side just missed out on the League One title, but they had nonetheless emulated Harry Redknapp's team of 1987 in securing promotion to the second tier of English football.

The match also saw Steve Fletcher enter the field for the final time as a Cherries player, his appearance as a substitute being his 728th outing for the club. His dedication and contribution to AFC Bournemouth had been immense, and one of the first things Eddie did then was to make certain that Steve would continue to be a presence within the club by appointing him as one of his backroom staff.

CHAPTER 8
'TOGETHER, ANYTHING IS POSSIBLE'

It's 21 July 2013. Real Madrid need a venue for a friendly after their game in Israel is cancelled for security reasons. Enter Tom Mitchell, our Director of Football. By sheer luck or divine intervention, he is in the right place at the right time and snags AFC Bournemouth the opportunity of a lifetime: hosting the mighty Real Madrid. Who wouldn't want to welcome football royalty to their doorstep?

Normally you're talking fees and logistics, but everyone mobilises to scrape together whatever funds necessary to host arguably the world's most famous club at the Vitality Stadium. As fate decrees, this match marks Carlo Ancelotti's first game as Real Madrid's manager, with none other than Zinedine Zidane as his assistant. Having these legends in town is miracle enough, and that's before we get to their all-star roster of players.

The ticket sales are, as you might expect, practically instantaneous. We discover fans we never even knew existed queuing for a glimpse. When you have talents like Isco, Cristiano Ronaldo, Angel Di Maria, Casemiro, and Gonzalo Higuain on the pitch, it's like basketball's Harlem Globetrotters paying a visit. The excitement is off the charts.

The day begins with a surreal lunch at the Haven Hotel in Bournemouth, where I find myself seated next to the legendary Florentino Pérez. As players stop by, my inner child leaps with joy, and I feel those boyhood autograph-collecting jitters, especially while chatting with Zinedine Zidane and Carlo Ancelotti. Knees slightly shaking, standing alongside such giants of the sport, is nothing short of a dream.

We are at this time still a humble Championship side, long before Premier League feats, and rubbing shoulders with the elite of world football is unheard of. While resisting the urge to ask for autographs, we indulge in the honour of photographs and revel in the moment like starstruck fans.

The game itself turns into a blur of excitement, and though I recall very few highlights, the 6-0 scoreline is forever etched in my memory. But honestly, the result is irrelevant. We have just played Real Madrid! In my whimsical recounts over drinks, I've often suggested this wasn't just a friendly. No, I've spun it as a grand competition that saw AFC Bournemouth against the might of Real Madrid.

This, my friends, was fantasy football at its most fantastical – and what a glorious fantasy it was!

* * *

The 2013/14 season marked a pivotal moment in our incredible journey at AFC Bournemouth. It was the season when things truly began to take off, following Eddie Mitchell's sale of his shares to Maxim Demin.

Maxim came in with two clear goals: first, to invest in players and ensure the team's success on the pitch under Eddie Howe's outstanding leadership; second, to build a cutting-edge academy. To help him achieve the latter, new state-of-the-art training pitches were built at the rear of the stadium and subsequently he would go on to purchase the land previously occupied by a golf course, six miles down the road near Canford Magna.

Recognising the importance of scaling as we climbed the football pyramid, I wholeheartedly supported Maxim's vision. Homegrown talent is the lifeblood of clubs outside the top six and finding that rare gem can fund the club for years. As we moved higher, Eddie became deeply involved in player development, ensuring all teams played with a consistent style to allow for seamless transitions. This could only be achieved by gaining control from the Academy upwards.

Eddie and I spent countless hours discussing his passion for the training ground. For him, matches were the result of five days' work. I knew if it ever came to choosing between a new training ground or a new stadium, Eddie's choice would be clear. The intimate stadium atmosphere was more than enough to motivate our team on a matchday. But a world-class training ground for the future was an opportunity not to be missed. Eddie's world is centred on the training pitch with his staff and his players; that's where he is in his element. I also know he has always had total sympathy for those loyal fans unable to get a matchday ticket due to our limited capacity.

As I commenced my second spell as chairman, I embraced the chance to further elevate the club's brand. Initially, Steve Sly and I were focused on keeping the club afloat, but now with Maxim's support, I shifted towards enhancing our off-field presence, including media interactions, public relations and league meetings. With Maxim's backing and in partnership with our CEO Neill Blake, we created a sustainable growth structure.

The essence of my chairmanship was to elevate the club's status, firstly by making it a beloved second-favourite club for supporters worldwide. Internally, I focused on empowering our team, providing continuous support and recognising their achievements – a crucial intangible asset. Working alongside each other, Eddie Howe, Neill Blake, Maxim and I sculpted a football culture interwoven with the effective business operations necessary for ongoing success. One of our first tasks was to ensure that Eddie had all the assistance he required alongside him, and we invested heavily in support staff by employing a team of analysts, sports scientists and medical personnel.

The season began with a surreal pre-season trip to Switzerland for a friendly against FC Zurich, a far cry from the days when we couldn't afford a lunch there! Stephen Purches had a testimonial match against West Ham, and shortly afterwards a conversation led to organising a friendly with Real Madrid – another dream come true. Seeing the likes of Ronaldo, Kaká, Özil and Benzema at our ground was unforgettable, as was the sight of manager Carlo Ancelotti and coach Zinedine Zidane in the away dugout. We lost 6-0, but the significance was monumental, signalling our departure from Third Division status and attracting national attention.

During the summer a temporary stand had been built at the south end of the ground, and named after one of our own legends, Ted MacDougall, who flew over from Florida to perform the opening duties ahead of the game against Real Madrid. This stand provided around 2,000 additional seats and increased the stadium's capacity to 11,450.

After Eddie had added some experience to his playing squad by signing defenders Elliot Ward and former Irish international Ian Harte, Andrew Surman returned for a second loan spell at the club, but the biggest signing came shortly before the summer transfer window closed. Just as Eddie Mitchell's shares in the club finally transitioned to Maxim, the seven-figure fee that was paid to Malmo for 22-year-old South African striker Tokelo Rantie, comfortably broke the club's previous transfer record.

CHAMPIONSHIP CHALLENGES

Life back in the second tier after a gap of twenty-three years was never going to be easy though, and as chairman I faced my share of challenges just as the team did on the pitch. A tough 6-1 loss at Watford in our first away game was soon followed by a 5-1 defeat at Huddersfield before three wins in our next seven games saw us rise up the table.

One of the season's iconic moments for me came during a spectacular comeback at Millwall after we had been two goals down within the first ten minutes. Despite the early setbacks we continued to drive forward and attack at every opportunity, and in the end we ran out 5-2 winners and provided further proof of the special character Eddie had in the side.

In goal that day was Stephen Henderson who was on loan from West Ham, but his stay was to be brief as he suffered a dislocated shoulder in the following game. Soon afterwards, Ryan Allsop went down with glandular fever and Eddie turned to West Bromwich Albion keeper Lee Camp, who, on loan, brought with him welcome Championship experience.

With Charlie Daniels and Marc Pugh providing a constant threat down the left, and Simon Francis combining well with the trickery of Matt Ritchie on the right, the team was certainly beginning to find its feet again, and by Christmas a ten-point gap had opened up between us and the division's bottom three.

A series of impressive performances prompted Eddie to make Camp's deal permanent when the window opened in January but at the other end of the pitch, Rantie was finding goals hard to come by since his arrival in September. Instead, it was Lewis Grabban who became the first of our strikers to reach double figures for the season. Both players were on the scoresheet in our first success of 2014, a 2-1 home win against Huddersfield, with Grabban netting for the 11th time on his way to his season's final tally of 22.

In the FA Cup, a deluge of rain saw our Third-Round fixture against League Two Burton Albion postponed shortly before kick-off. With the Burton team and many of their supporters already inside the stadium, our fans spent the next few days generously raising £3,000 towards their travel costs – a testament to our community spirit and a thank you for the way they had supported us when we gained promotion there in 2010.

The match was replayed ten days later, and a 4-1 victory brought a Fourth-Round tie at home to Brendan Rodgers' Liverpool side. The game was selected for live TV coverage, and although the Reds won 2-0, our courage and willingness to try and play our way forward earned praise from the Red's manager afterwards.

The January transfer window also saw Eddie fight off competition from several other clubs to complete the permanent transfer of Adam Smith, after the England Under 21 full-back had enjoyed a second successful loan period with us. Another player to join us was Charlton striker Yann Kermorgant, who had also been on our radar for some time, and the arrival of both players promised impactful futures at the club.

Strong in the air and skilful on the ground, Kermorgant was soon to provide us with a fine example of his ability when he marked his full debut with a hat-trick in a 5-0 home win against Doncaster. This helped set us on our way to a five-game winning streak during March and April which coincided with the news that Howe and Jason Tindall had each signed two-year contract extensions to keep them with us until 2018.

Despite far bigger ambitions at the start of the season, I knew that avoiding relegation would have to be regarded as an achievement in itself, but not only was this comfortably achieved, a draw at Ipswich on the final day meant that we actually finished 10th, which was then our highest-ever finish at second tier level.

We still had much to learn at this level, but our success that season hinted that our rise was far from over. Eddie and Jason had assembled a group of players which backed this up and we had also achieved a level of stability off the pitch and in the boardroom. Reflecting afterwards alongside Eddie, Maxim, Neill, Nick Rothwell and Richard Hughes, who moved upstairs and became Head of Recruitment at the club, I considered that we had forged a thriving football culture and operations system, and we were delighted to have been able to merge on-field success with effective business management. In fact, it sparked a new club motto – 'Together, Anything is Possible.'

CHAPTER 9
'I LOVE THESE F***ING BOYS!'

We are scheduled to visit Leeds United at Elland Road. Leeds are currently under the stewardship of Massimo Cellino, an Italian with a few quirky superstitions. One of his first actions upon taking the reins is to eliminate anything purple from the stadium, as it's considered unlucky in his native Italy.

So I can't help myself. I turn up at Elland Road donning a bold purple V-neck sweater. Naturally, it catches Massimo's eye, and he makes a point of keeping his distance from me throughout the match. Unfortunately, my fashion choice doesn't bring us any luck on the pitch as we fall to a 1-0 defeat.

Afterwards, in a gesture of unexpected hospitality, Massimo insists on personally driving me back to my hotel near the city centre. 'What a gentleman,' I muse as I hop into his car. Little do I know, this courtesy ride is about to turn into a car adventure. Massimo zips through the streets of Leeds at speeds that would give a Formula One driver a run for their money. By the time we reach the hotel, my complexion has shifted from playful defiance to ghostly white. I swear we overtook Lewis Hamilton on the way!

* * *

I must firstly apologise for using the expletive above for the chapter title; however, by the time you have completed reading this chapter, I hope you will understand why I feel it is appropriate to do so.

When Eddie and Jason signed their contract extensions, it brought a new wave of confidence to the club and the supporters. We saw some changes to the playing squad over the summer, with Lewis Grabban leaving for Norwich for a club record fee and Richard Hughes retiring to join our backroom staff. But most notably, 22-year-old striker Callum Wilson joined us from Coventry City, along with midfielders Dan Gosling and Junior Stanislas from Newcastle

The Chairman

and Burnley respectively. Each one of them would prove to be a significant signing and their presence considerably bolstered our squad.

We also took the opportunity to invest in our facilities at Dean Court, laying new training pitches directly outside and installing a top-quality pitch inside the stadium itself. The work cost around £750,000 and it showed signs of a sound financial footing, something not every club at our level could manage.

We brought Andrew Surman back to the club on a permanent basis from Norwich, having had him previously on loan from Southampton, and another noteworthy signing was experienced, Polish international, goalkeeper Artur Boruc, whose arrival from Southampton helped to stabilise the defence.

The 2014/15 season began at Huddersfield, where we had suffered such heartbreak three years previously. This time, Marc Pugh scored in the first minute, Wilson grabbed a brace and together with another from Kermorgant we won 4-0. It was the best possible start we could have hoped for in what was to become the most amazing season the club had ever known.

But in true AFC Bournemouth style, nothing was going to be that straightforward from the outset and we could only add two more League victories from our next eight games. Boruc took over from Lee Camp in goal at the beginning of October, and from this point on, everything began to come together. Callum Wilson's impact proved considerable as our front line gained momentum.

We started scoring more freely, and our defence stopped making the costly errors that had plagued us previously. The highlight of this period was an 8-0 victory over Birmingham City on 25 October. That day we tore the opposition apart after a red card had reduced them to ten men. Pugh hit a hat-trick, the only one of his career, Boruc saved a penalty and Tokelo Rantie scored twice to the delight of our travelling fans, who were able to go on and enjoy a club record 8-0 victory.

It was a day when amazingly everything went right, and I have been asked many times since how it felt to be present at St Andrews. Well, the simple answer is that I wasn't there! I was on holiday in Miami but celebrated each goal by knocking back pina coladas like there was no tomorrow! When I returned home a few days later, I was reminded by my fellow directors that my presence at any future away games might be under review. In all honesty, of course I regret not being there, but I do have a lovely memory of celebrating our success while on the other side of the pond.

That dominant win felt like a landmark moment, and we were also enjoying a good run in the Carling Cup, where a 2-1 victory against Premier League West Bromwich Albion saw us into the quarter-finals and another cup-tie against Liverpool. They had just been knocked out of the Champions League when they came down to play us but unfortunately were in no mood to exit a second cup competition anytime soon. Two goals up inside the first half-hour, they grabbed a third later in the game before Gosling grabbed a consolation.

By then, Eddie had been named as manager of the month for November after a sixth consecutive Championship win at Sheffield Wednesday took us to the top of the table for the first time. The club was in a position that was both thrilling and uncharted territory for us and the cup defeat was soon forgotten a few days later when we registered another amazing 6-1 win against Blackpool at Bloomfield Road.

As 2014 came to an end, our unbeaten run had brought eleven wins and saw us sitting at the top of the table, one point ahead of second-placed Ipswich. We were all enjoying this incredible journey and I think could be forgiven for wondering just where it might eventually take us.

In addition, Callum Wilson had earned a call-up to the England Under 21 squad, and the club had hosted its fifth England international match in eight years when England's Under 20 team met Canada at the Goldsands Stadium. It all added to the testament of how far we had come as a club since being on the brink of financial collapse.

Heading into 2015, sad to say our long, unbeaten League run quickly came to an end. In fact, two defeats in the first three games were followed by an FA Cup exit at Aston Villa. Back-to-back wins against Watford and Wigan reinforced our position at the top before defeats at Brentford and Nottingham Forest set us back, but the 2-1 loss at the City Ground on 25 February would prove to be our last defeat of the season.

Middlesbrough had briefly taken over at the top but, in early March, we returned after three consecutive wins, which included a tremendous away performance against Fulham. This proved to be a hugely pivotal game and our 5-1 victory, which was broadcast live on Sky, showcased our attacking prowess and fast-paced play.

Matt Ritchie and Brett Pitman each scored twice and our other goal at Craven Cottage came after a brilliant finish by defender Steve Cook. We always knew that 'Cookie' was solid as a rock as a stopper in the heart of our defence, but he again proved that he was an adept finisher in the other penalty area as well. One of Brett's goals came after he had run half the length of the pitch with the ball, and I believe the team's performance that evening signalled that we weren't just contenders; we were serious about securing our place at the top.

A clinical 3-0 win over Middlesbrough reinforced our position with seven games remaining and as Easter approached, we moved quickly to sign

Kenwyne Jones on loan from Cardiff City to add a new dimension to our play. The presence of the six-foot-two-inch Trinidad and Tobago striker was part of Eddie's Plan B, a more direct approach, having recognised that teams were learning how to counter our usual style of playing out from the back.

It worked perfectly when Jones headed home in a 1-1 draw at Ipswich before Bank Holiday Monday brought a 4-2 home success against Birmingham. Further wins against Brighton and Reading followed but then a determined Sheffield Wednesday held up our promotion charge.

Their visit to the Goldsands Stadium in April is one I can still vividly recall, partly for an absolutely brilliant goal by Matt Ritchie but also for a controversial late penalty awarded to Wednesday. We had fallen a goal behind in the first half, but Yann Kermorgant had equalised after the break before defender Simon Francis received a red card. We were back on course five minutes later when an absolute screamer from Ritchie blasted into the back of the net. Promotion was now tantalisingly close but with everyone on the edge of their seat or hiding beneath it, Wednesday equalised after a strongly disputed penalty decision five minutes into added time. Let me put it this way: had VAR (Video Assistant Referee), dare I mention it, been in existence, it would not have given it.

'WE ARE PREMIER LEAGUE!'

Despite this setback, we knew that with Norwich and Middlesbrough also slipping up, securing promotion was within our grasp if we beat Bolton in our last home game. The build-up to the game was similar to that for a cup final, which in almost every way it was. The press continually asked about my emotions and whether I believed we could get over the line. Most of them had expected us to implode well before we reached this stage, but we had kept on going out and winning games. Fortunately, I am the type of person whose glass is usually overflowing, and I was honestly convinced we would not miss out now. This was a once in a lifetime chance for the players to create history. Why wouldn't they?

My pre-match routine was much the same as always, although I made sure I was wearing my lucky clothes and tie. Rose and I took a taxi to the ground as I thought there was a chance I might require an intake of alcohol! Everything about the game was to prove unforgettable of course.

It was hard to believe that the club had journeyed this far from financial distress to the point of entering the Premier League. The atmosphere inside and outside the stadium was electric, so powerful that you could not sense anything other than that history was about to be made. I was immediately drawn in and any negative thoughts I may have had were eliminated by the strength of desire and determination on display from the manager to the players and the supporters.

When the game itself began, with nothing to play for themselves, Bolton were simply swept aside. Their goalkeeper produced a series of fine saves early on, but when Ritchie burst down the right six minutes before half-time and clipped over a cross for Pugh, he was never going to make a mistake with his left foot. Then, a minute before the break, Wilson sprinted clear and the move was completed by Ritchie, who gloriously struck the ball home on the half-volley.

As I made my way back into the boardroom at half-time, I was obviously elated after the events I had just witnessed. But, with visiting directors and guests inside, I made sure that I did not lose sight of my surroundings, and managed to remain composed and respectful towards my guests.

After the interval, as Kermorgant blazed a penalty over the bar, when scoring could have made the game safe, I felt a sense of familiarity. It was no slight on the Frenchman, but taking the easy route had never been the AFC Bournemouth way! However, when Wilson scored a third in the 78th minute the match was effectively over and it provided the cue for an outpouring of emotion, the like of which neither I nor the club had never experienced before.

'We are Premier League' sang our supporters at the top of their voices as tears of joy welled up in my eyes. Fortunately, the team at least managed to keep their emotions in check and see out the final minutes of the game before the celebrations rose to a crescendo at the final whistle. I don't believe anyone present could have imagined they would ever see such a moment at Dean Court. Supporters screamed in jubilation as they swarmed onto the pitch and carried many of the players shoulder high across the turf and towards the tunnel. Just six years after almost being relegated from the Football League, we had made it to English football's holy grail.

After accepting the congratulations of those around me, I set off at pace downstairs to the dressing room. By this time the players had managed to battle their way inside and Sky Sports were given permission to continue filming inside. Their floor manager burst in and told the lads that while they were recording they could pretty much do anything; but they should not swear on live television.

As you can imagine, I bounced in with my clothing and hair dishevelled from all the celebrations I had encountered along the way and promptly made my way to celebrate with the team. 'I love these f***ing boys!' I screamed for all and sundry to hear as I dashed towards them, looking rather like some sort of crazed professor. Aware of the fact that I had directly disobeyed the instruction they had just received, they decided to punish me by throwing me up in the air several times before giving me a damn good spanking while we were still live on Sky! Of course, I had received my share of spankings while at school, but I have to say I don't think I ever enjoyed one as much as this!

> **Jeff deserves huge credit**, together with Eddie Howe and the rest of the backroom staff, for what they did over the years. They created such a hardworking, selfless squad and gave us the platform to be able to make history for what was such a small club at the time. It truly does show that 'Together, Anything is Possible!'
>
> **CALLUM WILSON #THECHAIRMAN**

IN THEIR OWN WORDS ON JEFF

Callum Wilson
Former AFC Bournemouth Player

Well, Jeff Mostyn, where should I start really? What a human being!

From the moment I first arrived at AFC Bournemouth, Jeff's enthusiasm and energy was at the forefront of our relationship. Full of energy, he had so much passion for the town and the club that I felt as though I was joining a family.

Later, when I heard that Jeff and his beautiful family had saved the club over the years, I wasn't surprised at all as I knew, from the moment I met him, that AFC Bournemouth was his heart and soul.

When he adopted AFC Bournemouth by investing his own finances into the club, he did it out of the goodness of his heart. This, together with his armed forces commitments and work for numerous charities, mean that he affects so many people's lives for the better.

My football journey has never been straightforward, but AFC Bournemouth has had a huge part to play in my career, and without Jeff doing what he did, when he did, it would not have happened. Had he not helped the club progress to new levels, there might not have been an AFC Bournemouth, and I might not have ever got the opportunity to play in the Championship while he was chairman, then become a Premier League player and go on to make my full international debut. All it of may never have happened if Jeff Mostyn hadn't been a piece of my puzzle. Therefore, I'm forever grateful that people like Jeff exist.

Throughout my time with the Cherries, Jeff was known for his speeches. During any big occasion or event, he would always get up on the microphone and take to the stage to thank everybody, often, after a few drinks, outstaying his welcome up there while dropping the F-bomb numerous times! He would have the whole room crying with laughter while Rosie shook her head with a smile of disbelief. You did sometimes dread what he might come out with!

Of course there was one occasion that will always stand out. We had beaten Bolton Wanderers and got promoted to the Premier League, and after a pitch invasion and lots of celebrating, Jeff came

> into the dressing room. He was jumping up and down in front of the Sky cameras while dropping his famous F-bomb before he was picked up to receive a spanking live on television! It's something that will live long in my memory.
>
> If there's one thing I've learned from him over the years, it's to have a smile on your face at all times and spread positive energy in the room. It's something that he always has which is very infectious.
>
> He deserves huge credit, together with Eddie Howe and the rest of the backroom staff, for what they did over the years. They created such a hardworking, selfless squad and gave us the platform to be able to make history for what was such a small club at the time. It truly does show that 'Together, Anything is Possible!'
>
> Or in Jeff's own words… 'I love these f***ing boys!'

After we had celebrated in the dressing room, Eddie, Jason, the players and staff emerged through a haze of champagne to celebrate with the supporters on the pitch, many being carried shoulder-high across the turf. I took great delight in joining them and it was at this point Ryan Fraser placed on my head a sombrero hat with the word 'PREMIER' emblazoned across the front of it. Captured by the press, this became another image that was symbolic of what we had just achieved, and I made sure that I held on to that hat for as long as possible.

As you can imagine, the celebrations went on well into the night and no doubt the following morning too. When I arrived at the ground early the next day it seemed we had all become stars overnight. BBC, ITV and Sky camera crews had set up camp outside and multiple microphones were thrust in my face as I was asked for my reaction to our success as I walked from the car. I could only reiterate what I had said the previous evening, explaining that our success had produced unbelievable pride and joy not just for the club and its supporters but for the town.

My favourite quote of the night: 'If Hans Christian Andersen were to write a fairy story about football, it would have been AFC Bournemouth winning promotion to the Premier League!'

However, there was still one game to play and in the days that followed Eddie was certainly not going to allow the players to over-celebrate promotion when there was still a chance that we could become Football League champions. We were a point behind leaders Watford and if we could win at

Charlton, and Watford slipped up against Sheffield Wednesday at Vicarage Road, we would win the League.

I was late getting into the boardroom before the game at The Valley because I spent so long celebrating with our supporters outside. People who had supported the club all their lives were still shedding tears of joy and disbelief. I felt incredibly honoured by their welcome, as I still considered myself to be a relative newcomer and shed tears myself. It was another truly wonderful moment.

Whatever the outcome, the day was all about pride, and Rose and I were determined to ensure that our visit to The Valley would be embraced as a celebration off the pitch. But this amazing season still had one last twist in the tail. A goal from Harry Arter sandwiched between two from Matt Ritchie, meant that we were soon heading to a comfortable 3-0 win. Watford were a goal up and as both games went into stoppage time, the Hornets looked like they were taking the crown, but at least we had ended on a positive note on a beautiful sunny afternoon.

At that point, a tremendous roar from our supporters greeted news from Watford that Atdhe Nuhiu had snatched a stoppage-time equaliser for Sheffield Wednesday. It meant we were top of the League! Nuhiu had been the player who was allegedly brought down by Adam Smith in the passage of play that led to Wednesday's penalty and late equaliser against us the previous week, so perhaps this was some form of pre-VAR karma! The news was soon relayed to our players as with no further goals in either game, at the final whistle, AFC Bournemouth were Football League champions.

Fortunately, the Football League had the Championship trophy, medals and more champagne on hand, and before the game, the chairman of the EFL had asked me if I would like the honour of taking the trophy out on to the pitch. After another massive outpouring of emotion, I had made my way from the stand down to our dressing room and, soon afterwards, across the pitch. Along the way, I couldn't help thinking about the first time I made my way onto a pitch as chairman of the club back in 2007 and tried to take in the enormity of the journey that we had all undertaken to reach this point.

With the great support of everyone at Charlton Athletic, the after-match presentation took place in front of our large band of travelling supporters. I carried the trophy across from the side of the pitch and took the opportunity to lift it in front of them before placing it on its plinth in readiness for the official presentation.

It was another special moment for us all and yet another came when our captain Tommy Elphick received the trophy. The champagne corks popped, ticker tape flew into the air and the fireworks exploded. At this point, I took a position to the side of the stage because this moment was about Eddie, Jason, the players and the staff. Mind you, I did so while holding a large bottle of champagne in readiness to strike back at a moment's notice!

When I finally went back into the stadium, Rose and I excused ourselves from the boardroom, where space was limited, in order that we could celebrate further with our guests who were accommodated in a separate lounge. These were more of the people who had made all this possible and I was again grateful to Charlton's directors for enabling us to spend the rest of the afternoon together.

The celebrations continued of course in the days that followed and culminated in an open-top bus parade which saw around 80,000 supporters fill the town centre and promenade to pay tribute to Eddie and the players. I didn't realise we had that many supporters and had to wonder where some of them had been when we were in League Two, but I was delighted to see them nonetheless! Eddie was named as the League Managers Association manager of the year, Championship manager of the year and manager of the decade. If he had ridden a horse in the Grand National or sung in the Eurovision Song Contest, he would probably have won those as well!

CHAPTER 10
FROM CATCH OF THE DAY TO MATCH OF THE DAY

June 2015 marks my baptism by fire into the world of the Premier League Annual General Meeting (AGM). It's my first meeting, and the nerves are palpable. Anticipation has me more jittery than a goalkeeper on penalty duty. The prospect of presenting myself before English football's hierarchy is daunting, to say the least.

Arriving at the exquisite Rudding Park Hotel in Harrogate, I am ushered to my room. Trying to shake off the nerves, I recall Richard Scudamore's advice to come early and ease into the setting. Naturally, I made a beeline for the bar. Now, let's just say that the Sauvignon Blanc and I become fast friends, and by the time I am about to order my third glass, in walks none other than Sir John Chippendale Keswick, better known as Sir Chips, chairman of Arsenal.

My heart skips a beat as reality sets in. Sir Chips, I think! Really? Why not some lesser-known delegate to kick off my introduction to this world? But here he is, greeting me with a hearty, 'Hello, old boy, how are you?'

Summoning all my composure, I manage to respond, 'Oh, I'm fine, Sir Chips. Jeff Mostyn here, proud chairman of AFC Bournemouth.'

'Jolly good, old boy,' he replies. 'Come and join me for a glass.' Off we saunter down to the bar, and I join him for yet another Sauvignon Blanc, trying hard not to disclose it's my third.

Amid the drinks, Sir Chips casually asks how I arrived. 'I flew down, Sir Chips,' I say innocently.

'Absolutely right.' He nods knowingly. 'You're part of the Premier League now. You must have your own aircraft.'

Suppressing a laugh, I explain, 'No, Sir Chips, I flew Flybe this time.' He chuckles, but that slight misunderstanding tickles me immensely.

Retiring to my room shortly after our conversation, I call Neill Blake, our CEO,

Jeff Mostyn

brimming with amusement. 'Neill,' I declare, 'we've truly arrived. Sir Chips thinks I've got my own aircraft and believes I'm worthy of a seat at the Premier League table!'

* * *

I found myself living the dream as we entered the Premier League with a whopping £80 million budget. Of course, we quickly realised we needed to spend £10 million before a ball was kicked, just to meet the Premier League's membership requirement for mandatory ground improvements. It wasn't long before I was sticking my neck out during the Premier League Induction Course. That's when Richard Scudamore casually mentioned, 'Oh, and the final thing is the undersoil heating.' I just couldn't believe it. I raised my hand, and Richard acknowledged me, 'Yes, Jeff?'

With all the politeness I could muster, I questioned, 'Are you serious about the undersoil heating? You do know where we are? Bournemouth has its own microclimate, and we really don't need it.'

Richard's reply was succinct and to the point: 'Thank you for your question, Jeff. So, the final point is you will need to install undersoil heating!'

We had a brand-new training pavilion constructed behind the southeast corner of the stadium and all the club's medical staff were relocated nearby to free up space in the main stand area for other needs. Maxim made it clear from the start that we weren't in the Premier League just to fill in numbers. He wanted us to compete, which meant investing a substantial part of our budget into strengthening the team, hoping to extend our stay in the League for as long as possible.

Maxim prioritised player investments, and we were determined to try and ensure our Premier League success. Premier League maintenance was costly, and staying competitive was our top priority. Often, during a presentation, I joke about stadium seats never scoring a goal – players do. But that emphasis on players is why we prioritised investing in them over building a new stadium.

It meant that, as well as accommodating a new media suite in the main stand, a series of interview rooms had to be constructed directly off the main tunnel. We also faced the challenge of moving media seats back to the main stand due to League regulations – a change our season ticket holders were not too thrilled about. The pitch had undergone significant treatment, yet we still had to dig it up for the mandatory undersoil heating. And so, with a list in hand, we spent the summer working tirelessly to ensure we met every Premier League requirement, even the smallest details like the number of cubicles in the dressing room toilets.

"

Jeff and his enthusiasm helping you unlock potential is a privilege. What really comes to mind is fun, energising, human and quite simply a gift to the spirit.

RICHARD SCUDAMORE CBE #THECHAIRMAN

IN THEIR OWN WORDS ON JEFF

Richard Scudamore CBE
Former CEO of the English Premier League

I defy anybody not to remember the first time they met Jeff Mostyn: the cheeky smile, the warmth, the 'I think I have known you forever' approach. For me it was no different. Although I cannot precisely date it (somewhere around the spring of 2015), I recall it vividly.

Jeff had been asked to be part of a delegation (a posse more like) of EFL directors and senior club personnel sent to secure a better solidarity payments deal with the Premier League. Prior to the official meeting we had all met in the coffee area downstairs at Premier League HQ, deliberately located to break ice and where most of the meaningful work was done. The group moved up to my office and an impassioned plea from Sean Harvey (the EFL Chief Executive at the time) was followed by the 'Enforcer' Jeff closing the deal. I smiled, thanked them for their time and assured them that their proposal had no chance of adoption. Undeterred, Jeff tried again, and we continued our exchange. It was then that our friendship started, thus proving that life would be a whole lot better if people with opposite views could express them clearly and remain, or in this case become, friends.

This was Jeff – committed, impassioned, commercial, fighting for what he believed to be right but, when the dust settled, still the same charming, affable chap.

At the end of that 2014/15 season, AFC Bournemouth were promoted to the Premier League and so began the most engaging period between us. There are some strict ground criteria for Premier League clubs, so a visit to the south coast was needed to check out the 'Vitality'. Jeff showed us around and tried to convince me that there was no need for undersoil heating as Bournemouth benefitted from a 'micro-climate'! What a salesman. I thought I had heard them all, but this was new! It cut no ice with us and so the pitch had to be torn up and the heating installed. We laugh about that moment to this day; again, the tension brings you closer.

To see Jeff mixing it at the Premier League AGM and conference in June 2015 was something to behold! Immaculate as always, looking like this was where he belonged. Working the room, laughing and sharing stories with everyone. Then the 'serious' business started. All twenty clubs sit around a hexagonal layout and are seated alphabetically; therefore, Bournemouth should have been placed between Aston Villa and Chelsea. But not Jeff. He insisted that the club's actual name was AFC Bournemouth, so place names were moved, and he took his seat as the first club – ahead of Arsenal and right next to the Premier League Board representatives.

How proud he was, but we got the last laugh. The sensitive topic of Short-Term Cost Control (limits to player wage bills) was discussed, and I suggested that we should seek individual club views on this complex matter... starting with the first club around the table: AFC Bournemouth. Jeff gave me the look, smiled and blurted something out about 'not having any experience, it was difficult to analyse, but that the club would embrace it as they wanted to do something'. In that first intervention he showed all that is best about him: some humility, realism, solidarity and practicality. His reputation was sealed, the Premier League room enhanced by his presence.

And so, to the first home game of that 2015/16 season. Aston Villa were the opponents and the excitement was palpable. Jeff was bouncing, but it was the first time I had ever met his wonderful wife Rosie. You could instantly tell (and I have never stopped pointing out since) that his good fortune was not confined to business. A Gestede header on 72 minutes sealed the points for Aston Villa and Jeff was gracious in defeat. Over the next five seasons I visited many times and took on several roles during the match. These included Jeff's blood pressure monitor and referee assessor (instant critical feedback) to name but two. Jeff's passion never dimmed though, and the match was watched as a constant stream of fans walked by, Jeff finding a kind word or a gesture for all of them. I so admired the capacity he had for making others feel good about themselves.

Jeff took no time in settling into Premier League business, and the clubs elected him to represent them on the FA Council and FA Cup committee. For reasons I still fail to understand he absolutely loved it, thrived at being so involved and gave everything he could. He was dependable, reliable and, along with Peter McCormick, the

Premier League's long-serving Legal Counsel, did much to maintain excellent working relations between the two 'branches' of the FA: the National and Professional game.

But of course, there is much more to Jeff than blazers and badges. He doesn't dip his toe, he dives right in. Just like the fantastic work he has done with the armed services, his business career helping servicemen, leading to a personal commitment to service personnel in need. It is no surprise that so many charities have sought his help and engagement. What an ambassador to have on your side. No surprise also that the AFC Bournemouth Foundation grew from an acorn to a huge oak tree under his chairmanship, engaging with and helping young people in particular, using the power and influence of the football club to change people's lives for the better.

To know Jeff is to feel better; to have Jeff in your corner is a comfort; to have Jeff and his enthusiasm helping you unlock potential is a privilege. Impossible to sum up with one word; it would be inadequate. No, I don't mean that would be the word! What really comes to mind is fun, energising, human and quite simply a gift to the spirit.

A NEW FOOTBALL HOME

In July 2015, AFC Bournemouth's home experienced another transformative milestone with the announcement of a new naming rights agreement, ushering in the era of the Vitality Stadium. This significant change marked another step forward for the club, underscoring our growing presence and ambition within the football community. It was not merely a rebranding effort but a reflection of the club's evolution and the strengthening of its commercial partnerships. Vitality, a brand synonymous with health and wellness, aligned perfectly with the club's ethos and commitment to excellence both on and off the pitch.

Securing such a partnership was a testament to our progress and appeal in the Premier League, highlighting our determination to forge strong, meaningful alliances that resonated with our values and aspirations. The rebranded Vitality Stadium symbolised more than just a change in signage, it represented the vitality and dynamism of our journey, capturing the spirit of AFC Bournemouth's continuous rise and ambition.

To this day, our partnership with Vitality has significantly elevated the club's commercial status, thanks to its global respect and core values focused on community health. On a personal note, I value my relationship with chief executive Neville Koopowitz as much as any commercial agreement. Our core values have been perfectly aligned, and the mutual respect we have for each other has grown year after year.

As we stepped into this new chapter, the Vitality Stadium became a proud emblem of our identity, energising both players and supporters, and setting the stage for more memorable performances and experiences to come.

Another special moment for me was at the AGM Gala Dinner in Harrogate, in the presence of all twenty clubs, when Peter McCormick OBE awarded the club its Premier League Share Certificate, upon joining the competition for the first time in the club's history. I was incredibly proud of this moment and what it symbolised for our club's resilience and achievement.

Everyone in football values Jeff for his commitment, character, determination and sense of fun. Long may he continue!

PETER MCCORMICK OBE #THECHAIRMAN

IN THEIR OWN WORDS ON JEFF

Peter McCormick OBE
Former Chairman of the Football Association and Premier League

No one can forget their first meeting with Jeff Mostyn, and I am no exception!

It was over sixteen years ago that I attended a dinner sponsored by a lawyer colleague with whom I work closely, and it was taking place on the middle night of a football conference in London.

I arrived at a well-known Chinese restaurant in Knightsbridge, The Good Earth, and as I entered, I saw a dapper man holding court, surrounded by executives from the world of football. I was introduced and was struck immediately, not only by his charismatic personality and popularity but because he really knew his football! I was there in my capacity as chairman of the Legal Advisory Group of the Premier League and senior partner of a law firm doing the legal work for the Premier League and advising clubs and individuals in the sport – so we had plenty to talk about!

That evening AFC Bournemouth was nowhere near the Premier League and had been going through particularly difficult financial times. It was clear that Jeff had an undying passion for his club and for the game of football. Indeed, during those difficult days at Bournemouth, he was to be seen in the car park before matches, collecting money in a bucket to help keep the club afloat. Commitment and determination came with capital letters.

Over the years that followed, Jeff, as chairman, pushed the club onwards and, having found a benevolent owner who was prepared to back his ambitions, the Cherries were promoted to the Premier League. By this time, I had become more heavily involved there, serving as chairman in 2014/15 and then remaining as an executive, chairing the Football Board and continuing to chair the Legal Advisory Group. I was also appointed to represent the Premier League on the FA Board and the FA Council.

I served for my full term of nine years on the FA Board, and I continue to serve on the FA Council. Contact with Jeff became ever more frequent as I would be chairing or attending shareholder meetings of the League and Jeff would be the first name on the attendance list, benefiting from the fact that the initials AFC came before the name of the club and that put him immediately next to the top table at our meetings! As a result, we have come to know each other and our families extremely well.

Jeff loves his football, and during his time at AFC Bournemouth he was truly committed to the cause. His devotion, however, is as a family man and it has been a joy to see him with his beloved Rosie and to witness the love and affection that they hold and display for each other. For example, an away game at Norwich City would not be a journey from and to Bournemouth in the day. Unlike most football club executives, Jeff would make a weekend of it, arranging to stay in a lovely hotel in the centre of Norwich and treating Rosie to some sightseeing, food and wine, and time off. Then, as the pre-match lunch with Delia Smith and her husband, Michael Wynn-Jones, took place, he would revert to the 'football nut' but always in a gentlemanly and well-mannered fashion. Jeff remains a popular visitor at any ground at which he attends a match.

He volunteered to serve on the FA Council. The Premier League Rules specify a process for joining the FA Council. Six members are elected by the twenty Premier League clubs and the Board nominates the other two representatives. As soon as AFC Bournemouth were promoted back to the Premier League, Jeff, public-spirited as ever, stood for election and it was not a surprise to find that he returned the largest number of votes! He served on the FA Council and on sub-committees, such as the FA Challenge Cup Committee, with enthusiasm and distinction. His enthusiasm became infectious at Council meetings, which is a substantial tribute to his ability to make an impression because there would be 128 people in the room for such meetings!

Eventually, and very unfortunately, old Father Time caught up with Jeff and at a time when AFC Bournemouth was temporarily back in the Championship, despite an overwhelming vote in favour of him continuing to serve on the council, the age limit prevented him from doing so. His energetic and youthful approach to life would have meant that, without such a rule, he would have been able to stay on for many more years! I was delighted to be the chairman of the

> FA at the time his term of office came to an end, and we were able to obtain the approval of the FA Board for Jeff to join the Fellowship of the FA. He attends every major fixture at Wembley and is always given a friendly welcome by everyone involved.
>
> Everyone in football values Jeff for his commitment, character, determination and sense of fun. Long may he continue!

A GLOBAL SPOTLIGHT

AFC Bournemouth was suddenly very much in the spotlight, and I was thrilled when American broadcasting giants NBC approached us for permission to make a documentary about our rise to the Premier League. Their team was led by broadcaster, podcaster and filmmaker Roger Bennett, who I had met previously on a visit to America. Roger founded the Men In Blazers Media Network and I knew that his weekly programme, featuring all kinds of footballing passions had generated a cult following across the pond.

The Americans love an underdog and a rags-to-riches story, as do I, and ours was certainly one of those! The documentary was to be entitled *AFC Bournemouth – 'Together, Anything is Possible'* and we were delighted to give Roger and his team all the access they needed. In addition to myself, among the other people interviewed were our club 'legend' (his words) Steve Fletcher, manager Eddie Howe and our club secretary Neil Vacher. When it came to my turn to speak, I'm afraid my emotions got the better of me, and when Roger brought up the 'Gerald Krasner' moment and my nod of agreement I simply burst into tears.

After a glass of water, I was able to finish the interview but, embarrassed at having been unable to control my emotions, was relieved when Roger said afterwards that this piece would be edited out when he returned to New York. Imagine my surprise then to find this footage slap bang in the middle of the documentary when it was released. I contacted Roger to ask him what had happened, and he told me that his editor had insisted that this piece should remain in. Apparently, the editor's comment was, 'If Steven Spielberg was directing this, he could not have found an actor who could have better represented the emotion at the central core of this whole story,' so it stayed in.

Roger also asked me to explain the differences between the pyramid system used to govern football in this country and a franchise system such as the one used by the Major League Soccer (MLS). I explained simply that one major difference is that the pyramid system allows promotion and relegation while the franchise system does not. It's true to say that no matter how much money you might invest in a football club operating in the pyramid system, the club could still be relegated the following year, and you could be left regretting that you ever got involved. But on the other hand, without the pyramid system, how could clubs like 'Little Old Bournemouth' ever have an opportunity to rub shoulders with the likes of Arsenal, Chelsea, Liverpool, Manchester United, etc. That has to be better than a franchise system which would effectively take away such an opportunity.

Funnily enough, Roger asked me the same question when I went over to America to appear on his *Men In Blazers* programme the following year. This time I responded, with my tongue firmly in my cheek, in favour of a change in this country from the pyramid to the franchise system. Roger reminded me of what I had said twelve months earlier and then accused me of wanting to change 150 years of history to stop anyone else achieving what we had! I took a bit of stick about that at the time, but it was all meant in good fun.

Anyway, to return to our story, it was incredible to see AFC Bournemouth's name achieving global recognition. This publicity really pushed the profile of the club and the town onto the world stage.

I can recall feeling both pride and apprehension when I attended my first Premier League shareholders' meeting during the summer. I was desperate to make a good impression on behalf of the club as I walked into the auditorium. The tables appeared to be laid out in a chivalric order reminiscent of the Knights of the Round Table, so I quickly ingratiated myself with those people I already knew. Meanwhile, I could see some of those who had not previously met me looking at me somewhat quizzically, as they might without going quite so far as to check the bottom of my shoes!

Nonetheless, my tactile nature made sure that everyone received a hug as I made my way around the room before taking my seat at the appropriate table. The tables were apparently laid out in alphabetical order, and I felt it only right to remind the Executive that our club's official name was *AFC Bournemouth*, rather than simply Bournemouth. As a result, I was proudly seated on the first table next to the Executive. However, I soon discovered that this was a double-edged sword as it meant that whenever a matter was opened up for discussion, my opinion would be the one that came first! I was very careful in my responses at first but by the time we came to the final round, I had become more confident, and it was wonderful to hear many of the other representatives simply saying, 'I agree with Jeff.'

Following our promotion to the Premier League, I had an interest in forming a collaboration with an MLS Club to help raise our profile in the United States. Tom Glick, chief commercial officer of Manchester City, very kindly called Don Garber, the Commissioner of the MLS, while in his office in Manchester. Don very kindly agreed to see me in New York and introduce me to a number of MLS clubs who he believed had synergy with AFC Bournemouth.

During the meeting with Don in his office on Fifth Avenue in New York, I explained I had not come to try and sell 50,000 AFC Bournemouth shirts on Fifth Avenue (although, who knows, one day we might!).

I was hoping to identify clubs in America of a similar mind and status to ourselves, who we could work with to develop the best practices in medical science, sports science and recruitment. I hoped he might help me find such a club with whom we could exchange technical data as I believed we could offer the best practical advice on the game while the United States could offer the best medical and technical services. One of the clubs Don introduced me to was Philadelphia Union, and following my meeting with Don, I arranged to meet with the president of the club, Nick Sakiewicz, and we developed a strong relationship which ultimately led to a pre-season tour.

Before we returned to Bournemouth, I was delighted that we were able to reach an agreement of mutual support with Philadelphia Union, which was provisionally signed at a friendly match at the Union Stadium. To add to the spectacle, Nick Sakiewicz and I were even persuaded to parade our national flags around the pitch as a show of unity prior to the game.

Meanwhile, Eddie knew that he had Maxim's support to fund a competitive side, but typically, he would remain as loyal as possible to the players that had earned the club promotion. Despite this, one of our much-loved players, Brett Pitman, left before he could make a Premier League appearance, despite having played for us in every division of the Football League.

New arrivals included Joshua King, who signed from Blackburn Rovers to replace Brett, while Max Gradel returned from France to rejoin us. Goalkeeper Artur Boruc signed a permanent deal, and the experienced former Everton defender Sylvan Distin helped to bolster the centre of defence. Twenty-two-year-old Tyrone Mings joined us from Ipswich for another club record fee and Glenn Murray, someone Eddie had pursued for a long time, finally joined us soon after the season began. Eddie saw potential in him as a link to our style of play, though in reality, he became more of an alternative option.

A STARRING ROLE ON MATCH OF THE DAY

Our first Premier League season began with our game leading the BBC TV *Match of the Day* line-up. This wasn't merely remarkable; it felt unbelievable and was a huge milestone. As the first game broadcast of the new season, it wasn't just a continuation of our journey, more a defining moment where the reality of reaching the grandest stage truly hit. It was no longer a local endeavour; it was a recognition of all the hard work, commitment and dreams that had propelled us forward.

Making an appearance on *Match of the* Day felt monumental. It signified that we had truly arrived in the Premier League, an acknowledgement that transcended playing football. It was about stepping into the global spotlight, watched by audiences all over the world.

Additionally, being invited to the Premier League pre-season show was a remarkable affirmation of our journey. Typically, newly promoted clubs might not get much spotlight, but here we were, taking our place at the season launch. To occupy that space was an incredible experience, a powerful declaration that AFC Bournemouth was no longer just a rising team but a proud fixture in the Premier League tapestry. It was an experience that underscored our arrival and participation at the highest levels of the game, proving that hard work and determination really do pay off.

Each week, appearing on *Match of the Day* provided an opportunity to share our story with the world. It was a platform to build the AFC Bournemouth brand across continents, showcasing the heart, spirit and resilience of our club. This level of global exposure was beyond anything we had imagined when we started out.

Not only did it allow us to connect with football fans around the world, but it helped us grow as an organisation. It was a chance to show that we belonged, to depict our journey, and to foster pride among our supporters. Week after week, being part of *Match of the Day* bolstered our resolve to continue dreaming of bigger things. It gave us a platform to reach out and impact a broader audience, telling our story and inviting others to join us on our journey.

I vividly remember the first time BBC's Saturday lunchtime programme *Football Focus* was broadcast live from the stadium. It was there that I had my initial interview with the brilliant broadcaster, and now my dear friend, Mark Clemmit. The air was alive with buzz, fanfare and celebrations following our promotion.

Our Premier League debut was a home fixture against Aston Villa, a match that ended in a 1-0 loss, which was a reminder, as if we needed it, of the huge task ahead. It was followed by another 1-0 defeat at Liverpool, although this was a game in which we put in a great performance and were unlucky enough to have an early goal by Tommy Elphick disallowed.

However, we claimed victory in our third game with a 4-3 win at West Ham, where Callum Wilson celebrated his and the club's first Premier League hat-trick, and Marc Pugh achieved another club milestone by netting in all four League divisions. Recalling my mention of Marc earlier in the book, his £100,000 signing was undeniably a bargain, and his commitment to the club filled me with pride.

Our first Premier League win on home soil came in mid-September when goals from Wilson and Matt Ritchie brought us a 2-0 success but the month concluded on a sombre note when we lost at Stoke and, more significantly, lost our dedicated club photographer Mick Cunningham. He had been a lifetime supporter, not to mention a one-man media team at the club since the mid-80s. Sadly, Mick fell ill while working pitch side and passed away at just 55 years of age. It was a huge loss as he had given so much to the club and was an integral part of its fabric.

In the same game, Callum Wilson suffered an anterior cruciate ligament (ACL) injury and joined Max Gradel and Tyrone Mings who had also been sidelined with similar injuries. These were cruel blows and the team's resolve was severely tested. We suffered heavy defeats to Manchester City and Tottenham, lost to Southampton, and faced another loss at Newcastle, yet the team found a way to rally. We managed to pick up points, securing draws at Swansea and against Everton.

A pivotal moment came with our victory against reigning Premier League champions Chelsea at the beginning of December. Glenn Murray's 82nd-minute goal sealed our win, giving everyone a well-deserved morale boost. Just a week later, we faced Manchester United at home, and after a thrilling match, won 2-1 thanks to goals from Junior Stanislas and Joshua King, providing an unforgettable back-to-back victory experience.

By the year's end, we had lost just one of our previous seven games and shown we could hold our own at the top level. We had surprised many, made mistakes, and learned from them. To strengthen the squad during the January transfer window, a period that was always likely to significantly influence our season's trajectory, Eddie made two significant additions to his striking options. Lewis Grabban re-joined us from Norwich, and former Arsenal and England Under-21 striker Benik Afobe signed from Wolves on a four-and-a-half-year contract.

A point against surprise League-leaders Leicester City once again epitomised the character and collective spirit at Howe's disposal. Down to ten men, the team's overall display at the King Power Stadium made for an encouraging start to the second half of the season.

Ahile Afobe scored his first Bournemouth goal in our home success against Norwich, the game also marked the final Cherries appearance of striker Yann Kermorgant, who moved to Championship side Reading a few days later. Yann's ability both in the air and on the ground had been a key part of our promotion success the previous season, and his great personality, hard work and commitment had made him a firm favourite among our supporters. While he remained a threat to opposing defences in the Premier League, he had found the increased demand for speed and intensity at this level slightly more difficult and as a result he could no longer be guaranteed a regular first team place.

We continued to pick up points during February, yet the anxiety about our position never left me, as budgeting was always a delicate balancing act for a club like Bournemouth. Just four points above the relegation zone and looking over our shoulders once again at one stage, we had already prepared separate financial projections for the following season. To do so was essential given our position and the massive difference in income available as a Premier League club compared to one in the Championship.

Despite being favourites with the bookies to go down, the team, in Eddie's hands, continued to defy expectations and by the end of March, a first League success against local rivals Southampton in almost fifty years had been followed by another three points at Newcastle. This enabled us to open a nine-point gap between ourselves and the relegation places.

A third successive win came the following Saturday, and during the 3-2 success at home to Swansea we saw a wonderful example of the human side of the game. It came when Max Gradel ran over to celebrate emotionally with Eddie after scoring his first goal since returning from his early season injury. Callum Wilson was another player to make a successful return from injury before the season ended as we safely went past the forty-point mark ahead of a difficult April which brought defeats against Liverpool, Chelsea and Everton.

By then, we were safe, but our final game against Manchester United at Old Trafford was not without controversy. With most of the crowd already inside the stadium, the match was postponed shortly before kick-off due to a bomb hoax. Later it became clear that a dummy device had been left in one of the stands following a training exercise earlier in the week. As you can imagine, the United officials I met in the boardroom were obviously very embarrassed when it was discovered what had happened. However, it was sad that this unwelcome administrative howler ultimately hit us and, more significantly, our supporters in the pocket.

Manchester United were of course within their rights not to provide our supporters with refunds under the conditions of sale specified on their match tickets, but some recompense in view of their travelling costs would have been a nice gesture. Instead, the supporters were left with no choice other than to make their way up to Manchester again the following Wednesday if they wanted to make use of their match tickets. United deservedly won 3-1.

When the dust had settled though, I was elated that we finished sixteenth in the Premier League with forty-two points. For a club like ours, the smallest in the League, it was a monumental achievement to compete and survive in such a competitive environment. It was also remarkable for it to have happened at the end of one of the most exciting seasons in the competition's history, that saw rank outsiders Leicester City win the title.

We had also enjoyed a run to the last sixteen of the FA Cup, but with Premier League survival always being the priority, Eddie had chosen to rest some of his senior players, unlike opponents Everton, who progressed to the quarter-finals with a 2-0 win.

The club's rise to the Premier League had continued to attract huge interest locally, but the massive increase in television exposure meant that it had also captured the imagination of football followers much further afield, and the club could now claim to have a worldwide profile.

THE GREAT WALL OF CHINA

In the summer of 2015, a group of Chinese football coaches had visited us to participate in a coaching course with our Community Football Programme. The following summer though, it was my turn to make a visit to China. This came about after I had conversations with the British Chamber of Commerce in London and the British Consul in Beijing. I explained that I was looking to set up a collaboration between AFC Bournemouth and sponsors of some Chinese clubs and as a result I was invited across for further discussions.

The new Chinese Super League had just got underway and interest in football there was becoming massive. I spent a week in Beijing where I met with business leaders from a number of global companies. These meetings proved positive, and I was hopeful that further discussions could take place. However, soon afterwards, difficulties in exporting money out of China prevented any potential partnership reaching fruition. It was also during this visit to China that I had the great thrill and honour of being pictured holding an AFC Bournemouth shirt on the Great Wall.

Upon my return from the China visit, we were active in the transfer market. That summer, we signed Liverpool winger Jordon Ibe, for another club record fee. We also managed to secure defender Nathan Aké on a half-season loan from Chelsea, a move that proved to be quite significant.

In addition 22-year-old full-back Brad Smith arrived from Liverpool and midfielder Lewis Cook from Leeds United. The accent was firmly placed on youth – Cook was just 19 and Ibe 20, as were two of our other signings, US international midfielder Emerson Hyndman and Le Havre forward Lys Mousset.

To add some experience, Irish international Marc Wilson returned for a second spell with us from Stoke City, and near the end of the transfer window Arsenal's England international midfielder Jack Wilshere joined us on a season-long loan. Meanwhile, it was sad to see Tommy Elphick, a true leader, who had been a massive influence at the club, leave for Aston Villa. In his place, Simon Francis was appointed as the club captain.

Matt Ritchie was another to leave us in favour of joining a Championship side, in his case, Newcastle United, while Shaun MacDonald left for Wigan Athletic. Both these players had shown the club and the community the fullness of their character and personality, and had become well-loved as a result, quite apart from their abilities on the pitch.

"

You were a consistent source of **positive energy** that spread throughout the club!

MATT RITCHIE #THECHAIRMAN

"

IN THEIR OWN WORDS ON JEFF

Matt Ritchie
Former Player of AFC Bournemouth

Jeff, what a time we had! You long before me, but thanks to you and the immense impact you had on the club, I had the opportunity to express myself on the pitch.

Without you, we would not have had the success or memories we treasure today. I will forever be thankful to you for that!

Whenever I speak or reminisce of the best days of my life so far, my fond memories of those days with you are at the forefront of my mind.

The conversation in Steve Hard's office when I discovered the role you played in saving the club, the memories on the pitch and in the dressing room after Bolton, so many amazing times! You were a consistent source of positive energy that spread throughout the club!

What a man, Jeff! I'll be forever grateful!

WE'RE UP AND RUNNING

After the first team squad had enjoyed an early pre-season training camp in Chicago, the 2016/17 season kicked off with a 3-1 defeat against Manchester United on the opening day, followed by a 1-0 loss at West Ham. It was the first time West Ham had staged a Premier League fixture at the London Stadium, and although the result was disappointing from our point of view, I found the Hammers' new home to be extremely impressive behind the scenes.

The first thing I noticed upon entering an immaculately turned-out boardroom was a huge mural on the wall of their former captain and England's World Cup winning skipper, the late Bobby Moore OBE. While I was admiring it, I was joined by David Gold, then co-owner of the club, who pointed out that the portrait is made up of 3,500 images of former West Ham players.

It was not the first time that I had been in the stadium itself as Rose and I had seen our daughter Alex take part in the opening ceremony for the 2012 Summer Paralympics there. However, when David took me down on to the pitch, I had my first experience of looking across the stadium at this level. Unfortunately, my reaction was to move my hand towards my eyes in a 'binocular' fashion and this was duly captured by a photographer from *The Sun* newspaper. The picture then appeared in the following morning's paper with a caption that read something like, 'Jeff Mostyn confirms everyone else's view that you cannot see the other side of the pitch properly at the London Stadium!'

This was certainly not what I intended to convey to the media, although I must admit the football pitch did seem very distant from the stands and I believe the atmosphere suffered a little as a result. But I preferred to take pride in seeing our team embrace what is unquestionably a fine playing surface inside a superb arena.

A draw at Crystal Palace finally got us up and running and our first win of the new campaign came against West Bromwich Albion on 10 September. Callum Wilson scored his first goal since recovering from the ACL injury he had sustained the previous season, his 76th-minute strike securing a 1-0 victory over the Baggies.

Two games stood out for me later that season. The first was in October, a monumental 6-1 win against Hull City, during which Callum Wilson, Charlie Daniels, Steve Cook, Junior Stanislas and Dan Gosling all found the net. It was our biggest Premier League win to date. However, we did also succumb to defeats by Middlesbrough and Sunderland, both of whom were struggling near the bottom of the table, highlighting our ongoing challenge for consistency.

Nathan Aké had proved to be an outstanding acquisition, offering strength at the back and a goalscoring threat from set pieces upfront, and at the beginning of December, he was to play a significant part in the second outstanding match of the period: a win against Liverpool at the Vitality Stadium that was to prove a season-defining moment.

Such was Liverpool's dominance that we found ourselves two goals down at half-time, and our supporters could have been excused for wondering how many goals Jürgen Klopp's Reds might score. However, our team showed remarkable character, and Callum Wilson pulled a goal back soon after the interval. With twenty minutes remaining, Liverpool scored again, only for Ryan Fraser to this time step up and reduce the deficit. The 'Wee Man', as he was accustomed to being referred to, then set up Steve Cook for the equaliser, and in a dramatic finish, Aké capitalised on a mishap from the Liverpool goalkeeper to grab a memorable 4-3 victory. It exemplified the resilience and never-give-up attitude of our team.

By year's end, we had accumulated twenty-four points from nineteen games, but as we moved into 2017, we learned more lessons about the unpredictability of the Premier League. A home game against Arsenal saw us let a 3-0 lead slip, resulting in a 3-3 draw as Olivier Giroud netted in the 92nd minute. It was a reminder that no lead is ever a safe one in this league.

Our focus remained primarily on the Premier League of course, and we didn't fare too well in cup competitions. In the Carabao Cup, Eddie had made eleven changes before a 3-2 defeat against Championship side Preston, and another much changed side were defeated 3-0 at Millwall in the FA Cup.

Chelsea recalled Nathan Aké which left Eddie with a headache in defence, and although Tyrone Mings made a welcome return from injury, fourteen goals were conceded in the next five games as just one point was gained. I can recall a particularly difficult afternoon which brought a 6-2 loss to Everton, on top of the blow of Callum Wilson suffering another ACL injury in training.

I felt distraught for Callum, picking up a second injury of this type just as he was establishing himself once again. As always, the players and staff rallied around him and fortunately he once more showed us that he is a man of great resilience. Callum is someone whose outward facade always shows what he is feeling inside and his 'never say die' attitude at this time enabled him to retain hope of fulfilling all of his ambitions.

I was proud that the club did everything possible to ensure he received the best possible rehabilitation, some of which took place overseas. We engaged some of the world's leading consultants to work alongside our own rehabilitation and recovery teams, and his welfare remained under constant review. While Callum's unbelievable inner strength allowed him to train alone for many months as he sought to regain full fitness, it was wonderful to see how his fellow players rallied round him when he was back at home.

Despite all of these challenges, the team managed to produce results when needed and we went undefeated during March, with Eddie receiving the manager of the month award. We began to gain a reputation for being capable of troubling the top clubs. A draw at Manchester United confirmed this, although the match is remembered more for two incidents involving Tyrone Mings and United's Zlatan Ibrahimović.

The first incident occurred when Mings appeared to land on the back of the United forward's head as he lay on the ground, and then from a corner, Ibrahimović responded with an elbow into Mings. This was witnessed by Andrew Surman, who pushed the Swedish striker to the ground and was promptly sent off for a second bookable offence. Soon afterwards, he was joined in the stands by assistant manager Jason Tindall, whose protestations overstepped the mark.

Although both Mings and Ibrahimović escaped punishment on the pitch,

Mings was subsequently issued with a five-match suspension for the 'stamping incident' despite no proof of intent in his challenge, and Ibrahimović received a three-match ban for the second incident.

Despite feeling hard done by the ramifications of what happened at Old Trafford, we responded positively and came close to securing three consecutive wins. In fact, I'm sure we would have done so had Harry Arter not slipped as he ran up to take a penalty against Southampton. Despite lamenting our missed chances, however, we continued to learn and grow. We came back to take our first-ever point from Liverpool at Anfield. The season was a learning curve for everyone, not just the players but Eddie and Jason as well.

It was a pleasure to see some of the players who had shone in the lower leagues now stepping up to hold their own in the Premier League. Charlie Daniels, Marc Pugh, and others who had journeyed with us from the lower ranks demonstrated immense growth and belief in their abilities.

The side embraced its Premier League identity and continued to push on. To finish as high as ninth, marking our highest-ever League position, with a total of forty-six points, was a monumental achievement in the club's history. These were uncharted waters for us; being in this position was absolutely astounding.

It was truly remarkable how far we had come in such a short time: from the brink of relegation out of the Fourth Division to the Premier League. It was a constant thrill to see AFC Bournemouth in the national press and media, now mentioned in headlines, not just small match reports. Also our merchandise among the country's top brands and even one of our players pictured on a Panini sticker packet was surreal. After spending so many years in the lower leagues, it was nothing short of miraculous.

OPTIMISM AHEAD FOR 2017/18

The 2017/18 season for AFC Bournemouth marked another fascinating chapter in the club's ongoing tale of resilience and steady growth in English football's top tier. Under the charismatic management of Eddie Howe, the club embarked on their third consecutive season in the Premier League, aiming to consolidate their status and build upon past successes.

Following a strong ninth-place finish in the previous season, there were heightened expectations. Both Eddie and Maxim had agreed from the moment that we had reached the Premier League that the club's first priority would always be to invest as heavily as possible in the playing squad, and by doing so to try and keep the club in the Premier League for as long as possible.

However, it was not lost on them, or any of us, that whatever the length of the club's stay at the top table, some form of legacy should remain as a permanent reminder of its success. The importance of building a successful academy and state-of-the-art training facilities remained in our thoughts. In a step towards achieving this, the club had already purchased the land that had previously housed the Canford Magna Golf Club, some six miles down the road from the Vitality Stadium.

The long-term plan was to build a new multi-million-pound training complex which would include ten full-size pitches, three junior pitches and an indoor artificial playing surface, as well as sports science and rehabilitation facilities. When completed, it would bring first team, development squad, academy and pre-academy training operations and facilities into one location. These plans were now made public for the first time, and a few weeks later local councillors gave unanimous support for the project.

We believed this complex should take priority over any proposal to build a larger stadium, and it was decided to keep matchday ticket prices unchanged for a third year running. Meanwhile, the summer saw Eddie and the club's board working diligently to try and strengthen the squad. Key acquisitions included Nathan Aké, who broke the club's record transfer fee when he rejoined permanently after his successful loan spell the previous season, and Jermain Defoe, whose vast experience was seen as invaluable for the young team. Asmir Begović also joined as a reliable presence between the posts.

Despite the optimism, the season began on a challenging note. The team struggled to find their rhythm, facing a string of tough fixtures that tested their mettle early on. The demanding nature of the Premier League was all too evident as we battled to secure points and build momentum.

The visit of newly promoted Brighton & Hove Albion brought back memories of numerous south-coast derbies between the two clubs, stretching back to when we first entered the Football League in 1923. The big difference this time was that the clubs were meeting for the first time in the Premier League, providing us with another reminder of just how far we had come. The game also brought our first League win of the season, with Defoe and Andrew Surman leading us to a 2-1 success which was followed four days later by a 1-0 victory when the Seagulls returned in the Carabao Cup.

Nonetheless, we had only accumulated four points from our first seven League games played, and Eddie had come in for some criticism regarding his team's expansive style of play. But as autumn set in, a significant first away win came at Stoke and the boys began to show glimpses of their true potential. Their usual resilience was evident once again in their ability to rally from setbacks, and they gradually climbed up the League table.

Boxing Day provided another pivotal moment after a dramatic 3-3 draw against West Ham United, where the team's attacking flair was on full display, earning them plaudits for their determination and fighting spirit. Moments like these underlined our reputation as a team that could punch above its weight, and it marked the start of an improved run that went on to see us remain unbeaten in the League through January and February, a run that included a notable first-ever win against Arsenal, a point against West Ham at the London Stadium and an away success against Chelsea.

Vitality Stadium, known for its vibrant atmosphere, became a fortress where we often found the extra push needed to gain crucial victories. Again, this period of success was characterised by the team's spirit and Eddie's tactical astuteness, which often caught opponents off guard. His philosophy of playing attractive, attacking football continued to be a hallmark of our approach. The team's fluid style, coupled with strategic adaptations, often kept them competitive against even the most formidable Premier League sides. Players like Callum Wilson and Ryan Fraser emerged as key attacking threats, while Nathan Aké was again showing what a superb player and person he was: a joy to have at the club and a source of increased stability in defence. It was no surprise that he was later named as our player of the season. His stature in the dressing room was immense, and he played a significant role in our games.

The winter months tested the squad's endurance, but key performances, particularly from seasoned campaigners like Jermain Defoe, ensured that the team remained cohesive and competitive throughout testing stretches. According to a Deloitte report, AFC Bournemouth was now the 28th richest club in the world, so it was important that we continued to solidify our Premier League credentials. Captain Simon Francis made the 600th appearance of his career and both Steve Cook and Stanislas completed their 100th Premier League outings as a series of strong performances in the final months underscored the team's progress. This culminated in a satisfying finish that further established their status in English football's elite league.

Another historic moment for the club came on 27 March when Lewis Cook became the first serving AFC Bournemouth player to represent the England senior side, after being introduced as a substitute in the friendly international against Italy at Wembley. He was also rewarded with a new four-year contract at the end of the season.

While we were steadily climbing the table, our neighbours at Southampton were still in danger of facing the drop. Our visit to St Mary's at the end of April was a tense affair which included both our first-ever goal at that stadium and our first goal away to the Saints in thirty-one years. A 2-2 draw earned both sides a point, although Southampton celebrated it rather more than us, as they finally assured themselves of safety.

We ended our third Premier League season in 12th place with forty-four points, two points fewer than the season before. With a better goal difference, we could have finished as high as tenth, but I believe the final league standing was reflective of the strategies implemented by the management and the collective efforts of the team, who embraced the challenges of top-tier football with courage and skill.

The season had been significant not merely for its results but more so for the lessons learned and the strength of character displayed by the squad. The team had gained twenty-one points from games in which they had been in losing positions and, not surprisingly, the media had christened them as the 'Comeback Kings'!

The team's successes laid down a strong foundation for the club to build upon in the following seasons, as we looked to further cement our position and aim for greater achievements. As always, the synergy between the club's management, the players, and the loyal fanbase continued to be the backbone of our journey, embodying a spirit of unity and ambition that motivated everyone to aim higher with every passing season.

While working hard to ensure that AFC Bournemouth took the opportunity to make the most of its growing worldwide profile, Maxim, the directors and I did not lose sight of the importance of the club's strong standing in the local community. We wanted to make the most of the incredible support we had witnessed by making the club as inclusive as possible. Already, in May 2018, our women's team had played at the Vitality Stadium for the first time on their way to achieving promotion to the Southern Regional Premier Division. It was a success we looked to build further upon in the coming years. Our Head of Community, Steve Cuss, also oversaw the introduction of a walking football team and the club's first powerchair side. In addition, our well-established Ability Counts teams offered opportunities to people of all ages and abilities to play football.

For some years Steve had been working on a very limited budget and a very small staff, but our Community Sports Trust had now grown to such an extent that its staff touched the lives of around 4,000 local people each week, from schoolchildren to seniors, on projects ranging from healthy living to road safety. Each project was also allocated a first team player as its ambassador.

For me personally, I was proud to become the board's Equality Champion and also patron of the Community Sport Trust. Appointing me, the chairman, as the patron of the Trust, tied the two bodies together seamlessly and it was a sheer joy to be able to take all these initiatives further forward together. At the start of the 2018/19 season, we also launched our 'Everyone Together' scheme, the aim of which was to make all supporters welcome at the club and embrace the diversity of its fan base.

On the playing side, the summer transfer window was a crucial period for strategic planning. We focused on strengthening our line-up by reinforcing key positions to ensure our squad not only had the necessary depth but also the quality to remain competitive at the highest level.

While fostering growth across every aspect of the club, both on and off the pitch, our on-field goal remained clear. Under Eddie Howe's astute management, we were determined to build on our previous successes. We brought in three new players, including Levante's 23-year-old Colombian international midfielder Jefferson Lerma, the fee involved even surpassing that which had brought Aké from Chelsea twelve months earlier. Another signing was an exciting 21-year-old named David Brooks, who joined after showing impressive form in the championship for Sheffield United. Both would prove to be significant choices albeit for totally different reasons.

We kicked off the season with enthusiasm and optimism. Our initial ten games were solid; we won six, drew two, and lost two, setting a positive tone. We also made good progress in the Carabao Cup and our fourth-round win against Norwich City also saw the multi-camera network system, VAR, put to use at the Vitality Stadium for the first time to assist Hawkeye in providing further information to an additional match official.

Callum Wilson enjoyed his best-ever start to a Premier League season and scored his seventh goal of the campaign in a 2-1 defeat against Manchester United at the beginning of November. Later that month he was able to mark his first start in a full International for England with a goal in their win against the USA later that month. It was a fitting reward for all the hard work and dedication Callum had shown in regaining fitness after his two cruciate ligament injuries and he became the first serving AFC Bournemouth player to start a game and score for England.

For some reason, as a club we never seemed far away from our next injury of this type. During the last three weeks of 2018, both Lewis Cook and Simon Francis were to suffer this same fate, and their ensuing absence was a heavy blow. The only consolation we could take was that both injuries occurred before the January transfer window which would give us a chance to seek replacements.

Striker Dominic Solanke and defender Chris Mepham joined us. Both just 21 years old, they were already full internationals with England and Wales respectively and fitted in with Eddie's plans to try and reduce the average age of his squad.

As the season progressed, we faced challenges typical of Premier League football. Injuries continued to test the depth and resilience of our squad, requiring players to step up and contribute significantly when needed. Despite these hurdles, the team's spirit remained unbroken, demonstrating the camaraderie and determination that has become a hallmark of the club.

There was also a significant change in the club's ownership at this time, which saw Maxim Demin regain full control of the club by purchasing back a 25 per cent shareholdings that had been sold to Peak6 Football Holdings in 2015.

Mepham's first appearance came as a substitute during a standout home win against Chelsea at the end of January. Artur Boruc was recalled in goal in place of Asmir Begović, and he was initially kept busy as Maurizio Sarri's team dominated the first half but, immediately after the interval, Joshua King scored against the run of play on the counterattack. David Brooks then doubled our lead before King struck again, and a wonderful evening was crowned when Charlie Daniels added a fourth goal in stoppage time.

Solanke made his first start in a 2-0 defeat at Cardiff which was played only days after the tragic death of City striker Emiliano Sala. The outpouring of emotion that greeted us all upon arrival at the Cardiff City Stadium could not fail to have touched supporters and players of both clubs and a difficult afternoon was inevitable. Sala's death in a private plane while travelling across the English Channel was to serve as a reminder that as we move around the world at great pace to try and meet deadlines of one sort or another, life itself remains the most valuable possession of all.

Each setback continued to be met with renewed focus and grit, and the unwavering support of our amazing supporters also played a pivotal role in propelling our team to reach a position of relative safety during tough times. By the end of the month, we had the comfort of a ten-point cushion above the final relegation spot. Before the season came to an end though, there were still some memorable moments to be enjoyed, particularly at Brighton where we achieved a remarkable 5-0 success and also a thrilling finish against Tottenham Hotspur which brought a 91st-minute winning goal from Nathan Aké to give us our first ever Premier League win over Spurs. The match also saw a surprise debut for 19-year-old goalkeeper Mark Travers, who made a series of fine saves. I had first met Mark when he came across from Ireland to sign his first contract a couple of years earlier, accompanied by his lovely family, and I was delighted for all of them that his first senior appearance for us had turned out so well.

Before the season was over there was a reminder of the long journey Eddie and I had travelled together since those difficult days in League Two when he reached the milestone of the 500th game of his managerial career. It was an opportunity to celebrate not only his remarkable achievements during this time – a testament to his incredibly hard work and talented leadership – but also the high regard in which he was held by our loyal supporters, dedicated staff and the larger community.

To mark the tenth anniversary of Eddie's first season in charge, the club's media team undertook production of a feature-length documentary entitled *Minus 17*, which chronicled events of the 2008/09 'greatest escape' campaign. This was first seen at a red-carpet premiere at the Odeon at Bh2.

Reflecting on the 2018/19 season, it stands out as yet another remarkable chapter in the story of AFC Bournemouth. Once again, I had the privilege of witnessing at first hand the continued growth of our club as we navigated our fourth consecutive season in the Premier League. We had secured our status in the Premier League, finishing in a respectable 14th place with forty-five points and, in addition, we reached the quarter-finals of the Carabao Cup before being narrowly defeated by Chelsea.

We had experienced a season of two unequal halves with twenty-six points coming from the first eighteen games and nineteen in the second half of season, but the long- and short-term injuries incurred by the players naturally had a dramatic effect on performances. Nonetheless, the resilience, ambition and unity displayed throughout the season continued to be significant in our journey towards being a sustainable, competitive club.

CHAPTER 11
TOUGH TIMES DURING THE GLOBAL PANDEMIC

It's early, around 7.30 a.m., when I receive a call from Clare Gallie, the CEO of Lewis-Manning Hospice Care. They are in dire need of a space for a giant mobile clinic for hospice patients during lockdown. After a few quick phone calls, by 8.15 a.m., we have arranged for the mobile unit to park in the players' car park at AFC Bournemouth. By 9 a.m., patients are being attended to.

I'm immensely proud of the AFC Bournemouth team for making this happen. It serves as a powerful reminder that football can be a tool for uniting and supporting the community, bringing people together in times of need.

* * *

During the summer transfer window, we aimed to bolster our squad with strategic signings to complement our existing group of players. At the same time we wanted to retain the services of players of the calibre of Aké and Wilson, whose performances continued to impress and not surprisingly made them targets for other clubs. We successfully achieved while allowing players like Tyrone Mings and Lys Mousset to move on for considerable fees, to underscore our strategy of reinvesting in talents who could make a significant impact on the pitch.

After a terrific first season in the Premier League, David Brooks signed a new long-term deal, but the club said farewell to two players of long standing. Marc Pugh left after 274 appearances that began in League One, while Harry Arter joined Nottingham Forest initially on a season-long loan before joining them permanently.

Notable signings were Bristol City's England Under 21 defender Lloyd

Kelly, Danish international midfielder Philip Billing and a promising Dutch winger from Club Brugge named Arnaut Danjuma. However, preparations for the new season took a blow when Brooks suffered an ankle injury in pre-season which sidelined him for several months before it was found a second operation would be necessary. Little did anyone know at that time of course that an even more serious health issue lay a little further ahead for this young man.

Harry Wilson's arrival on a season-long loan from Liverpool softened the blow of losing Brooks a little, but the 2019/20 season was to prove one of the most challenging and pivotal periods in our recent history. As we entered our fifth consecutive season in the top flight, we were again hopeful and determined to consolidate our position in the Premier League. However, what unfolded was a rollercoaster of emotions that tested everyone involved with the club.

The season began with flashes of promise, but it quickly revealed challenges that would persist throughout. Eddie Howe had at least appeared to solve his goalkeeping dilemma by handing England Under 21 international Aaron Ramsdale his Premier League debut in the opening match. He proved to be a brilliant young custodian, and the early weeks of the campaign turned out to be Bournemouth's best spell of the season.

A 3-1 win at Southampton in September was our first away win against the Saints since 1953 and we moved up to third place overnight. However, the team's performances then became marred by inconsistency, and despite having a squad capable of producing much attacking flair, results were hard to come by. This began to put considerable pressure on both the players and Eddie Howe's tactical strategies.

A well taken goal by Joshua King brought a welcome 1-0 home success against Manchester United at the beginning of November but this was followed by a run of five successive defeats. The last of these, a 3-0 reverse against League leaders Liverpool at home on 7 December, came at a huge cost. First, Nathan Aké overstretched in an attempt to intercept a long through ball and had to be substituted, then Callum Wilson pulled up with a hamstring injury, to become the ninth senior player to be put out of action in another all too familiar injury scenario.

After sixteen matches, we had slipped to 15th place and only one point above the relegation zone before a steadfast defensive performance and a dramatic late winner from Dan Gosling ended our miserable run in a game against Chelsea at Stamford Bridge. But subsequent defeats against Burnley and Brighton meant that by mid-season, we were in the throes of a relegation battle.

It was a stark contrast to the stability we had previously enjoyed. The series of injuries to key players had naturally added to our difficulties. This challenging period often saw us fall to narrow defeats, highlighting the fragility of maintaining Premier League status amid fierce competition.

January saw skipper Simon Francis return from injury only for us to lose the services of Chris Mepham with a serious knee injury. Meanwhile, a relatively quiet transfer window saw Sam Surridge recalled from loan at Swansea and an unwelcome very late attempt by Manchester United to sign Joshua King politely declined. A 4-0 defeat at West Ham was further compounded by losses at home to Watford and away at the bottom club Norwich before home wins against Brighton and Aston Villa lifted spirits briefly.

Once again, we were unable to build upon these successes though, and at times lady luck certainly appeared to be against us. This was especially so against Burnley when VAR wiped out a goal from King at Turf Moor and instead awarded the home side a penalty. After at first believing we had drawn level, we then found ourselves two goals behind and eventually lost 3-0.

Little seemed to be going right and even after a second-half fightback against Chelsea had seen us lead 2-1 at the Vitality Stadium, a late equaliser from the visitors meant another two points were dropped. Callum Wilson then put us ahead at Liverpool, but after Steve Cook was forced off the pitch through injury, Jürgen Klopp's team went on to claim a narrow victory. The 2019/20 campaign was highlighting the brutal realities of the Premier League, where fine margins often shape destiny.

COVID PUTS THE SEASON ON HOLD

The Covid-19 pandemic then added an unforeseen layer of difficulty, bringing an abrupt halt to the season in March. The break offered a chance for re-evaluation and recovery, yet the uncertainty about football's return weighed heavily on fans, players and staff alike. This unprecedented pause complicated our quest to secure top-flight survival.

There were a number of logistical issues we had to immediately address; training in groups was suspended, and players were asked to exercise on their own; social distancing guidelines need to be put in place for players and staff; those staff who could do so were asked to work from home rather than attend the stadium and anyone showing symptoms of the virus had to go into isolation.

A restart was tentatively scheduled for 20 April, but with the extent of the virus still increasing, this proved to be impossible. As more and more time elapsed, it became a real possibility that the season would not recommence at all. I became increasingly of the opinion that the season should be abandoned, and all results annulled if this was to be the case. In fact, this was something that was discussed at a Premier League shareholders' meeting. When I agreed with the suggestion I was accused of demonstrating self-interest given our precarious position in the league table. After a moment's silence, I thanked the individual who made the comment, as it demonstrated I had upheld my duty as chairman to work for the benefit of my football club. My response was greeted with much delight from my allies around the table, who realised I had turned the criticism on its head. I rest my case.

The League finally resumed in June, albeit with matches played behind closed doors and no supporters present, and this caused a number of contractual issues with players. With the season now not due to be concluded until 26 July, like many clubs, we had players who would be out of contract from 1 July, and temporary extensions were agreed with Simon Francis, Andrew Surman, Artur Boruc and Charlie Daniels, while the Harry Wilson loan from Liverpool was also duly extended.

One player who refused to sign was Ryan Fraser. The diminutive Scot had enjoyed his best-ever season during 2018/19 and had been linked with a host of top clubs during the summer, after he turned down our offer of a new contract. A move did not materialise, however, and Ryan instead made it clear that he wanted to leave when his original contract expired at the end of the 2019/20 season.

I have often been asked my opinion about Ryan's decision and my reply has always been to say I was hugely disappointed for Eddie, Neill Blake, who had conducted the negotiations, our supporters and myself. Ryan had been offered a new contract at another club the following season that was hugely beneficial for him and he chose not to put that at risk by playing for AFC Bournemouth beyond his original contract period. In effect he had chosen not to help the club further in its fight to retain Premier League status. Other players who also had offers lined up fortunately chose to do the opposite. It is not my style to bear grudges so I leave it up to you to make your own decision about whether Ryan was right or wrong to act as he did.

Like all other clubs, AFC Bournemouth took every precaution possible to ensure that staff, players and match officials remained safe during the pandemic. There was staggered entry on to the pitch for players and no handshakes were allowed before kick-off. Corner flags, goalposts, substitution boards and match balls were deep cleaned before and after each fixture and other measures were taken to ensure that players and coaching staff could maintain social distancing rules when travelling to and from games.

But without the presence of our incredible supporters who regularly acted not just as our 12th man, but the 13th and 14th as well, we faced an uphill struggle. Each remaining fixture was crucial, every match became a do-or-die situation in our quest to retain Premier League status. As chairman, I was one of very few people privileged to be able to attend matches, but the absence of supporters created a surreal matchday experience as the shouts and screams of players and staff were left to echo inside the grounds.

We had gone into lockdown in 18th place, with nine fixtures remaining. Despite still occupying a relegation position, the team was playing well and had rediscovered its momentum, which could not be said of most of the other teams around them. Understandably, the players now required time to get back into their playing rhythm and to adjust to matchdays where there was no atmosphere in the stadium, but unfortunately, this took too long.

I felt that while the absence of our wonderful supporters impacted us negatively, other sides that had been receiving far more criticism seemed to now benefit from the absence of most of their detractors. Nonetheless, as the season neared its conclusion, we showed commendable tenacity and spirit. Our key performances against strong adversaries occasionally rekindled hope and revealed glimpses of the skill and determination our squad truly possessed. Despite our best efforts, however, crucial points slipped away in vital matches.

On the final day of the season, the situation was clear. To have a chance of staying up, we had to win at Everton and hope that Aston Villa and Watford both lost their final games. An impressive performance followed at Goodison Park. Joshua King's penalty gave us an early lead and despite conceding an equaliser, further goals from Solanke and Stanislas had us 3-1 ahead after 80 minutes. It looked likely then that our fate would ultimately be decided by matters which were no longer in our own hands, and that was to prove exactly the case.

We comfortably held on for the win at Goodison Park only for news to come through confirming that although Watford had lost at Arsenal, Villa had drawn at West Ham to save themselves, and we were to be relegated, together with Watford and Norwich after a five-year stay in the Premier League. We finished the season in 18th place, falling just a single point short of survival.

Ironically, the team directly above us, Aston Villa, had been the benefactors in an incident during the first match upon the League's resumption in June, between themselves and Sheffield United, which turned out to have a bearing on the final outcome. A lapse in the goal line technology system meant that a goal for United was ruled out, and the point that Villa gained that day proved enough for them to stay up at our expense.

24. Rosie and I with the Championship trophy

25. With my wife, Rosie. She made saving the club possible with her love, passion and support

26. A father and daughter moment with Janine. I am so proud of her influence in the sports industry.

27. A true AFC Bournemouth legend. Alongside Ted MacDougall at the opening of his stand at the Vitality Stadium

28. A special moment as Chair of the FA Cup Committee with Manchester City Chairman Khaldoon Al Mubarak

29. Welcoming the England Women's National Team to the Vitality Stadium alongside Steph Houghton MBE and Kelly Smith MBE

30. Angside a true football legend, Sir Bobby Charlton, 70 years on asking for an autograph at the YMCA club

31. Roy Hodgson CBE, a true gentleman, enjoying a match at the Vitality Stadium

32. Sir Gareth Southgate, one of my inspirational mentors during my time as FA Council, England team ambassador

33. Debbie Hewitt MBE, FA Chair, a true leader and someone I am proud to call a friend

34. One of my dearest friends, the late great voice of football, John Motson OBE, with his iconic coat

35. At the 2017 Premier League Conference with Paul Barber (left) and Tony Bloom (right), on the day I suffered my heart attack

36. With my two Manchester City heroes, Mike Summerbee OBE (left) and Denis Law (right)

37. The late Bill Kenwright, Chair of Everton, a dear friend and inspiration to me

38. Neil Vacher, 'Mr Bournemouth', a gentleman and a friend. I am proud to have shared the journey with him.

39. The now famous dressing room scene re-mastered by my EFL colleagues

40. Steve Parish, Crystal Palace Chairman, a friend and one of my Premier League mentors

41. An iconic moment on the Great Wall of China as I complete an interview holding the AFC Bournemouth shirt

42. The world's oldest ball boy at Sir Gareth's England training camp!

There was no means available to us afterwards that could change the result of that game, although there were suggestions that we should make a legal challenge at the end of the season. Interestingly though, this incident led to an increase thereafter in the number of cameras used for deciding if a ball had crossed the goal line.

It had been a season unlike any other in English football history. Whatever the ifs and buts, at the end of the day we had been relegated because we had one fewer point than the team directly above us. Relegation marked the end of an incredible five-year journey in the top tier for AFC Bournemouth, prompting deep reflection on our successes and shortcomings.

One thing I continued to be certain of was that the most important people in football are the supporters. They create the atmosphere that provides an essential part of the product which can then be sold to and enjoyed by millions of people across the world. Without them, the game is not the same.

Whether or not football should have continued to have been played during the pandemic remains a relevant question and is one on which I have been asked my opinion many times since. My own view is that the live televised screenings brought pleasure to viewers throughout the world and provided them with a respite from the devastation caused by Covid-19. Many of them had sadly lost loved ones or had loved ones in hospital whom they were not allowed to visit due to the regulations that had been imposed. Life and health had to come before anything else, but if watching professional football helped to ease the pain for some people, then I believe it was worth continuing.

This, though, truly was the end of an era, a fairy tale woven by Maxim Demin, myself, Neill Blake, Eddie Howe, Jason Tindall and Richard Hughes. From League Two to five seasons in the Premier League, our progress had been both inspiring and extraordinary. I recall a moment with the legendary John Motson, whose unparalleled football knowledge illuminated many conversations in our boardroom. He once suggested I might not fully appreciate the magnitude of what we had accomplished due to my humble nature.

In Premier League history, only a few chairmen have navigated clubs through all four divisions; I was privileged to be among this exclusive group. Yet, the unique partnership Eddie Howe and I fostered in driving the same club from Division Two to the Premier League, stands alone. In football's storied legacy, this achievement highlights our extraordinary journey, a testament I believe will remain unmatched.

CHAPTER 12
THE FAIRY TALE COMES TO AN END

As I sit here reflecting, I can't help but feel incredibly grateful for having known the late, great voice of football, John Motson. Over the span of more than fifty years, he was not only an icon in the football world but also a dear friend who enriched my journey in the sport. His presence was one of the most respected globally, and it was an honour to have him as a frequent guest at the football club.

Imagine, if you will, sitting beside the voice of football during a live match. Closing my eyes, I'd listen to John narrating the game in his legendary style. Although the commentary was directed straight into my ear instead of a microphone, it was nothing short of a delight. One particular match stands out vividly in my memory; it was when John, after enjoying a glass of red wine post-game, handed me his notes from a Bournemouth match. Scribbled with alterations and substitutions, those sheets are treasures I hold dear.

John was an extraordinary character. His knowledge of every event over five decades was as vivid as if it happened yesterday. After one memorable game, back in the boardroom, John – affectionately known as Motti – tapped his glass to get everyone's attention. He rose, graciously thanking me and Rosie for our hospitality, and then, surprising us all, he shared a few incredible facts about me.

According to John, I was one of only four chairmen to have led a club from Division Two to the Premier League. He mentioned, too, that along with Eddie Howe, I was one of the few to have been both chairman and manager of the same club across all four divisions. The room erupted in applause, and I was nearly moved to tears by his kind words and astonishing knowledge.

John's wisdom and generosity made me feel part of a unique history in football, and those moments with him will forever be cherished.

* * *

Five days after the season ended, Eddie Howe, by now 42 years old and the architect of our remarkable rise through the divisions, parted ways with us in mutual respect, closing a memorable chapter in our club's history. Eddie's departure was a deeply emotional moment for me personally, given everything he had achieved with the club.

Eddie had been with the club since he was a child, a player beloved by all, before his transfer to Portsmouth. I first met him in a rather unassuming manner. It was a simple introduction from Kevin Bond, 'This is Eddie Howe, and this is what he does…'. At the time, Eddie was just a young lad, assisting Kevin and his assistant Rob Newman with first-team affairs. I certainly didn't grasp the monumental impact Eddie would soon have on my life, and on AFC Bournemouth.

Eddie seemed inconspicuous then, but there was something about his presence that was intriguing. I didn't know it at the time, but I was witnessing the early days of a remarkable talent.

When I acquired the football club in 2006, my relationship with Eddie was informal, although he was aware of my role in saving the club. It wasn't until post-administration that our professional bond truly started, his respect for me deepened, and our rapport grew.

Eddie's passion for personal development was unmatched. This drive earned him the respect of everyone – players and staff alike. He wasn't the kind of manager who rested on past accolades; he was relentless in his pursuit of growth. His dedication inspired me, even as I embarked on my own new career at an age when many thought of retirement. Eddie's drive pushed me to learn continually, fostering a culture of improvement and resilience within the club.

My admiration for Eddie extends beyond professional respect; it is personal. Even today, when Eddie returns to AFC Bournemouth, he is greeted as 'Gaffer', a testament to his enduring legacy. Similarly, I am honoured when he refers to me as 'Chairman', a title that maintains its significance among those who were part of our journey.

Eddie's work ethic has always been a source of admiration for me. I vividly remember our flights to places like Philadelphia, where he would be engrossed in his work before we even took off.

Watching him with his laptop fired up, analysing tactical aspects, asking for specific clips from our head analyst, Garvan Stewart, was truly inspiring.

Eddie insisted on evaluating these clips first, forming his own judgements about players rather than relying solely on others. Eddie's focus and dedication were unwavering. This commitment to constant growth and understanding is one of the things that make Eddie exceptional. His return to the club and his performance during the 'Minus 17' season was phenomenal, as he achieved what many deemed impossible. It was this resilience that set the foundation of success for AFC Bournemouth, instilling a siege mentality that became part of the club and gave birth to our motto 'Together, Anything is Possible'.

Eddie created a sense of unity in our dressing room that defied the odds time and again. Despite originally having no managerial experience, within a year of his appointment, he had crafted his own path, and his appetite for personal growth was insatiable. This mindset is a lesson in persistence and self-belief.

The outcome of his approach was that the team exceeded their perceived limitations, played beyond their supposed capabilities and climbed from League Two to the Premier League in just seven seasons.

What still stands out about Eddie is his intolerance of egos. He would never allow any staff member or player to become self-important, maintaining that ethos of development and humility among his team. Despite attracting experienced players at various stages in their careers, Eddie's standards ensured they remained leaders, not egotists, in the dressing room. His respect commanded theirs, reinforcing the culture he built.

His strength continues to lie not only in his managerial skills but in his ability to improve players with limited resources. At AFC Bournemouth, he honed the existing talent and elevated the team through sheer innovation and effort. The respect he garners, from players and beyond, continues to this day as a testament to his incredible attributes as a leader and a person.

I remain completely in awe of his capabilities and look upon him as I would a son. To be the first person to arrive at a football club and the last to leave each day takes its toll, especially when you are someone like Eddie who truly values this aspect of his life enormously. He made the most tremendous sacrifices in this regard for the benefit of the club and for that reason his legacy here is set in stone and he will always have the respect of everyone connected with AFC Bournemouth, players, staff and supporters.

"

'Together, Anything is Possible.' Jeff epitomised those words, and having given AFC Bournemouth a future, he then helped propel it to the Premier League.'

EDDIE HOWE #THECHAIRMAN

"

IN THEIR OWN WORDS ON JEFF

Eddie Howe
Head Coach of Newcastle United and
Former AFC Bournemouth Manager

Back in 2008, with my playing career at AFC Bournemouth coming to an end due to injury, our then manager Kevin Bond had unexpectedly given me the chance to join his backroom team and with it an opportunity to take a different path in my life. Around the same time, Kevin had also introduced his long-time friend Jeff Mostyn to the club, as the latest in a long line of people who had the passion to try and help with its perilous financial problems.

I'm not sure I knew what I was getting myself into when I started down the road of coaching, and I'm absolutely certain Jeff had no idea what was in store when he walked through the door at the club for the first time. Very quickly he got involved, taking AFC Bournemouth to his heart, investing his own money in the club and eventually becoming its owner.

A turbulent period of time followed, during which Jeff funded the club through administration and kept on giving to keep the club alive. This period should never be forgotten as he continued to fight for the club when it needed it the most. His perseverance paid off as he eventually sold his shares to enable Maxim Demin to give the club the financial security it needed.

After I returned to Bournemouth from Burnley, Jeff also returned to the club as chairman, and what followed was a journey which was beyond all of our wildest dreams. The club's rise through the leagues is one of the greatest and most unlikely journeys in the history of English football, and while the players on the pitch deserve so much credit, so do the team behind the scenes led by Jeff.

At its heart there was a simple ethos that ran through every layer of the club: 'Together, Anything is Possible.' Jeff epitomised those words, and having given AFC Bournemouth a future, he then helped propel it to the Premier League. He was incredibly supportive towards me, the coaching staff and each of the players, and represented the

> club so well throughout football, from boardrooms to the corridors of the FA, where he is universally loved and respected.
>
> Most of all, his friendship, love and loyalty, together with his amazing wife Rosie, made the impossible feel possible. His energy and integrity filtered down to everyone who was lucky enough to work with him, and the end result was a magical period of time which brought joy to so many people, made a million memories and will never be forgotten.

THE SHOW MUST GO ON

After Eddie's departure, a new manager was appointed – Jason Tindall, someone who had worked closely with Eddie and understood the club's ethos intimately. Although I was still the very public face of the football club and continued to have a voice in the boardroom, decisions in the football department were now left in the hands of owner Maxim Demin, Neill Blake and Richard Hughes our Technical Director who also was responsible for player recruitment. Maxim had witnessed Jason as a loyal deputy to Eddie and knew he would now like a crack at being a No1. rather than a No.2. It was easy to see therefore that Jason's appointment was strategic. His deep-rooted connection with the club offered continuity, which we all hoped would be key as we navigated our way through this critical transition period.

The same could also be said of first team coach Stephen Purches, another of our former players, who now became assistant manager, while former Luton manager Graeme Jones arrived as first team coach.

As we braced ourselves for life in the EFL Championship, our focus shifted to constructing a robust foundation for a potential return to the Premier League while we adapted to a new set of challenges, both on and off the pitch. Despite the setback of relegation, our commitment to a sustainable and competitive future remained steadfast. We believed that our loyal fan base, proven resilience and lessons from past experiences would enable us to find the path towards redemption and revival in the seasons to come.

With this in mind, we entered the Championship with a renewed sense of purpose and determination. Our goal was clear: we aimed to reclaim our place in the top tier of English football while overcoming the numerous challenges that the 2020/21 season would bring.

Maintaining a strong and competitive squad was a crucial priority. The realities of relegation meant that we faced significant player changes and Nathan Aké, Aaron Ramsdale and Callum Wilson each made moves back into the Premier League, while Artur Boruc and Andrew Surman also moved on, and Simon Francis ended his playing career. Although we were sad to lose players of such quality, the club could at least take some comfort from the transfer fees received, which, together with the 'parachute payment' from the Premier League, would help to offset some of the loss of income brought about by relegation.

Despite inevitably losing some key players, our focus remained on retaining others like Jefferson Lerma and Dominic Solanke, while also integrating promising new talents who could bring fresh energy to the team. During the summer transfer window, we decided to mix experience with youthful dynamism, thereby setting ourselves up for what we hoped would be a competitive campaign. With this in mind, two players arrived on season-long loans, Tottenham's US international defender Cameron Carter-Vickers and 20-year-old winger Rodrigo Riquelme from Atlético Madrid. Meanwhile, goalkeeper Asmir Begović was back with us after completing loans with Qarabağ and AC Milan the previous season.

The new campaign did not commence until 12 September, but the intensity and demands of the Championship soon became apparent. Each game brought its own set of challenges, and maintaining consistency was vital. Despite the global pandemic preventing supporters' attendance, the mood at the Vitality Stadium remained positive, and I felt the spirit of our fans resonating with every match.

We remained unbeaten in the Championship throughout September and October, and despite suffering our first loss against Sheffield Wednesday in November, we climbed steadily up the table and into second place. In early December, a loosening of restrictions enabled 2,000 home supporters to be welcomed back to the Vitality Stadium for the visit of Huddersfield. It was wonderful to see the fans back and spread out though the stadium. I couldn't help but smile when it was pointed out to me that not so long ago this would have been considered a decent attendance!

I don't think it was any coincidence that the team responded by recording their biggest win of the season, two goals from Dominic Solanke and others from David Brooks, Junior Stanislas and Sam Surridge completing a 5-0 success. Three days later, a similar attendance saw a 1-0 win against Wycombe, but when a new variant of the Covid-19 virus brought another sudden rise in infections, the country reverted to lockdown, and games were back behind closed doors once more.

Without wishing to put myself in the frame for any retrospective speeding fines, one benefit I enjoyed during lockdown was the speed at which you could travel from one end of the country to the other and not see anyone else on the way. My usual approach was to share the driving with my long-time senior accounts team member Mark Luther. I would drive to the stadium and my co-pilot, Mark, would drive home.

I remember after a particularly early arrival at Blackburn, being asked if we had flown up there, to which my co-driver's response was 'Yes, in 2 hours and 50 minutes we flew in a car not a plane!' It was also nice to be out of the car park and on our way home within two minutes of the final whistle. In all seriousness, I was always very respectful of the conditions under which we were travelling to these games. There was no hospitality provided at the stadiums of course and on one occasion, at Watford, I had the entire stand to myself. It was a truly bizarre experience, the impact of which was not lost upon me.

In the January transfer window, we added more quality and experience to our squad with the permanent signing of former Arsenal, West Ham and England midfielder Jack Wilshere. But just one Championship success during the month was accompanied by three defeats,, which began to cause concern.

First team coach Graeme Jones left to take up a similar role at Newcastle, before another reverse at home to Sheffield Wednesday at the beginning of February led to a reassessment of our approach and the decision to part ways with Jason. It was a difficult call for Maxim and Neill given Jason's outstanding commitment to the club, but sadly necessary to reignite our push for promotion. Like many previously relegated clubs, some of our players were clearly finding it difficult to come to terms with the Championship and I'm afraid that is what did it for Jason. Although we thought we had all our ducks lined up in a row at the beginning of the season, Jason was not the first manager to see those hopes, dreams and aspirations brought down by performances on the pitch.

Jason had been an integral part of our journey from League Two to the Premier League and I was disappointed to see him go. I remain deeply grateful for everything he helped us to achieve and treasure the relationship I continue to share with him to this day.

Jason was always willing to step up to the plate when needed, and I will always remember the memorable moment when he not only helped Eddie by playing when there was barely half a fit squad to choose from but also got him his first away win as a manager back in 2009 on that cold evening at Dagenham and Redbridge with his iconic assist!

The camaraderie I have shared with Jason has also been shaped by our personal relationship, particularly during pre-season and warm-weather trips. While Eddie often immersed himself in tactical planning, Jason had the ability to switch gears and engage with the team more casually. This balance between their professional and social dynamics underscores the perfect partnership, which drove AFC Bournemouth and now Newcastle United both on and off the pitch. Their working relationship remains a key factor in both clubs' accomplishments.

A few days before Jason departed, former England international defender Jonathan Woodgate had arrived to replace Graeme Jones as first team coach. The 41-year-old former Middlesbrough manager, initially appointed in an interim capacity, brought with him a fresh perspective and was a tactical shift aimed at revitalising the team's performance. His emphasis on regaining momentum and consistency seemed to be exactly what we needed for the challenging road ahead. Jonathan's first game in caretaker charge was a 3-2 success against Birmingham and his position as Head Coach was soon made permanent.

March saw former Liverpool Under 23 coach Gary O'Neil join our backroom team as first team coach as we continued to hover just outside the play-off places. The speedy Arnaut Danjuma was scoring regularly and proving a handful for most Championship defences, but on the downside, Lewis Cook's fine season was ended by a cruciate ligament injury in a 1-1 draw at Preston.

Despite the loss of Lewis, six consecutive wins in April lifted us into the Championship's top three and once again we were challengers for automatic promotion. But defeats in each of our final fixtures meant a sixth-place finish and if we were to make an immediate return to the top flight, it would be via the play-offs.

For the first time since the previous December, Covid-19 conditions had been eased enough to allow a limited number of home supporters to attend each of the play-off semi-final matches and a crowd of 2,000 was at the Vitality Stadium to see us face Brentford in the first leg. While the global pandemic continued to pose a threat to public safety, it was understandable that this should of course take absolute priority, but the financial cost across all levels of English football was now being counted in millions of pounds. We were not at threat of extinction ourselves, but I felt for the owners of clubs at a lower level and could understand their increasing concerns.

Danjuma scored the only goal of the game early in the second half and once again the atmosphere generated by the supporters clearly helped the players. Although we created the bulk of the chances, we could have found ourselves going into the return leg all square had Bryan Mbeumo not missed from six yards out with the goal gaping, or Emiliano Marcondes not been denied by a smart block from Asmir Begović.

It was Danjuma again who no doubt stunned the 4,000 Brentford supporters permitted in their new Gtech Community Stadium for the second leg when he doubled our advantage after an early counterattack. However, from that point on, events seemed to conspire against us as a series of hotly disputed decisions went in favour of the home side.

I believe that the Australian referee, Jared Gillet, was officiating in his first match in English football and his inexperience was clear to see. First, Brentford were awarded a penalty kick when Lloyd Kelly was harshly adjudged to have handled a cross that rolled up his leg and onto his arm while he was on the ground. Deliberate handball it certainly was not, but Ivan Toney was given the opportunity to step up and strike the penalty past Asmir Begović to level the leg at 1-1.

However, the tie really turned upon the sending off of our defender Chris Mepham in the first half. Chris brought down Mbeumo when the Brentford winger was barely over the halfway line. To say he was clean through on goal from that distance was at the very least questionable. Mbeumo still had half the pitch to run unless he was going to try an ambitious chip over our goalkeeper's head. He had missed a similar opportunity in the first leg, and I think it is reasonable to say that this may well have also been going through his mind.

Chris was under immense pressure, playing against his former club and he made the call to stop Mbeumo and paid a heavy price. In this case, I believe it was the wrong call as we were still ahead in the tie at that time and there was no guarantee Mbeumo would score. Whatever the outcome though, we would at least still have had eleven men on the pitch for the rest of the game. Having said that, it should be remembered that Chris did what he thought was best and I have never missed a shot or misjudged a tackle while scoring every goal from my seat in the stand!

Brentford went 2-1 ahead early in the second half to draw level on aggregate and as extra-time loomed, our dreams of an immediate return to the Premier League were shattered when the Bees scored again in the 81st minute to make their way to the final.

While Brentford went on to beat Swansea at Wembley and gain their first-ever promotion to the Premier League, we were left with another reminder of the fiercely competitive nature of the Championship. Despite this, I believed that our hard work towards the end of the season had laid a sturdy foundation for future aspirations. In Dominic Solanke and Arnaut

Danjuma, we had strikers of exceptional quality, and this was further supported by each of them hitting fifteen goals in the Championship. Looking at the bigger picture, we also learned valuable lessons, both strategically and operationally, that would inform our planning moving forward.

Aside from our exploits in the Championship, we had also enjoyed a run in the FA Cup which took us to the quarter-final stage of the competition for only the second time in the club's history. Without the presence of supporters, there was nothing like the level of excitement we had enjoyed upon the previous occasion in 1957, when we beat Wolves and Tottenham before losing to Manchester United, but it was a considerable achievement, nonetheless. I could only imagine the electric atmosphere that would normally have been created for a tie at home to Southampton in the last eight. I really do not believe that Saints would have been quite such comfortable 3-0 winners as they were, had the match been played in front of a packed Vitality Stadium.

I must acknowledge at this point the exceptional Asmir Begović who had a fantastic season, and became a pillar of brilliance for our club with over 100 appearances since his initial loan move from Portsmouth back in 2007. Asmir was featured in all but one Championship match this season, achieving eighteen clean sheets across all competitions. A moment that particularly stood out to me, aside from his outstanding goalkeeping abilities, was on 13 March against Barnsley. In that match, he authoritatively caught a free kick in the box and, with a monster throw from the box over the halfway line, set up Junior Stanislas on the right side of the pitch. Junior then ran on to set up Arnaut Danjuma for an easy tap-in goal. It was a fantastic counterattack goal, and even though we lost the game 3-2, Asmir's abilities in goal were of the highest quality that season. As a result, he was named in the Division Team of the Year and also received the Bournemouth Echo Player of the Year Trophy.

Throughout it all though, the steadfast support from our fans was invaluable. Even when they couldn't be present physically, their passion and commitment were unwavering, driving us to continue pushing forward. Looking ahead, I remained optimistic and what we saw as our journey back to the Premier League continued to be fuelled by a strong resolve to learn, adapt and strive for excellence in every aspect of our club operations.

"

A truly kind and special person and **very much an icon in the footballing world.** He is someone I look up to and really appreciate. Jeff, you are a legend and thank you for everything.

ASMIR BEGOVIĆ #THECHAIRMAN

"

IN THEIR WORDS ON JEFF

Asmir Begović
Former Goalkeeper at AFC Bournemouth

Jeff Mostyn is one of the best people in football I have ever met. One of the most genuine and caring gentlemen you can ever come across. In an industry that is very ruthless, cutthroat and difficult to build a relationship in, Jeff was the complete outlier. A man that would unify a football club and all of the people associated with it. I remember his warm welcome to myself and my family when I joined Bournemouth. These are little things that we will never forget and was so refreshing in this industry.

One of my favourite dealings with Jeff was when he joined my *Season of Sports* podcast on a mid-season trip to Portugal with the AFC Bournemouth first team squad. His contribution provided a great insight and at that time it was one of the first interviews of its kind. This just sums up the man.

A truly kind and special person and very much an icon in the footballing world. He is someone I look up to and really appreciate. Jeff, you are a legend and thank you for everything.

CHAPTER 13
GETTING BACK TO THE PREMIER LEAGUE

Tuesday 3 May is no ordinary day. As we face Nottingham Forest at home in our penultimate match of the season, the stakes are sky-high. Fulham are set to be promoted as champions, but a win for us will guarantee our own ticket back to the Premier League as runners-up.

The air is thick with anticipation, and just when we think the atmosphere can't get any more charged, we receive the best news imaginable: David Brooks is clear of cancer and ready to resume his playing career. If ever there was a boost we needed before such a crucial game, this is it.

The stadium is electric, buzzing with energy that only heightens as the tense match begins. Unlike our memorable fixture against Bolton in 2015 when we first ascended to the Premier League, every moment is edge-of-the-seat intense. Drama fills the play: our former striker Sam Surridge hits the crossbar, and we see the referee wave away Forest's strong plea for a penalty in the second half.

The game remains on a knife-edge until the 83rd minute. Then, substitute Kieffer Moore turns an opportunity into a celebration with a sharp finish after being on the end of a low free kick unmarked in the box. As the ball hits the net, sealing our victory and return to English football's top tier, a wall of noise erupts around us.

The culmination of our hard work has paid off, leading to a double celebration of sorts, especially after the frenzy Forest had caused over the original postponement. It is a moment of sheer, unbridled joy. To secure a second promotion to the Premier League is beyond anything I could have dreamt back in 2007 when I bought the club. I stand there for a moment, overcome with disbelief and happiness, thinking back to that time. Who would have thought we'd achieve not one, but two promotions to the Premier League? Absolutely incredible!

Jeff Mostyn

* * *

After narrowly missing out on promotion the previous season, our ambitions for returning to the Premier League were bolder than ever. The club rallied under a strengthened vision, and changes made during the summer saw the departure of Jonathan Woodgate together with Stephen Purches and several of the backroom staff who had previously served under Eddie Howe. Woodgate deserved credit for the job he had done in difficult circumstances, but we were determined to make the 2021/22 campaign count.

The appointment of 40-year-old Scott Parker as our new Head Coach marked a fresh start with a strategic vision. Coming from Fulham, the former England international midfielder brought a wealth of experience and a keen tactical mind, aligning with our ethos of competitive and attractive football. In his first season in charge of Fulham, he had guided them to promotion to the Premier League, although they had been relegated back to the Championship shortly before he joined us. Gary O'Neil remained as first team coach while Scott brought with him several of the staff he had worked alongside at Craven Cottage, including assistant manager Matt Wells.

Scott's leadership promised to galvanise the team, injecting both discipline and creativity into our approach. Before the transfer window closed at the end of August, he had been forced to reshape the side. Both Begović and Danjuma had been named in the Championship team of the previous season, but they were now keen to move on, Danjuma making an expensive move to Villarreal, while Begović returned to the Premier League with Everton.

Despite these and other departures I was confident we again had a squad capable of competing at the top of the Championship. The transfer window was a busy time, with the arrival of key players to reinforce our ambitions. Midfielder Ryan Christie joined us from Celtic and former Portsmouth striker Jamal Lowe came from Swansea, while among those arriving on free transfers were former Everton and England defender Gary Cahill and Brentford's Emiliano Marcondes, who had scored the Bees' winning goal at Wembley in May. I felt that Gary's arrival was particularly significant for us, as he brought with him the invaluable experience from his international career with England and his successful tenure at Chelsea.

Thankfully, supporters were able to fully return to stadiums at the start of the 2021/22 campaign but there was one very significant absentee on the pitch. That was our Colombian midfielder Jefferson Lerma, who was serving a six-game suspension after being found guilty of a misdemeanour the previous season.

I was thankful that Jefferson had stayed with us after relegation from the Premier League when others chose to move on. He never gave less than 100 per cent to the cause but, unfortunately, the passionate nature of his play sometimes made him a soft target for opposition players and match officials, and as a result he collected more than his fair share of cautions.

Scott Parker's style of play placed the emphasis on controlling possession of the ball, passing it out of defence and switching play from right to left. It may not have set supporters' pulses racing but it would prove to be key in gaining promotion.

Remarkably, we secured eleven wins and four draws in our first fifteen Championship games. It was an incredible start, marking our best opening to any season in our history. Leading the charge was Dominic Solanke, who was instrumental in our success, scoring twelve goals in these initial fifteen games.

After returning from suspension, Lerma once again became a strong influence in midfield, but the undefeated run finally ended with a 2-1 home defeat by Preston at the beginning of November. The team's response was perfect though, with two goals each from Solanke and Jaidon Anthony bringing a 4-0 home victory over Swansea. Jaidon and fellow Academy graduate, left-back Jordan Zemura, produced some impressive performances with both benefitting from the understanding they had developed together in the Under 21s.

However, David Brooks looked just a shadow of the player we knew him to be, and he missed a number of games through illness. When test results revealed the terrible news that he was suffering from Hodgkin's lymphoma, it came as a great shock to us all, and the hearts of everybody associated with the football club went out to him. The football family came together as one with messages of encouragement and support as the 24-year-old began his remedial treatment.

David was a credit to himself in the way that he dealt with this blow, knowing he faced a lengthy period of treatment and recovery. Irrespective of how much time it would take, the level of support we could provide was our first concern while we all hoped and prayed there would be a positive outcome.

Although a sticky spell saw us go six games without a win and fall behind leaders Fulham, these crucial moments were defined by our ability to rally and respond. The squad's spirit and determination shone through in critical matches to ensure that our aspirations for promotion remained alive. We were boosted by the addition of former Burnley winger Robbie Brady, together with the return of Lewis Cook from injury, and now more determined than ever to gain promotion. The Christmas period saw us return to the top of the table, after wins against Queens Park Rangers and Cardiff City.

Determined to seize upon the progress made during the first half of the season we took the opportunity to add as many as eight players to the squad during the January transfer window and among those joining us on a permanent basis was Cardiff striker Kieffer Moore, while Liverpool defender Nat Phillips and Norwich midfielder Todd Cantwell arrived on loan. One long-serving player to leave the club, however, was Steve Cook, who moved to promotion rivals Nottingham Forest after making 356 League appearances for Bournemouth.

Although we had strengthened our numbers considerably, as the weeks passed, we were still to experience the usual ups and downs of a typical Championship season. Injuries and the relentless pace sometimes tested us to the full, but resilience was the hallmark of our approach. Fortunately, there was no hangover after an FA Cup slip-up at home to National League side Boreham Wood. Instead a positive response came in a 3-1 win against Birmingham City, although this was offset by Moore breaking his foot within five minutes of coming on as a second half substitute. Another of our January signings, Siriki Dembélé, then proved to be the matchwinner in a last gasp 2-1 success at Blackpool before Jamal Lowe produced a dramatic late winner at home to Stoke. It might have been a struggle at times, but nobody could question the team's work rate over 90 minutes.

Meanwhile, Fulham continued to set a fast pace at the top of the table and were in the process of opening up a very healthy lead. As if we needed another wake-up call, a defeat at Preston and a disappointing home draw against the Championship's bottom side, Peterborough, left us fourteen points behind the Cottagers, although we did have two games in hand. Teams were often defending deeply against us, and we struggled to break them down at times, but the great adaptability of the squad played a key role in achieving victories in three of our next four games with the other drawn, and we at least remained firmly in second place.

Dominic Solanke struck his 24th goal of the season in a 3-0 success at Huddersfield and while he continued to excel in attack, Nat Phillips and captain Lloyd Kelly were proving hard nuts to crack at the back, and Mark Travers was proving to be a colossus in goal and was on his way to a clean sweep at the end of season awards as well as winning the Championship's Golden Glove.

As the season drew to a close, we were grateful to Solanke once again for a last-minute equaliser against Fulham and a few days later to Kieffer Moore for another comeback point at Swansea. Having only just returned from injury, he came off the bench with the Welsh side 3-0 up at half-time and proceeded to score twice during a remarkable second half fightback which saw the game end 3-3. Although by now we were heavy favourites to finish as runners-up, there were occasions when we needed to keep a look-out over our shoulders as Nottingham Forest were making a late bid for automatic promotion themselves. We had been due to play them at home in February, but the game was postponed after damaging winds and severe weather conditions had caused structural damage to the Vitality Stadium and the general public were advised not to travel unless absolutely necessary.

At the time, Forest thought we were trying to pull a fast one as they believed we had a couple of players out through injury, but of course the decision to postpone was finally made by the Football League on grounds of public safety, after they had sought the advice of the police and the local authorities.

The revised date was set for the evening of Tuesday 3 May and Kieffer Moore's late goal proved enough to secure three points and with it a return to English football's top tier.

The players had performed at an incredibly high level during the sort of long, hard season so typical of the Championship, and securing automatic promotion was a testament to the hard work, dedication and unwavering belief within our club. It was a moment of immense pride, not just for the players and staff, but for every one of our wonderful supporters who were present and all those with the club at heart who were unable to be present. Throughout the season, maintaining a strong home record and harnessing the electrifying atmosphere at the Vitality Stadium were pivotal to our campaign strategy and with the target achieved, our Bubbles champagne lounge was certainly rocking again that night!

It's crucial to understand that bouncing back to the Premier League is no small achievement. Just consider that Leeds United took sixteen years to make their first comeback. Although ours was very much a team effort, I must mention the remarkable success enjoyed by Dominic Solanke. After receiving criticism in the past for his modest career goal-scoring record, Dominic provided the perfect response, and it was a delight to see him end the season with a total of thirty goals in the Championship and cup competitions.

The culmination of the season came after a home win against Millwall in our final game, when the players received their medals and the runners-up trophy. When I found a moment of solitude to relax afterwards, I simply put my hands together, looked up to the sky and whispered words of thanks.

There was so much to be pleased about throughout the club. In addition to the first team's success at the end of the season, Alan Connell's Under 18 side secured the EFL Youth Alliance title in February. The women's team, who had stepped up to the National League for the first time in 2021/22, played their first ever competitive game at the Vitality Stadium in April, which was watched by a crowd only just short of 1,600.

We had also staged the England Under 21's European Championship Qualifier against Andorra in March and launched our 'Hate Hurts Everyone' campaign focusing on the effect of abuse and discrimination on people in the community. This followed our award-winning 'Everyone Together' campaign, which had been centred upon tackling prejudice and promoting understanding. All these achievements augured well for the club's future well-being, and I truly believed we were heading in the right direction both on and off the pitch.

Jeff has always had the ability to bring it all together, and when I think of AFC Bournemouth, Jeff Mostyn – Mr Chairman – is always at the forefront of my mind and always will be. We all have a lot to thank Jeff for, both in the past and present, because if it wasn't for his actions in the past, the present might look very different. Up the Cherries – in all departments!

ALAN CONNELL #THECHAIRMAN

IN THEIR OWN WORDS ON JEFF

Alan Connell
Head Coach, AFC Bournemouth Development Squad

Mr Chairman or just Jeff, it didn't matter how you addressed him, or how you knew him, you would instantly feel his love and support when in his company.

For me, this was encapsulated ironically after I left AFC Bournemouth as a player and was playing for Bradford City. Having been beaten in the 2013 League Cup Final at Wembley, I was extremely disappointed but as I walked up the famous steps to collect my runners-up medal, I was very surprised to be greeted by a friendly face on the front row of the Royal Box who was representing the Football League. It was Jeff, a hug, a smile and an encounter neither of us have forgotten and one we still smile about now. His personal love and support to my family and I is something I will always be eternally grateful for.

Recognised for his achievements, leadership and most notably his wonderful character both internally and externally, Jeff has lived and breathed the highs and lows of AFC Bournemouth over many years. Leading the club from administration, relegation and minus seventeen points in League Two to the Premier League reflects on his love and unbelievable commitment to the club.

The football club is special and it's hard to explain how much it means to so many people, me included. I guess it's the familiarity, the feeling, the stadium, the memories, the journey we have been on and then the most important part in my opinion, the people. There are many groups of people that are the history and fabric of our club; supporters, players, staff, and Jeff stands tall among them all (well nearly at five foot six!). Jeff has always had the ability to bring it all together, and when I think of AFC Bournemouth, Jeff Mostyn – Mr Chairman – is always at the forefront of my mind and always will be. We all have a lot to thank Jeff for, both in the past and present, because if it wasn't for his actions in the past, the present might look very different. Up the Cherries – in all departments!

"

The people of Bournemouth owe you so much, Jeff, not just for saving our football club but also for keeping this unlikely driving instructor off the streets!

NEIL VACHER #THECHAIRMAN

"

IN THEIR OWN WORDS ON JEFF

Neil Vacher
Former Club Secretary of AFC Bournemouth

Firstly, may I say what a privilege it is to be able to pay this tribute to Jeff.

For a moment though, I would like to take everyone back to November 2006. Times were tough at AFC Bournemouth. The club was strapped for cash, its staff and bills were not being paid on time and creditors were circling for whatever they could get. The club was struggling to survive, and like most of the staff, I feared the worst.

Into this scenario came Jeff Mostyn to address the small number of us remaining at Dean Court. It was not the first time we had been introduced to a prospective new investor in the club, and, in all honesty, we did not expect to hear anything we had not heard before.

However, as Jeff spoke eloquently in his measured tone, the mood among us began to change. He kicked off by expressing his respect for everyone and offered thanks for the 'incredible job we were doing in very difficult circumstances'. There was a warmth and sincerity in his words, and it soon became clear that we were listening to a man with considerable business acumen, strong moral beliefs and, equally importantly, someone whose heart had already been won over by the club and its supporters.

Family meant everything to Jeff, and he clearly wanted AFC Bournemouth to become an extension of his own. But he soon hit the nail on the head – the club was in a financial mess and much as he would like to, he could not personally guarantee its short-term future, never mind anything long-term. He was clearly not someone who entertained unrealistic prophecies or promises, and he admitted that administration remained a possibility. But he left us in no doubt that his intention was to do everything within his power to try and keep the club alive.

We welcomed his straight-talking and could not fail to notice his emotional tone. Here was someone who had gained our respect, appeared to have the club's best interests at heart and made us all feel we had an important part to play in its future. Furthermore, Jeff was someone that you wanted to help succeed.

It was never going to be plain sailing of course and there would be plenty of rough waters to navigate along the way, well before Jeff's famous nod to Gerald Krasner two years later. At one point, winding up had seemed inevitable and, fearing redundancy, I even began to train as a driving instructor in case I needed to find another occupation. But Jeff remained true to his word and once again stepped forward to save the day.

In the years that followed, he provided the inspiration for others to come on board and became an irresistible force which enabled the club to push on and eventually achieve the seemingly impossible. He passionately believed that there were two dressing rooms within the club, one downstairs for the players and football staff, and another in the offices upstairs for the support team. Furthermore, he considered it his responsibility to ensure he was there when either one or both needed to be congratulated or consoled, never shying away from what he considered to be his duty, whatever the circumstances.

When Eddie Howe became manager in 2009, he and Jeff formed a bond which began in extreme adversity with the club desperately battling to retain its Football League status and eventually saw AFC Bournemouth in the unchartered heights of the Premier League. Incredible! But it was not just Eddie and the team that Jeff had inspired to achieve success. Whether you were a first team player or an admin assistant, a coach or a cleaner, in Jeff's eyes you played an important part in the success of the club. Hence the strapline 'Together, Anything is Possible'.

As club secretary during much of his tenure at Dean Court, I learned so much from Jeff about football, business and life. I very much admired the way in which he presented himself when addressing people from all walks of life. He became the face of AFC Bournemouth in good times and not such good times, but his polite and professional manner throughout did much to raise the esteem in which the football club was held, both within the game itself and across the local community.

I was honoured that Jeff entrusted me to look after his beloved boardroom on the rare occasions when he and Rosie were away on home matchdays. I could never hope to fill the shoes of someone with such a presence and persona of course, although one or two guests did at least enjoy hearing some different jokes! Jeff knew that I was operating slightly outside my comfort zone in this environment, but with his encouragement and faith, I became more assured whenever I hosted or on the occasions when I needed to speak in public.

When the team were playing away from home, it fell to me to make appropriate ticketing arrangements for our directors and whether the game was on a sunny Saturday on the south coast or a bleak Tuesday night somewhere in the far north, I knew that Jeff's would be the first name on my list to attend. Usually, Rosie would accompany him, although I was lucky enough to do so myself on a number of occasions. He was always good company, and it enabled me to witness the high esteem in which he was held in other clubs' boardrooms up and down the country.

Administratively, Jeff provided me with great support when dealing with delicate matters at the EFL, the Premier League and the FA. As you can probably imagine, I became a frequent caller during the club's transfer embargoes and cash flow difficulties and was often grateful for Jeff's expertise in helping to find ways forward. I will always consider myself to have been extremely fortunate in spending a large part of my career at AFC Bournemouth working alongside him and am proud to have been able to play a small part in the success of 'my club', the one I have supported for over sixty years.

In addition, it has been my privilege to be able to assist Jeff in the preparation of this book and to revisit with him some of the many memorable moments during his time at AFC Bournemouth. Our conversations have stretched on for many hours and at times have been very emotional. The enormous depth of feeling he has for the club remains clearly evident and I know these memories are dear to him. It is a truly wonderful story, beyond the dreams of all our supporters, and one both of us will never forget.

The people of Bournemouth owe you so much, Jeff, not just for saving our football club but also for keeping this unlikely driving instructor off the streets!

PART III
GIVING BACK

'Knowing that I could help change lives by collaborating with charitable organisations filled me with immense pride.'

CHAPTER 14
TIME TO STEP ASIDE

As I prepare for my final official duty as chairman of AFC Bournemouth, I can't help but feel the weight of a full-circle moment in my life. Before stepping down in favour of Bill Foley and transitioning out of my role, I will be honouring a great woman, the late Queen Elizabeth, at a match against Newcastle United. It is a day set for deep reflection across all Premier League and EFL clubs, following a week of postponed games in respect for Her Majesty.

Our club historian, Neil Vacher, approaches me with the request to lay a wreath at St James's Park. It is an honour I cannot refuse, with the arrangement made by Newcastle United and their chair, Amanda Staveley, whom I've met before at Premier League meetings. Before the match, we are briefed on the protocol: walk to the centre circle, lay the wreath, and join the players and officials in a moment of commemoration.

In the boardroom, Amanda and I share a few words before making our way to the tunnel where the wreath awaits us. She is incredibly reassuring and kind, understanding the significance of the task before us. The presence of the armed forces transports me back to my two decades with them; their pomp and ceremony are familiar and comforting.

Standing at the back of the tunnel with the wreath in hand, Amanda outlines the procedure – where to walk, where to stand. As we await our turn, the teams led by their captains begin to emerge. Unexpectedly, the atmosphere lightens as familiar faces from Newcastle greet me warmly. Eddie Howe, Callum Wilson, Matt Ritchie – they are all my men. The camaraderie is palpable, and Amanda humorously remarks on how well-loved I must be. I joke back about my seventeen-year head start, and with that, some of the pressure eases.

As we step onto the pitch, the roar of 55,000 voices reverberates around me, sending chills down my spine. In that moment, the sheer magnitude of the occasion hits me. Words feel inadequate to capture the honour of laying that wreath for the club in memory of the Queen. Eddie later tells me he hadn't expected to see me walking out to the centre circle amid the standing teams, which adds a layer of surprise and meaning to the event.

After the match, I spend time with Eddie in his room, remembering our shared journey and the significance of that day. Matt Ritchie, with open arms, embraces me for a moment. It is a day filled with solemnity and profound honour, one I will never forget, and a deeply poignant and personal milestone in my life.

* * *

Returning to the Premier League after a year in the Championship was both a challenge and an opportunity, but I did not know that the 2022/23 season would turn out to be my final season as chairman at AFC Bournemouth. From the very beginning, our goal was clear: to strengthen our status in top-flight football while building upon the solid foundations laid in previous seasons. This was characterised by meticulous planning, as we sought to ensure our playing squad was prepared to meet the Premier League's rigorous demands.

Our approach focused on strategic acquisitions to strengthen the team, welcoming players who could deliver both impact and resilience on the field. It was crucial to blend seasoned Premier League experience with youthful vigour, thus creating a balanced and dynamic line-up.

Significant departures in the summer transfer window were Gary Cahill and Robbie Brady, but their absence was offset by the arrival of former West Ham full-back Ryan Fredericks and Blackburn midfielder Joe Rothwell. Middlesbrough's exciting young winger Marcus Tavernier was another to join us. Soon after our 2-0 opening-day success against Aston Villa, Brazilian goalkeeper Neto arrived from Barcelona and Argentinian central defender Marcos Senesi joined from Feyenoord.

I felt a profound sense of responsibility to ensure that our tactical objectives were aligned with safeguarding the club's long-term vision. We knew we were a little short in certain areas of the pitch and expected that it would take a little time for the team to settle at the higher level, although the opening day's win gave us much encouragement. We understood that the Premier League's hallmark intensity and unpredictability meant that once again, each match was an opportunity to learn, adapt, and demonstrate our growth.

However, we did not look competitive during a 4-0 defeat at reigning champions Manchester City nor in a 3-0 reverse at home to Arsenal. Worse was to follow though in the shape of a club record equalling 9-0 defeat against Liverpool at Anfield.

After the game, our Head Coach, Scott Parker, made comments in a television interview which were disrespectful towards the club and the playing squad. As a result of these and other comments made around the same time, Scott was subsequently dismissed and left immediately, together with several of his backroom staff.

I do not feel that it would be right for me to say anything further as matters regarding football operations were no longer in my jurisdiction. However, it would be remiss of me while writing this book not to praise Scott in his role as Head Coach, together with his backroom team, for leading the football club back to the Premier League after just one season in charge.

It was vital, though, that the club should remain aligned in the manner that had brought us so much success in our recent history, and with this in mind, first team coach Gary O'Neil was placed in interim charge, assisted by fellow coaches Shaun Cooper and Tommy Elphick. The players had been left somewhat shell-shocked, particularly goalkeeper Mark Travers, whose confidence had inevitably been shaken. Neto took over between the posts at this point and a hard-earned 0-0 draw at home to Wolves four days later showed the real character of the squad.

I was particularly impressed with Gary, Tommy and Shaun who, together with the players, displayed such a high level of adaptability and professionalism in difficult circumstances. Their approach underscored our collective commitment to see AFC Bournemouth thrive at the highest level.

A 3-2 home win against Nottingham Forest, who had gone on to achieve promotion by winning the previous season's play-offs, was another benchmark before the following weekend saw matches postponed as a mark of respect after the sad passing of Queen Elizabeth II. Seven days later, on 17 September, came a first meeting with former manager Eddie Howe since his appointment as Head Coach at Newcastle United.

The 1-1 draw on Tyneside meant that the team was still unbeaten since Parker's departure, and this run was extended to six before a 1-0 home defeat against Southampton in mid-October. As a club, we had quickly adjusted to the pace and competitiveness, and it was inspiring to watch the team rally together, displaying remarkable tenacity and courage. Our ambition remained unwavering: securing our place in the League and laying firm groundwork for future successes. Every point we earned during this run was a testament to the hard work and dedication of our entire team, both on and off the field.

By the time we reached an extended international break for the World Cup Finals in Qatar in late November, we had risen to 14th in the Premier League table and progressed to the fourth round of the Carabao Cup. At the finals themselves, Kieffer Moore and Chris Mepham became the first active AFC Bournemouth players to take part in the finals since Colin Clarke in 1986. At the same time, Gary O'Neil took the rest of the playing squad for some hot-weather work in Dubai.

MY FINAL SEASON

It had now become clear to me that this would be my final season as chairman. With the club's remarkable growth, Maxim Demin had sold his full stake in the club to Bill Foley of Black Knight Football. After discussions with Neill Blake and Jim Frevola, who was soon to become the club's first President of Business, it was made clear to me that Bill would take over as chairman, just as he had done at each of the businesses he owned. I respected that and agreed to take on a new role as club ambassador when the sale had been completed.

By the time the season resumed on 20 December the deal had been completed. Nobody with the club's interests at heart would ever forget the massive debt of thanks owed to Maxim Demin for the achievements he had made possible, but he, Neill Blake and I believed that Bill, an American businessman and philanthropist, could provide the investment necessary to sustain and build on the club's remarkable growth in recent years.

On 22 December 2022, I stepped down, entrusting the helm to Bill as the new chairman and wished him the utmost success. In the meantime, I continued to host in the boardroom and ensured that visiting directors and guests received the respect they were entitled to, while also looking after members of the Foley family, and other guests from America. In fact, I was honoured and proud to be able to do so and did my best to make everyone feel special.

Remembering my final day as chairman, I am overwhelmed with emotion. Words can scarcely convey the depth of my feelings about the previous seventeen years. Serving in this role has been an immense privilege, but it was undeniably the right time to step down.

We still found results difficult to come by on the pitch as the new year dawned, until a 1-0 home win against Liverpool in mid-March set us on a run of six wins from nine games which saw us move up to 13th in the table. During this period, we were overjoyed not just to welcome David Brooks back to the side after his recovery from illness but also to see him receive such a wonderful reception from supporters up and down the country. I cannot praise him enough for his courage, endurance and determination.

Further wins over soon-to-be-relegated Southampton and Leeds United all but mathematically made us safe with four games remaining, which was a remarkable achievement. Gary, Tommy and Shaun together with the players and backroom staff had every right to feel proud of their achievements.

It was fitting for me that our last game should be at Everton, a club I have always held close to my heart due to my friendship with, the now sadly passed, Bill Kenwright. Bill was an absolute gentleman and one of my great mentors, and it was always a great honour to sit alongside him in the boardroom at Goodison Park. Mind you, Bill never forgot to mention an occasion when I was supposed to be looking after him at the Vitality Stadium soon after our first promotion to the Premier League. I had been delayed due to an important meeting and it was after 2 p.m. when I bounced into the boardroom and started to make my introductions and apologies. Bill's response was to tell me that my dear wife Rose had already taken over such duties in my absence, that she was a much better host than me, had delivered a delightful welcoming address and in his eyes was now chairman, so I could *** off! I think he repeated that story every time I met him afterwards!

I can remember talking to Jeff after his first Premier League chairman's meeting and he expressed the pride that he felt attending on behalf of AFC Bournemouth. Did the prestige of being chairman of a Premier League club change Jeff in any way? Definitely not. He still continued to be the same person we knew and loved.

RICHARD OSBORNE #THECHAIRMAN

IN THEIR OWN WORDS ON JEFF

Richard Osborne
Lifetime Vice President of AFC Bournemouth

I have been a supporter of AFC Bournemouth since the mid 1960s and a vice president of the club since 1994. I am a retired chartered accountant and my firm regularly sponsored matches in the 1990s and 2000s. It has also sponsored the club's Business Club and related events since its inception in 2011.

As a lifelong supporter I have experienced many ups and downs, culminating with the club being promoted to the Premier League at the end of the 2014/15 season. However, in my opinion, this would not have happened if it wasn't for the club's previous chairman, Jeff Mostyn. I remember Jeff arriving at the club in 2006 and joining a consortium to own the club. This I understand involved Jeff investing significant sums over a period of time, but despite this, the club was placed in administration in early 2008. I can clearly remember a press conference called by the administrator, Gerald Krasner, who advised that unless he was given a cheque for a six-figure sum at the end of the meeting to meet impending debts, he would have no option but to liquidate the club. The consequences of this would have been unthinkable, i.e. no football club. Only one person was willing to inject such a sum: Jeff Mostyn, and this he did. As a result, the club continued and the rest is history! For the decision Jeff made that day I am forever thankful, and also to his wife Rosie for supporting him during that difficult time and for being at his side ever since.

When Jeff joined the club, he was running a very successful financial services company providing advice to members of the armed forces, and I am sure that the experience gained owning and managing that business would have helped greatly in carrying out his duties at AFC Bournemouth.

Over the years, I would talk to Jeff and Rosie frequently while attending matches and also at commercial events held at the club, such as lunches and dinners. I would like to think that Jeff and I have become good friends during his time at the club.

What soon becomes apparent when you meet Jeff is his passion for the club and his ability to make you feel comfortable in his presence. His infectious humour enlightens any conversation that you have with him. As chairman of the club he was personable to everyone, the players, staff and most of all the club's supporters, for whom he would always make time for a friendly conversation.

During my time supporting the club I have got to know many of the club's staff well, particularly those in the Commercial Department and I know that they all have the greatest admiration for Jeff. Indeed, the approach to his chairmanship appeared to create a visible family atmosphere within the club.

He also had a fantastic relationship with the manager Eddie Howe and would always visit the dressing room before the game to wish the players well for the match; he would also visit afterwards, win or lose. Who can forget the scenes in the dressing room after the Bolton promotion game when the players were giving him the bumps? It showed the rapport that he had built up with them and the respect that the players had for him.

On a personal note, I was delighted to be invited into the boardroom on a matchday from time to time, and Jeff and Rosie were such excellent hosts. They would always afford such a friendly welcome to away directors and their guests, many of whom have become close friends to them.

I was also invited to join Jeff as his guest at away matches on one or two occasions, and I remember a game at Hartlepool, I think it was in 2012, when we were playing in Division One. The game was played on a Sunday and shown live on television due to an international break, meaning that there were no Premier League or Championship matches. Four of us flew to Newcastle Airport and travelled to Hartlepool by car. We thought that lunch in Newcastle would be appropriate and this was arranged. During the lunch 'My Way' was played on the sound system. As we had consumed a few glasses of red wine we started to sing along. On the next table there were two couples having lunch and the ladies showed their appreciation with a round of applause! In reply to that Jeff stood up and armed with the pepper pot as a microphone went over to their table and serenaded them. It was hilarious and this perfectly summed up Jeff. He could endear himself to all!

In recent years the football club has partnered local charities, one of which was Lewis-Manning Hospice Care. I have written these notes the day after attending a charity event, held by Lewis-Manning, at which Jeff was the guest speaker. Not only did he talk about his time at AFC Bournemouth but also his life prior to that, and the passion in his speech was inspirational to everyone present. At the end of the meeting Jeff was appointed a patron of the charity and his involvement going forward is bound to be such an asset to the charity.

How can you sum up Jeff's time at AFC Bournemouth? It was a momentous journey. From his financial commitment to the club in the early years, to him being chairman under Maxim Demin's ownership, Jeff showed such passion and loyalty, and quite rightly gained respect in the world of football, particularly after the club gained promotion to the Premier League. Could you say that Jeff being chairman of a Premier League club was reward for his financial commitment in earlier years? Possibly, but equally I believe that Jeff played a huge part in the success that the club has enjoyed and also in promoting AFC Bournemouth worldwide.

I can remember talking to Jeff after his first Premier League chairman's meeting and he expressed the pride that he felt attending on behalf of AFC Bournemouth. Did the prestige of being chairman of a Premier League club change Jeff in any way? Definitely not. He still continued to be the same person we knew and loved.

Is it possible to sum up Jeff in one word? Extremely difficult, but if I had to it would be 'inspirational'.

I take this opportunity to thank you, Jeff and Rose, for what you have done for this fantastic football club and for putting a smile on my face on so many occasions. You both have my very best wishes for the future and my wife Gill and I look forward to seeing you at Dean Court for many years to come.

❝

Jeff always stayed true to himself, which was a great lesson to me. He believed that authenticity was key and not feeling intimidated by those with more seniority or influence.

ROB MITCHELL #THECHAIRMAN

❞

IN THEIR OWN WORDS ON JEFF

Rob Mitchell
Commercial Director at AFC Bournemouth

In 2008 I had the privilege of meeting Jeff for the first time while attending an AFC Bournemouth match as a hospitality guest. The club was in League One at the time, so very different from the AFC Bournemouth of today. Despite the pressure Jeff faced as chairman and owner at that time – working through financial difficulties and the looming threat of relegation to League Two – his charm, positivity and energy were unmistakable, at least outwardly. I'm sure inwardly he was feeling very emotional and stressed by the precarious position the club was in at that time!

What I first noticed was how Jeff went out of his way to make everyone feel welcome, whether you were a hospitality guest like me who he'd never met, or one of the important main sponsors helping to fund the club. This was one of many lessons I learned from Jeff; to treat everyone with equal respect and professionalism, no matter who they are, or their background. As Jeff would say, 'In life, it's important to win friends and influence people.'

Whether you're a fan or work in football, it is very emotional. When working in the sport, you experience how much goes into the business on and off the pitch to prepare for each matchday. The team winning or losing, which is out of all our control, can massively impact the following week at work, and even job security or progress in your career depending on how the team ends a season. From Jeff I learned the importance of maintaining composure in front of fellow staff and clients. Win, lose or draw, Jeff always stayed professional and level-headed in public. However, behind closed doors, if a result hadn't gone our way, there would understandably be some expletives from both of us!

We all remember that unforgettable night when AFC Bournemouth were promoted to the Premier League for the first time in the club's history. Jeff, in true iconic fashion, burst into the dressing room to celebrate with the players, with his hair wild, looking like a mad professor! The moment was broadcast live on *Sky Sports*, showing him being lifted by the team and spanked on the backside by Callum Wilson, while shouting, 'I LOVE THESE F***ING BOYS!' Hilarious and a moment many of us will never forget!

If I had to describe Jeff in one word, it would be 'charismatic'. He has a way of drawing people in and making them feel like they belong. This quality, among many others, made him a great figurehead for AFC Bournemouth during his time as chairman. He was incredibly proud to undertake this role, and his passion extended beyond the club itself as he was always deeply committed to helping the local community. Through his charitable work, Jeff brought the club closer to the people of Bournemouth, connecting even with non-football fans. It is clear that community engagement is more than just a responsibility to him, it is also personal passion.

Working with Jeff was a rewarding experience. He has the knack to bring energy and humour to pretty much any situation. His light-heartedness would ease the atmosphere, but he always remained professional and was a great support for me when it came to building relationships with both new and existing business partners. I admit there were times when I'd hold my breath, unsure how one of his jokes would land, but he has a real gift for making people laugh, no matter their background or who they are.

Throughout my time working with Jeff, I learned countless lessons. He taught me the importance of listening – reminding me that, 'God made us with two ears and one mouth.' I took on board how he conducted himself with grace and confidence around people from all walks of life, including those with celebrity status and in high positions.

Jeff always stayed true to himself, which was a great lesson to me. He believed that authenticity was key and not feeling intimidated by those with more seniority or influence. And when it came to public speaking, his advice was simple but profound: 'No one knows your script.' This is advice I take with me when I undertake public speaking, and I have also passed on these wise words to my colleagues.

One of my fondest memories is being invited to Jeff's honorary doctorate ceremony at Bournemouth University. I attended with my colleague at the time, Alice Jeans, and we had our photo taken stood alongside Jeff in his gown and mortarboard. Jeff won't mind me saying this, but with both Alice and I being slightly taller than him, the picture came out looking like Alice and I were the proud parents at our son's big graduation day, albeit a son who must have had a tough, uphill paper round, looking somewhat older than his 'parents'!

Another great memory of good times and professional support from Jeff was when I was in Dubai preparing to deliver workshops to commercial and operations staff from clubs and governing bodies from across the UAE. It was the first time I'd been to Dubai, and I travelled on my own, so I was feeling pretty anxious about the days ahead. It was good timing that Jeff and Rose happened to be on holiday there at the same time and invited me over to their hotel the day before my first workshops.

True to form, Jeff was great at helping me relax! We spent the afternoon on their hotel beach, laughing, drinking and enjoying some shisha, which I quickly learned is a traditional thing to do while in Dubai! I was very grateful to him and Rose giving up their holiday time to spend with me and for putting me in a positive mindset!

It has been a pleasure to spend time and get to know members of Jeff's friends and family in the boardroom at AFC Bournemouth over the years, including his wife Rose, daughters Alex and Janine, and sons Blake and Darren. I would like to express my heartfelt gratitude to Jeff for the support he has given me during my time at the club. I'm also honoured that you've asked me to contribute a piece to your book – thank you for this wonderful opportunity.

CHAPTER 15
MY CHARITY WORK IN THE COMMUNITY

From a very young age, giving back was woven into the fabric of who I am. Even in my earliest years, before my sister contracted polio, my parents instilled in me the importance of supporting others, teaching me more through their actions than words.

As chairman, my goal has always been to unite the Bournemouth community by celebrating everyday heroes and charities, and supporting those who endeavour to overcome adversity, showcasing the profound influence of football beyond the pitch.

This deep passion for community involvement led me to work with various charities and to proudly serve on the FA Disability Committee. Thinking about my sister's life and the impact she had on me, I realise how much her journey influenced my dedication to charitable endeavours. Her story fuels my commitment to making a difference, using the power of football to bring people together and inspire positive change.

* * *

My involvement with five charities happened organically, step by step. But why did I feel compelled to engage with charitable work? Whenever I speak publicly, I emphasise two key institutions that I believe are pivotal in any city or town. First, universities, which are centres of learning excellence. Second, and equally important, are football clubs – the epicentres of influence within communities.

Given this influence, I believe those of us involved in football have a duty to the community. As chairman of a football club, I embraced this responsibility with utmost seriousness. I never expected that I would become a centre of influence myself. Yet, knowing that I could help change lives by collaborating with charitable organisations filled me with immense pride.

THE CHERRIES COMMUNITY SPORTS TRUST AND CHERRIES COMMUNITY FUND

The Cherries Community Sports Trust has been central to my journey since I bought the club in 2006. Steve Cuss, the head of the Trust, had to explain to me that the Trust operates independently as a charity. This separation is crucial to maintain its integrity and purpose. We've been fortunate to receive substantial funding from the Football Foundation and the Premier League, which plays a vital role in our success in the community.

Since stepping down as chairman at the football club, I am now ambassador for the Trust, which has allowed me to continue my support.

Steve Cuss oversees the distribution of the community fund. The fund is generated from our club supporters through the matchday lottery. Fifty per cent goes to prize winning and fifty per cent goes to the community. During my time as chairman, Steve, Marc Pugh and Marcus Tavernier and I selected the beneficiaries.

Requests weren't limited to infrastructure. Some sought equipment – a modest but vital need – and we'd provide footballs, cones or mini goal posts, etc., ensuring their immediate requirements were met. Others would request support for fundraising campaigns, like marathons for causes such as prostate cancer. We supported them generously, recognising their broader impact by empowering individuals motivated by their personal convictions.

An aspect I truly cherish is involving players beyond the pitch. Players like Marc Pugh and Marcus Tavernier have had extraordinary influence in the community. Their visits to schools were nothing short of magical, with students listening in awe, utterly captivated.

In one memorable instance, Mark and I visited one of Care South's residential homes, where he engaged residents by kicking a football around, a simple yet profound interaction. It's remarkable witnessing a player's effect beyond the game, especially considering how challenging it can be to secure their presence away from their familiar confines.

Reflecting on my journey, I never envisioned this aspect of my responsibility as chairman, where the community dimension adds such invaluable richness. It's an honour I cherish deeply, aware that not many chairmen partake in such immersive roles. Our club's recognition, such as earning the Advanced Equality Standard on our first attempt – a feat only one other

Premier League club has achieved to this date – speaks volumes about our commitment.

Garth Crooks, chair of the Equality Independent Football Commission's racism and equality issues committee, once acknowledged this dedication, noting how I was the sole chairman actively participating in team presentations. His words, acknowledging me as a true equality standard bearer for the club, still resonate deeply. This recognition reaffirms why this role is more than a job; it's a calling enriched by unsparing community service.

DORSET CANCER CARE FOUNDATION

I was introduced by Eve Went, co-founder of Dorset Cancer Care Foundation by Rob Mitchell, my Commercial Director, to discuss potential commercial opportunities. Meeting Eve was transformative – she explained that the Dorset Cancer Care Foundation exclusively supports local people in Dorset. A hundred per cent of the donations to Dorset Cancer Care Foundation go directly to those in need.

What I found most compelling about this charity was its comprehensive support structure. When people think of cancer charities, they often focus solely on the patients. While supporting cancer sufferers is crucial, this charity also aids their families, assisting with mortgage payments, rent, utility bills and transportation costs. Many families endure financial strain because a loved one might have to stop working to provide care, exacerbating the impact of this dreadful disease.

I once organised a fundraising event at the football club, aptly named 'An Evening with Jeff', where we raised £25,000. This fund was used to send a cancer patient to the United States for treatment that was unavailable in the UK. Sadly, despite two treatments, the intervention did not yield the hoped-for results. However, we found solace in knowing that we were able to relieve the financial burden on the family, allowing them to pursue this last hopeful avenue of treatment without incurring unmanageable debt.

Every step of my journey with the Dorset Cancer Care Foundation has underscored the importance of community support. It's about empowering families when they need it most, ensuring they do not face insurmountable financial hurdles. Providing these layers of support, from helping with everyday expenses to facilitating crucial medical treatment abroad, reaffirms my belief in the power of charitable work and the profound impact it can have on people's lives.

"

Thanks to Jeff's **infectious energy and determination**, the Dorset Cancer Care Foundation is gaining momentum, offering vital assistance to those battling cancer.

EVE WENT #THECHAIRMAN

"

IN THEIR OWN WORDS ON JEFF

Eve Went
Co-Founder of Dorset Cancer Care Foundation

In 2012, as a co-founder, I initiated the establishment of the charity. Our inaugural patron, Harry Redknapp, lent his support early on, marking a significant milestone for us. However, as the Dorset Cancer Care Foundation expanded, we recognised the need for another influential figure to champion our cause within the community.

Despite my lack of connections in the football world, I was determined to secure a patron deeply rooted in our local fabric. Jeff emerged as the perfect fit. I persistently reached out, bombarding him with messages until he finally relented. Well, perhaps not bombarded, but I did make persistent efforts. When we finally met, I shared my personal journey behind founding the charity and emphasised the critical role it played in alleviating the financial burdens faced by cancer patients – a struggle I knew all too well. Jeff was genuinely moved by our mission and readily agreed to lend his support.

Navigating the charity landscape proved challenging for me, with my background primarily in nursing and entrepreneurship rather than non-profit management. However, Jeff's unwavering enthusiasm and support breathed new life into our endeavours. His active involvement, particularly in ensuring the success of our fundraising auctions, has been invaluable. What's truly endearing is his genuine care and attention to everyone, not just the VIPs, at our events. Together with his wife, Rosie, Jeff stands steadfastly by our side, amplifying our efforts within the Dorset community.

Thanks to Jeff's infectious energy and determination, the Dorset Cancer Care Foundation is gaining momentum, offering vital assistance to those battling cancer.

On a lighter note, there's a humorous anecdote involving Jeff and our black-tie event last year. Despite an unforeseen circumstance preventing his physical attendance, Jeff lightened the mood by sending a cardboard cut-out of himself – a gesture that brought laughter and camaraderie to the evening.

LEWIS-MANNING HOSPICE CARE

Last year marked a significant milestone in my involvement with Lewis-Manning, as I moved from being an ambassador to becoming a patron. My journey with this remarkable charity began under the inspiring leadership of Clare Gallie, their dedicated chief executive. Throughout my time as an ambassador, I seized every opportunity to support their fundraising efforts, often donating signed football shirts or boots for their auctions. My presence at various events was aimed at boosting their profile, as just having 'Jeff Mostyn, chairman of AFC Bournemouth' in attendance could significantly enhance both the event's success and the charity's visibility.

Lewis-Manning's focus on end-of-life care is a cause that resonates deeply with me. As someone holding a position of influence, both as chairman of AFC Bournemouth and ambassador of the Community Sports Trust, I could not contemplate declining the role of patron. While it comes with more responsibilities than being an ambassador, as Clare now often reaches out for assistance with fundraising efforts or newsletter contributions, my affection and respect for Lewis-Manning and their Dorset-wide network of care homes have only grown. Their ability to continue fundraising amid the financial challenges post-pandemic and during widespread austerity is essential.

The collaborations between Lewis-Manning and AFC Bournemouth were highlighted when we helped with logistical hurdles related to parking a large mobile clinic during the Covid pandemic. Recognising the urgency, I worked closely with our general manager, Liz Finney, to resolve the issue swiftly.

This scenario brought to mind a personal philosophy I've subconsciously lived by: say yes, and figure out the details later. It's a strategy I've applied throughout my career, and in this instance, it proved effective. With Liz's adept coordination, the arrangements were handled with remarkable efficiency, preventing potential disruptions to essential health services.

Facilitating the parking of the mobile testing unit was, to me, an act of goodwill rather than a traditional charitable endeavour. Although providing the space didn't fit into the usual framework of charity work, it was an inherently kind gesture that highlighted the profound impact of extending goodwill – a fundamental aspect of charity.

Upon reflection, among the various charitable initiatives we've undertaken, this particular effort stands out for its significant impact. It underscores the importance of leveraging influence to foster acts of goodwill, which, in turn, profoundly benefit the wider Bournemouth community. This approach not only fulfils our charitable commitments but also reiterates the intrinsic value of using one's influence for a greater good, impacting countless lives in a meaningful way.

"

Jeff, you are a man who puts himself out for others, who listens and acts in the interest of others, and those are rare qualities indeed.

CLARE GALLIE #THECHAIRMAN

IN THEIR OWN WORDS ON JEFF

Clare Gallie
Chief Executive Officer Lewis-Manning Hospice Care

In my role as chief executive officer at Lewis-Manning Hospice Care, Dorset, I am lucky to have so many amazing opportunities to meet different people, from all walks of life, backgrounds, ethnicity, of all ages, children and young people, adults and the elderly. It's so diverse and that's why I love the role and the hospice so very much.

Having the opportunity to meet Jeff on that first day was, in my head 'nice', a planned meeting between two people, at AFC Bournemouth (I'm not a huge football fan, but again 'nice') where I was due to go along, thank the chairman (Jeff) for adopting our local hospice charity as the football club's charity partner, shake hands and smile a lot. No problem, do it all the time, I got this.

What I didn't realise at that time, was quite how much that one meeting with Jeff would help so many local Dorset and west Hampshire cancer patients with life limiting illness in the months to come!

So off I trot in the winter of 2020, amid the turmoil of Covid lockdowns followed by breaks of short-lived freedom, to meet with Jeff Mostyn and thank him for his support. And it was as imagined, a 'nice' meeting, in his very nice office, with even nicer pastries, which I didn't eat but were packed in a box for me to take back to the hospice for staff at the end of the meeting (tick!). A lovely chat with a thoroughly lovely man who was so welcoming, most obviously really kind and passionate about our cause and helping others (double tick!) and at the end of the meeting he gave me his mobile number, saying if your charity ever needs anything that I can help with, do let me know (triple tick with knobs on!).

Now what I should mention at this point is that as we all know the pandemic was more than horrendous for so many, worldwide. For some in the UK furlough was an option, although for many, again not an easy option. But for hospice charities in the UK the pandemic was beyond madness for so many reasons; lack of funding as our events programmes were cancelled, our charity shops were closed; staff issues due to sickness (yes nurses and doctors get Covid too!); the NHS needing all the support it can get from local organisations such as ours, an increase in death, people shielding at home, the operational side of continuing to support patients in hospice, at home, virtually, by phone and in some cases in clinic because these patients are ill, some are dying and we needed to carry on.

These patients *cannot*, not be seen. The worry, the concern, the stress.

Question – for those hospice patients who need to be seen in clinic, who were finding it increasingly difficult to travel to us, especially in the middle of a pandemic on public transport, what do you do? We decided to try something different, a pilot using what we described as a mobile unit, 'clinics on wheels', much like the breast screening units that travel around the UK but in this instance 2/3 clinics, in the back of an articulated lorry that could be sprayed down with coronavirus *de-bugging* solution in between appointments and could rock up more locally across our geographical area, taking up around twelve car parking spaces when fully set up and our cancer patients could get to us and get safely treated by our amazing specialist nurses so much more easily. The unit was hired from another charity in Wales who were doing something similar, was quite beautiful in its shiny clinical cleanliness, came down to Dorset each week for the clinics to begin. Just one issue, where to park the beast. Well, given the empty council car parks and the lack of travelling allowed at the time the obvious choice was to ask our local council for free space with them. I mean, what charity wants to spend huge sums on twelve car parking spaces all day? Happily our local council BCP agreed, giving us space in a large car park once a week, right next door to the AFC Bournemouth football ground.

Our hospice work continued, as did our mobile clinics, with great reviews, our Closer to Home Strategy in action with excellent patient feedback and safety. All running well and cancer patients getting the lymphedema treatment they need, in a place that they could travel to easily, so what mattered to them, at that time was working well.

BUT one morning a phone call very early from our contact at the Council: 'Travellers have moved into the car park, so sorry, your mobile unit and patients can't come today or indeed again until the travellers have moved on, nowhere for your lorry and nurses to park, sorry.'

It was an imminent disaster in my mind, with a giant articulated lorry already on the A34 heading down to Bournemouth, clinics booked in, patients to be seen and nowhere for them to be seen, what to do? Then a thought, Jeff Mostyn, I have his mobile number and he did say those words, *if your charity ever needs anything that I can help with, do let me know.*

So, with a very deep breath, and at around 7.30 in the morning, I called Jeff's mobile, and guess what – he picked up. Once again kindness and understanding shone through, having explained our dilemma and the importance of finding a solution Jeff was on it. By 8.15 a.m. he had arranged for our mobile unit lorry to park in the Players Car Park at AFC Bournemouth that day, and what a huge relief this was. Patients received the treatments they needed, the Lewis-Manning service was unaffected, the lorry/clinic had simply moved slightly, parked in a different place, but within 100 yards of the agreed, planned space – yippee!

Now, a few years on, I still feel so hugely grateful to Jeff and to all at AFC Bournemouth who helped Lewis-Manning Hospice Care to deliver our services, from their car park for some months following that first near disaster day. The Closer to Home clinic pilot proved a success both in and out of Covid times, so much so that our charity has since opened three local clinics in the Bournemouth area of Dorset, outside of the main Poole hospice centre and closer to home, based on patient feedback and what matters to them. Our friends at AFC continue to support our charity in so many ways and everyone at Lewis-Manning Hospice Care was delighted when Jeff Mostyn kindly accepted our Board of Trustees invitation to become a patron of our charity in January 2024. Thank you, Jeff, you are a man who puts himself out for others, who listens and acts in the interest of others, and those are rare qualities indeed.

JULIA'S HOUSE CHILDREN'S HOSPICE

Each Christmas we have a tradition at the football club that truly reflects the spirit of giving. Having been split into two groups, players and staff, one half visits Julia's House, and the other goes to Poole Hospital.

Rather like Father Christmas, loaded with merchandise from the club store, at Julia's House, in particular, the experience is profoundly moving. We usually gather in the garden, and there is never a dry eye among the staff or players when we leave. These are children with life-threatening or life-limiting conditions, which is incredibly difficult to talk about without feeling overwhelmed by emotion. The impact of these visits is profound, reminding us of the real joys and sorrows of life. The suffering of others puts football into perspective. I express gratitude for their contributions to the community, their selfless work elevated far above my role as chairman.

These experiences resonate with my past work with the Army, particularly visiting rehabilitation centres like Selly Oak and Headley Court. Witnessing the resilience of injured soldiers taught me invaluable lessons about humility and the human spirit. These visits often left me reflecting deeply and emotionally, impacted by the soldiers' incredible motivation despite their injuries.

Ultimately, the more people we can uplift, the more profound the impact on the community.

FOOTBALL FOR PEACE

My involvement started with Football for Peace when Kashif Siddiqi, the founder and one of the first Asian professional footballers in Britain, invited me to present an award to Jermain Defoe and his mother. The award recognised their outstanding charitable work, particularly related to Jermain's friendship with Bradley Lowery, a young Sunderland fan who tragically passed away from neuroblastoma, a rare and aggressive childhood cancer, at just six years old.

This event was the charity's first Golden Ball at the Corinthia Hotel in London, and aimed to raise a quarter of a million pounds. I attended with limited expectations, not knowing many people there, but ended up on stage giving a major presentation. One of the patrons is Prince William, President of the Football Association.

Currently, Football for Peace focuses on addressing global water shortages, with noteworthy backing from the United States Government. Their efforts centre around alleviating droughts, especially in African nations. Climate change and its consequences – ranging from droughts to other catastrophic events – remain at the forefront of global conversations.

In 2019 I had the privilege of representing Football for Peace, speaking to delegates from the United Nations General Assembly in New York about issues such as radicalisation, highlighting how AFC Bournemouth educates five thousand children weekly on crucial issues.

Being part of this organisation is something I am immensely proud of. I had the great honour meeting HRH Prince William at Boxpark for a Football for Peace event. During our introduction, I was flattered by Prince William's awareness of my involvement at AFC Bournemouth. Together with his knowledge of the recent transfer of Tyrone Mings to his beloved Aston Villa, which was both surprising and delightful.

"

Jeff and Rose are quite the team – energetic, enthusiastic, and always ready to lend a hand. Their support for our foundation has been unwavering, proving their commitment reaches far beyond the football pitch.

KASHIF SIDDIQI #THE CHAIRMAN

"

IN THEIR OWN WORDS ON JEFF

Kashif Siddiqi
Co-Founder of Football for Peace

I'll never forget the first time I met Jeff. There he was, fresh off the stage at the Soccerex Conference in Manchester, walking through the crowd like he was Tom Cruise making his way down the red carpet.

I was chatting with HRH Prince Ali Bin Al Hussein, one of our patrons, and figured I'd seize the moment to introduce myself.

Expecting nothing more than a polite nod, I was taken aback when he greeted me with a hearty handshake and a warm hug. 'Call me,' he said, slipping me his business card. That brief encounter was the start of nearly a decade of collaboration, from Manchester all the way to the United Nations (UN) in New York, with support from notables including HRH Prince William.

Jeff and Rose are quite the team – energetic, enthusiastic, and always ready to lend a hand. Their support for our foundation has been unwavering, proving their commitment reaches far beyond the football pitch. Jeff's down-to-earth approach has not only won him legions of fans at Bournemouth but has also earned him a hat tip in communities worldwide.

He's the kind of guy who's as comfortable in a boardroom as he is in the stands – genuine, approachable, and always looking to make a real difference. As an athlete, I've learned a lot from Jeff about the importance of forging strong relationships and being a mentor. He's the real deal.

If I had to describe Jeff in one word? Humble.

Speaking of humble, one of our standout moments together was at the UN during the 67th General Assembly. After our speeches, we found ourselves cracking jokes with Erkut Sogut (Mesut Özil's agent) and other dignitaries. There we were, laughing a tad too loudly in the hallowed halls of the UN, a surreal but grounding reminder of our modest beginnings.

Jeff's like the football dad of Bournemouth – supportive, guiding, and hugely influential both on and off the field. His legacy is as deep as it is broad, touching lives and inspiring fans and players alike.

JAAQ (JUST ASK ANY QUESTION)

My journey with JAAQ began through a dear friend, Matt Corica, who sponsored our football club through his business, Michael Matthews Jewellery. Matt introduced me to John Reynolds, a remarkable entrepreneur, philanthropist, and the host of the *Extraordinary Life Stories* TV show, that I had the honour to be a guest on. I asked John, 'What is JAAQ?' John explained that it stands for 'Just Ask Any Question', and I instantly loved the concept.

JAAQ was founded by Danny Gray, known for his appearance on *Dragons' Dragon's Den* where he pitched his male cosmetics line, War Paint. Danny's story is inspiring: motivated by his personal experiences of bullying due to his appearance while he was at school, and with support from his sister, he developed War Paint.

The company became a huge success, and drew attention and funding from all five dragons on the show. His accomplishments fuelled his passion to address mental health issues, leading to the creation of JAAQ (and www.JAAQ.org), which aspires to be the 'Google of mental health'.

Recently, John reached out to reconnect, reminding me of the importance of staying engaged with these impactful projects. Interestingly, John shared a story with me about a plumber working in his house who asked about me during a phone call. The plumber was thrilled to learn John knew me, highlighting how my role and efforts have made unexpected impressions. Moments like these remind me of what I've been told: how my work affects people beyond what I can see, emphasising the broader influences of kindness and leadership.

As of now, I serve JAAQ in an advisory capacity to the board. This role allows me to lend my experience and insights to help steer an initiative that holds great promise. Being part of JAAQ is not just a role for me; it signifies a commitment to elevating mental health discourse worldwide.

"

Empathy is a key trait of Jeff's success... Making those around him feel loved, empowered and special is a gift, made possible by his natural positive energy and genuine desire to help others.

JOHN REYNOLDS #THECHAIRMAN

IN THEIR OWN WORDS ON JEFF

John Reynolds
Relationship Director at JAAQ

The first time I met Jeff was away from football, which might make our relationship and friendship more unusual than that of others who contributed to his book. I got to know Jeff Mostyn as the individual rather than the chairman of AFC Bournemouth. I met a man I already respected from a distance, and I loved his genuine interest in me, what I was doing in my life, and how we could help each other. The timing of our meeting was incredible as we were both experiencing a total change of identity, and we opened up about that straight away, which I know was of real help to both of us. We both possess a lot of empathy, and it was almost like therapy, talking about something raw and very emotional with someone who genuinely cared and had perspective – both ways.

We are both very happily married; however, we later laughed because after that first meeting, which we later referred to as a date, our subsequent meetings were just as engaging! We shared so much about ourselves, and time flew – two hours of talking disappeared in what felt like seconds because we were enjoying getting to know each other so much!

The qualities Jeff exhibits, like his professionalism, character, loyalty to AFC Bournemouth, the Premier League, EFL and the FA, and his commitment to the armed forces and charities, are highlighted in the following story. My wife and I have had the pleasure of getting to know Jeff and Rosie over the past year, and it's clear that Jeff knows he's only been able to achieve so much within football and his charitable work because of Rosie's love and support. He has someone by his side who adores him, making them not only a formidable team but also a lovely couple.

I know Jeff tries to reach and influence as many great causes as possible, potentially stretching himself too far with his incredible bandwidth! Jeff is an incredibly valuable adviser to www.jaaq.org with so much experience in business, and on an emotional level, helping to make a positive social impact. His decision to get involved was made at a time when he was already busy and dealing with an emotional change of identity, which spoke volumes about his desire to make a difference where he knew he could.

(On Jeff's discretion, I think it's worth sharing): I have huge respect for the professionalism and respect Jeff demonstrated when he left the club, putting the interests of the club, fans and new owners first. During our conversations at the time, Jeff was dealing with many thoughts and changes, many of which were out of his control or liking, yet he never complained or had disputes. The lack of ego involved publicly and the fact that he graciously wished the new owners well and showed full support publicly is admirable and rare in the ego-driven world of top-level sport. I have the utmost respect and admiration for Jeff and Rosie for that.

Jeff treats EVERYONE with respect, from the kit boy to the chairman of Manchester City and top people in world football, making them all feel they matter. His authenticity in being present for those in his company is genuine. To achieve what he has and have stories recounted by fans, staff at every level, and those at the top of the football world is surely unique.

Empathy is a key trait of Jeff's success. For someone who has been chairman of a Premier League football club with such a success story, his ability to empathise and show genuine interest in those around him has undoubtedly been a massive contributor to his success. Making those around him feel loved, empowered and special is a gift, made possible by his natural positive energy, genuine desire to help others, and, of course, to win! But always fairly and with a big smile.

One meaningful and emotional conversation with Jeff was at our first meeting, where we didn't talk about football at all! I remember saying goodbye and walking to the car, amazed at how much we had shared on an emotional level, having only just met. Both of us teared up at one point, discussing very personal experiences I hadn't shared with others at the time. I knew then that I had a friendship at a deep level of trust that meant the world to me, and I couldn't wait to meet up again. It's not an experience that happens often.

For a bit of fun, Jeff and I discovered that during buffets, we both take a banana as a snack for later! We've exchanged pictures, including from holidays in Barbados – a mutual favourite holiday destination – of a banana on the table. It's a bit of a laugh given the incredible holiday pictures we could be sharing, and I might be the only friend who's called him 'banana man' a few times!

CHAPTER 16
MY ROLE WITH THE FA AND INSPIRATIONAL MANAGERS

Stepping into my role as an ambassador for the England national team filled me with a profound sense of pride. It was more than a personal achievement; it was the fulfilment of a childhood dream. As a kid, I dreamt of being a footballer one day, wearing the Three Lions.

Standing with the England youth team, watching them receive their kits, felt surreal. Being measured for my own England suit, adorned with the Three Lions, was a moment I never imagined possible. Though it wasn't an England football shirt, it was my own way of representing my country, and it filled me with immense pride.

Everywhere I went in that suit, I carried AFC Bournemouth with me, a reminder of our shared journey. Arriving in foreign lands, matching outfits with the England staff and manager, I often wondered at the reality of it all. Was this truly my life?

From a Manchester boy who left school at 15 without qualifications, my journey to representing the FA at an international level was remarkable. It was a testament to the power of dreams and determination. Standing there with the emblem of the Three Lions was not just a personal milestone, but a tribute to the young boy I once was, and the extraordinary journey that got me here.

* * *

My journey with the FA began in a somewhat unexpected yet deeply rewarding way when I was elected to represent the EFL on the FA Council. Looking back, this initial step marked the beginning of an incredibly fulfilling chapter in my life. It thrust me into the heart of football governance, a realm where passion for the beautiful game meets the responsibility of maintaining its integrity and legacy.

The FA Council itself has undergone many transformations over the years. It was fascinating to be part of an entity that had to evolve with the times. Today, the council embraces a more modern role, adapting to new challenges and ensuring compliance and governance across all levels of English football. It operates as a sort of check-and-balance system, able to veto decisions made by the board of directors and senior management. This functional dynamic ensures that football remains not just a sport, but a beacon of fair play and community spirit.

The council is composed of various councillors who bring diverse perspectives from across the football spectrum. They primarily represent the national game, which encompasses everything outside the professional leagues. These include local county leagues and various interest groups, like the armed forces, whose interests are represented by dedicated members such as Neil Hope, a dear friend. My role within this structure was firmly based within the professional game, which governs the four major divisions: the Premier League, Championship, League One and League Two.

Being one of six representatives from the EFL was an honour and, admittedly, a little intimidating. At that time, our league was situated within League One. The representation structure was inclusive; League Two had one representative, while the Championship had two. I was elected by the clubs – seventy-two of them to be precise – and suddenly found myself thrust into the intricate and prestigious world of the FA's decision-making panel. It felt like entering the lion's den of football's governance, and it was both a challenging and exhilarating experience.

Once I was part of the council, my responsibilities rapidly expanded. I was elected on to various subcommittees that played crucial roles in shaping different aspects of the sport. I began with the Youth Committee, where I focused on nurturing young talent and developing youth football programmes. This role allowed me to witness the growth of young England teams and support the grassroots of the sport. Equally rewarding was my involvement with the Disability Committee, which emphasised supporting different forms of disability football, including deaf, blind and wheelchair football.

Another notable responsibility was serving on the FA Membership Committee. This committee handled the distribution of Golden Shares among clubs, essentially decisions about club membership contingent on compliance with FA rules. I even had the challenging duty of representing my own club during membership deliberations, when I had to abstain from voting to maintain impartiality during our club's application for reacquisition of its share.

One of the pinnacle moments of my service was being elected as the chairman of the FA Cup Committee. This committee is the crème de la crème of all FA committees, traditionally offering the honour of joining Prince William on the Cup Final day to greet teams – a moment steeped in prestige. Unfortunately, my chairmanship coincided with the pandemic, which meant many of these traditional rituals were altered, with limited stadium access. However, my efforts were recognised with an honorary fellowship of the FA Council, a recognition that I proudly hold today.

TWO INTERNATIONAL MANAGERS WHO INSPIRED ME

Two England managers stand out as profound influences on my personal and professional development: Roy Hodgson CBE and Sir Gareth Southgate OBE.

Roy Hodgson CBE

I first met Roy Hodgson when I had the honour of being an ambassador for England during the infamous match against Iceland in Nice. Despite the outcome, my time with Roy before the game was unforgettable. He was a true gentleman, his demeanour balanced and respectful towards everyone, from the kit man to the England captain. His manner of speaking – gentle yet powerful – left all in awe, myself included. I had the privilege of getting to know him further as chairman of AFC Bournemouth, where he often attended matches. Sitting next to him in the director's box offered me a new perspective on the game. Roy's insights into the technical and tactical aspects went beyond the basics, enhancing my understanding and enjoyment of football. His profound knowledge and achievements in the sport earned him my deepest respect.

Sir Gareth Southgate OBE

I first met Sir Gareth Southgate through his role with the England youth teams. Like Roy Hodgson, Gareth was thoughtful and articulate, much like my own manager, Eddie Howe. His ability to convey complex ideas with such clarity made every interaction a learning experience for me.

One memorable encounter was during my involvement with the Youth Committee, which took me on various tours with young England teams. At the Toulon Tournament in France, I crossed paths with Gareth, who was then the England Academy manager. We developed a professional rapport

43. Eddie and I enjoying a moment together, a relationship I treasure to this day

44. Always fun with Mark Clemmit (Clem), a dear friend and a top sports presenter

45. A picture paints a thousand words. Promotion to the Premier League

46. An honour and a privilege to meet the great Sir Alex Ferguson, one of the greatest managers in the English Premier League

47. The iconic red and black ribbons signal our return to the Premier League.

48. With my great friend Cliff Crown, Brentford Chairman

49. Celebrating promotion to the Premier League with my friends from the EFL

50. Sharing a match day with my PA, Alice Jeans (left), and my wife Rosie

51. Enjoying a photo with the AFCB team at the EFL awards dinner

52. A reflective moment with my friend and advisor David Hinchcliffe

53. In bed with the Championship trophy

54. With (from left to right) comedian Jimmy Tarbuck, Liverpool legend Sir Kenny Dalglish and Lawrie McMenemy MBE.

55. I was so proud when Callum Wilson became the first AFC Bournemouth player to represent the England Men's National Team.

56. A very proud moment – being presented the Premier League Share by Peter McCormick OBE

56. My 'Ballon d'Or' player at the club, Marc Pugh won hearts and minds at AFC Bournemouth

58. With 'Mr Premier League', Richard Scudamore CBE. We still laugh about my negotiation skills on the undersoil heating.

59. Enjoying a celebration with James Beattie, a dear friend and neighbour

60. The journey begins with Ed Bowers, my book manager, who promised me this story would not be in the Mr Men book section!

based on mutual respect, a connection that naturally grew over the years. Travelling with the England team offered us rich opportunities to exchange ideas and insights that broadened my perspective.

Another significant trip was to Lithuania in 2017. Sir Gareth took time during the flight to sit next to me, and we spoke about my family heritage and life before football. It's hard to put into words how this was a defining moment for me in our relationship. To have the England National Team Manager join me on a flight, in the midst of planning for a qualifying tournament. It shows how much respect he had for me and what I represented.

This journey was deeply personal, as it led me to Vilnius, where my family's roots lie. Walking through the historic ghetto, alongside Cliff Crown, the Chair of Brentford, retracing my grandfather's footsteps, added layers of personal reflection to this professional journey.

Sir Gareth Southgate has always embodied the essence of a true gentleman. Our conversations often touched on personal aspects, such as when he acknowledged my achievements at AFC Bournemouth. His words were candid and complimentary, highlighting his genuine humility and character. Time spent with Gareth is always filled with camaraderie and joy, such as our memorable visit to Seville for England's historic victory against Spain.

Both Gareth and I share an insatiable appetite for self-development. This trait has been a guiding force in my career and personal life, helping me navigate the complexities and demands of football governance and beyond. This desire for continual improvement has shaped my interactions with others in the sport and deepened my appreciation for the broader, impactful narratives of the game.

> **An attentive host, a warm and charismatic man**, Jeff is one of the game's great characters and one of many people who quietly put the hours in, to allow their clubs and English football to function as well as they do.
>
> **SIR GARETH SOUTHGATE #THECHAIRMAN**

IN THEIR OWN WORDS ON JEFF

Sir Gareth Southgate OBE
Former England Men's Senior Football Manager

I first met Jeff when he travelled as an FA ambassador to the Nordics tournament with our under 16s. I must say his willingness to 'muck in', enthusiasm for the game and support of our development pathway was evident throughout, as well as his customary dry humour!

Over the subsequent years, he joined Under 21 and Senior team trips, always finding the right balance of supporting while not impeding what we were trying to do. I found him an important advocate for what we were trying to develop at St George's Park.

When I saw him at various Bournemouth matches, I admired the way he always supported his manager, despite the pressure of relegation at times. He kept perspective, still hated losing, but took any defeats with dignity. A difficult balance to find.

An attentive host, a warm and charismatic man, Jeff is one of the game's great characters and one of many people who quietly put the hours in, to allow their clubs and English football to function as well as they do.

WORKING ALONGSIDE THE FA CHAIR DEBBIE HEWITT MBE

My initial encounter with Debbie Hewitt MBE was during a Premier League shareholders' meeting, a formal assembly usually filled with robust discussions about the future of English football. Debbie, as the chair, often attended these meetings, which required a certain ceremonial knowledge and astuteness to navigate through topics relevant to both the Premier League and the FA.

Our introduction was immediate and genuine. I approached her, expressing what a pleasure and a privilege it was to meet her, offering my assistance whenever needed, along with my card. I also extended a warm invitation to join me at the Vitality Stadium for any meeting or match. This gesture sparked the beginning of a meaningful relationship.

Debbie's background was outside the traditional realm of football, having carved out a distinguished career as a business executive in the public sector. What struck me most was her instant willingness to learn and adapt to her new environment, a characteristic I admired deeply. Having met her for the first time, I was already contemplating what lessons I could glean from her vast business experience. My ever-present appetite for self-development drove my interactions, and I was eager to absorb any knowledge that would enhance my understanding and skill set.

As our relationship developed, I found myself supporting her during some challenging transitions within the FA. For instance, Debbie initiated significant changes, most notably the introduction of a mandatory retirement age of 75 for FA Council members. This decision aimed to infuse new perspectives and vitality into the council, which was often criticised for its outdated practices.

The proposed changes, while sounding radical to some, only mirrored how those on the board of directors were required to step down at 75. I'd often joke that, entering council meetings, I felt one of the youngest present. Truth be told, I was one of the oldest.

During a meeting to discuss the proposed changes amid the Covid pandemic, most council members participated via Zoom, but I chose to attend in person at Wembley alongside Cliff Crown the Brentford Chairman. Debbie initiated the discussion by asking for my thoughts on the proposed changes.

'For the avoidance of doubt for everybody online and in the room, we are not here to vote, we are here for a discussion,' I said. 'Therefore this is just my opinion. I'm going to be voting in favour of the changes.'

'Jeff, can you explain why you support the motion?' Debbie asked.

'All I can say is, Debbie, at my age, I pray every day to God that I'm still alive in ten years' time. Secondly, when I'm 90, will I want to go through the carnage of trying to get to Wembley to even get into the Royal Box to exercise my rights as a council member!'

Debbie just burst out laughing.

'Jeff, only you could articulate it in that unbelievably respectful way.'

'There is always a right time to leave the room for others to follow in your path,' I replied.

Reflecting on my unexpected yet deeply fulfilling journey with the FA, I am filled with a sense of pride and gratitude. Being elected to represent the EFL on the FA Council marked the beginning of a transformative chapter in my life. This role positioned me at the heart of football governance, where my profound love for the game converged with the crucial responsibility of upholding its integrity and enduring legacy.

My near decade of service to the FA as a Council member was special in so many ways. To work alongside the hierarchy of English football's heritage was such a privilege for me. Serving on the Youth Committee, Membership Committee, Disability Committee and last but by no means least the prestigious FA Cup Committee – as both Vice-chair and Chairman – taught me so much about the game, especially grass roots football. When you work daily in the professional game you can easily forget about the thousands of individuals working to improve football for all.

I'm grateful to everyone associated with the FA for embracing me during my time representing the organisation. The warmth of the reception I still receive when returning to the Royal Box on a matchday means a great deal to me and Rosie. It is a privilege that I will never take for granted.

As I look back on those extraordinary experiences and towards future endeavours, I am committed to using my insights to inspire others. I hope that these stories ignite the same passion and determination within you, encouraging you to seize every opportunity with open arms and an open mind. In the next chapter, I will share the four key aspects that have guided me throughout my business career and my tenure as chairman at AFC Bournemouth.

"

It's hard to do justice to the many good qualities in Jeff. More than anything, I admire his boundless energy to make the world a better place. It's a privilege to call him a colleague and a friend.

DEBBIE HEWITT MBE #THECHAIRMAN

IN THEIR OWN WORDS ON JEFF

Debbie Hewitt MBE
Chair of the FA

Where do I start? Probably with our first interaction. I had the pleasure of meeting Jeff at a Premier League shareholders' meeting in June 2022. Although I had only been in my role six months, I had heard his name and knew of his incredible reputation for overseeing AFC Bournemouth's 'rags to riches' journey from Division Two to the Premier League. Everyone in football knows Jeff but many outside too, as his story is one which is often told as an example of 'anything being possible'.

Being relatively new to my own role, I was conscious at my first Premier League meeting of being one of only a few in the room who knew the names and faces of everyone but not the individuals. Jeff was one of the first to introduce himself (although of course he needed no introduction) and made me feel so at ease. No surprises that he asked me about how I was finding my relatively new role, listening intently, before he modestly went on to describe his own journey.

From that first interaction I learned much more of the Bournemouth story, and it explained why he is such a legend, in particular how he joined a consortium of people to pay the club's outstanding and mounting tax bill. What I hadn't appreciated was the fact the others gradually dropped out, leaving him to become the 'sole owner'. His courage, commitment and dedication to the club is extraordinary but more impressive is the modest way he describes what he did.

When you hear Jeff tell his story, it's clear just how much he cares, and how much personal sacrifice he has had to make along the way. I've not yet met Rosie. I get a sense that she has been long-suffering, but beside him the whole way on the journey. It's noticeable how much he ascribes what he has achieved to her unwavering support.

Jeff followed up our initial meeting by inviting me and my family to a Bournemouth game.

The family invite says so much about his values as does the fact that he always asks me about my family whenever we meet. I am a mum of teenage twins, and you can imagine the challenges! They often remind me of the time they met Jeff at an England football game and were told by him how he left school with a 'qualification in truancy'. Funny but true and significantly impressive that he went on to successfully create his own company.

Jeff's business success is something I truly admire, especially given his humble beginnings. It's clear that he approached his working life as he did owning a football club, with hard work and resilience. It's that success that gave him the opportunity of buying the club, and unlike many who would sit back and enjoy their success, Jeff took on the challenge of the club, combining his business expertise with his lifelong love of football. Thank goodness for the club that he did.

Jeff's knowledge of the football pyramid is incredible, and he always has a common-sense answer to the many challenges that come our way. Although football can be a tribal sport, Jeff somehow manages to be balanced and respectful in his views. Watching a game of football with him is priceless, as he combines his passion and respect in equal measure. One of football's gentlemen, he is a welcome visitor to all other grounds.

Among all his great qualities, the trait that is stand-out for me is his strength and ability to fight for a deserving cause. His influence on the FA's work on disability through his participation in our Disability Committee cannot be underestimated. Nor can the fact that he is a familiar face in the local community, having driven AFC Bournemouth's Community programmes, and acts as patron and ambassador to several local charities, as well as being committed to various armed forces charities. His contribution to those whose lives are less fortunate is admirable and, through his involvement in football he brings to life the vision of making 'Football For All'.

It's hard to do justice to the many good qualities in Jeff. More than anything, I admire his boundless energy to make the world a better place. It's a privilege to call him a colleague and a friend.

CHAPTER 17
INSPIRING THE NEXT GENERATION OF BUSINESS AND FOOTBALL PROFESSIONALS

Before wrapping up this book, I want to reflect on the journey that led me to write it. Encouraged by Brigadier Andrew Griffiths OBE and in collaboration with my book manager, Ed Bowers, I embarked on this project with a clear mission: to share what I consider one of football's greatest untold stories and my personal life experiences to inspire you and the next generation of business and football industry professionals.

Over seventeen years, I've witnessed incredible shifts in the football industry, especially regarding educational opportunities and professional development. When I began, there was no clear path for pursuing a career in football. Today, however, there are countless educational programmes and insights from top experts available to help individuals grow both their careers and themselves within this dynamic field.

Reflecting on my time with AFC Bournemouth, one of my greatest joys has been inspiring and guiding the next generation of football professionals. During my tenure as chairman, I've seen the commitment and passion that drives people to careers in this vibrant industry, and it's been a true privilege to watch young talents emerge and flourish, both on and off the pitch.

At AFC Bournemouth, nurturing potential is a core value, whether in players, coaches or the myriad other roles that support the game. Our commitment is evident in our youth programmes, where aspiring footballers develop not only their skills but also learn essential values like teamwork, perseverance and sportsmanship.

But the growth of the next generation doesn't stop with players. It involves creating an environment where professionals can excel in various capacities, from management and coaching to marketing and media. At AFC Bournemouth, fostering an inclusive and empowering workplace is paramount, ensuring every individual feels valued and inspired to contribute to the club's success. This holistic approach underscores our dedication to developing talent for the future of football.

* * *

There are four parts that have guided my journey throughout my business career and during my tenure as chairman at AFC Bournemouth:

Part 1. The Art of Communication
Part 2. My Ten Principles of Running a Successful Football Club
Part 3. The JFK Decision-Making Method
Part 4. The Power of Mentors in Business, Football and Life

PART 1. THE ART OF COMMUNICATION

Communication has always been my strongest asset, a skill honed through diverse experiences in sales, my time collaborating with the Army, and as chairman of AFC Bournemouth. From all these arenas, I've learned that calm and concise communication plays a crucial role and can significantly de-escalate tension while capturing attention.

One of the essential techniques I employ is the 'mirror technique'. This involves reflecting the desired behaviour to the audience to guide their response. Whether it's making eye contact to build trust or using body language to convey confidence and sincerity, these non-verbal cues are vital. I've seen first-hand, from interactions with passionate supporters to engaging with players, that clear and respectful communication can transform situations.

Throughout my career, humility in leadership has been equally pivotal. It's not just about directing but about embodying the values I wish to see – the ability to remain poised and approachable, whether in triumph or defeat. For instance, at challenging matches, I chose to be present with the team, regardless of the outcome. This commitment to leadership in adversity helps in cultivating trust and rapport with the team, coaches and backroom staff.

During my sales journey, I found that making individuals feel special is increasingly rare today, largely due to the digital age's communication barriers. I've always believed that text can never replace the warmth of a human connection. Speaking calmly and thoughtfully allows you to lower the room's temperature, drawing others in and encouraging them to listen genuinely.

This approach, imbued with humility, fosters genuine interactions that are foundational to effective leadership. In every interaction, it's crucial to leave the door open. Acknowledging mistakes and inviting further discussion in a calmer setting affirm true leadership and integrity.

Communication is the love of my life, and I've consistently found the power to win friends, influence people and nurture lasting relationships through its simple yet profound art. Embracing the following tips has been pivotal in enhancing my ability to connect meaningfully, especially in a sales environment or as a chairman of a football club. Here are my three action steps to apply:

1. Practise calm and intentional speaking

By focusing on speaking calmly and deliberately, I've been able to lower tensions and captivate interest in various settings – be it meetings, presentations or personal conversations. This approach consistently encourages others to listen more closely and engage positively, enhancing my effectiveness as a communicator.

2. Employ the mirror technique

Using my actions and body language to guide others' responses has been indispensable. By modelling behaviours such as eye contact and open gestures, I've created more synchronised and connected interactions. This technique has proven invaluable in fostering openness and engagement from clients and colleagues alike.

3. Incorporate empathy and humility in interactions

Understanding others' perspectives by actively listening and demonstrating empathy has anchored my communication style. With humility and admitting mistakes leaves the door open for continued dialogue – I've been able to build a rapport that fosters genuine connections and trust.

By being mindful and deliberate through these three action steps, I've not only elevated my communication skills but have also significantly strengthened my capacity for meaningful interactions, ultimately supporting my success and influence as a sales professional.

Jeff's Iconic Hug

When writing this book and reading all the book perspectives, one theme consistently stood out: my iconic hug. Hugs are a meaningful part of my identity, helping to forge connections and break the ice. My iconic hug has, over the years, become an authentic way to communicate trust and allow others to feel comfortable being themselves when interacting with me.

PART 2. MY TEN PRINCIPLES OF RUNNING A SUCCESSFUL FOOTBALL CLUB

People often see a football club merely as an entity that plays football, but I take a different view. A football club, like any business, must manage finances, marketing and operations, while also navigating the unpredictable nature of sport. Some might still perceive the Premier League as solely sport focused. However, it's actually a vast business, one of the largest globally, and a significant contributor to Britain's Gross Domestic Product (GDP). It's beloved by over 3 billion people worldwide, evoking passion and rivalry. Although we cherish this game and travel far distances to be part of it, at its core, it's still a business.

In my role as the chairman of a Premier League club, I viewed myself as a business leader who established community values. We regularly held meetings at our AFC Bournemouth business club to network and learn from each other. Through these interactions, I learned that failure often teaches more than success because success can feel elusive. Running a football club means pursuing near perfection, and over time, I've honed my approach into ten key principles.

I have one important message before outlining my ten principles. Owning or running a football club is like no other business. There is one fundamental difference. For understandable reasons you actually have a football team, which is your product, and on matchdays you have no control over the outcome.

The success or failure of the team has a major impact on the success or failure of the business. No matter how much business expertise you have, you cannot affect the result once the whistle has blown on match days. As a consequence, sustained failure on the pitch will undoubtedly result in potential losses of income from your commercial activities. I sincerely hope these ten principles will be of benefit to you.

Principle 1: *Active Listening*

Active listening is vital in any business, including football. I often remind others that we have two ears and one mouth for a reason: to listen more than we speak. Many in football tend to talk more than they listen, but truly understanding challenges requires attentive listening. At AFC Bournemouth, I focused on understanding the issues at hand, internally and externally. For example, when considering a new sponsorship deal, listening to the marketing team's concerns allowed us to adjust our strategy successfully.

I frequently use a technique that involves repeating questions to ensure clarity of understanding and to give myself time to formulate thoughtful responses. This skill showcases the importance of truly listening before reacting. Active listening also builds meaningful relationships within the industry. Once, during a conversation with Sir Chips Keswick, the Arsenal Football Club chairman, in the Emirates boardroom, he nostalgically mentioned Uncle Joe's Mint Balls. Later, when we visited Wigan for the Carabao Cup, my mission was to find Wigan's famous Uncle Joe's mint balls. To my delight, upon arrival, bowls of mint balls awaited us, and I was given a jar to bring back.

When I next visited the Emirates, I gifted the mint balls to Chips, whose affectionate response highlighted the impact of active listening. Remembering a conversation from a year earlier enabled me to turn the interaction into an opportunity for a deeper connection. Active listening is not just about hearing; it's about comprehending and valuing what's conveyed, thereby fostering stronger bonds.

Principle 2: *Respect*

Respect isn't just a term; it's a powerful concept that empowers those around us, instilling them with the confidence to fulfil their roles and supporting them in their efforts. Unfortunately, many lack this kind of empowerment, which hinders their personal and organisational growth. From a young age, my mother instilled in me the significance of respect, a principle I've adhered to throughout my life. At AFC Bournemouth, every role is important – from the car park steward to the delivery personnel. Empowering everyone, regardless of their position, fosters a unified and supportive atmosphere. This isn't just about assigning tasks, but about trusting others to make decisions and contribute to the club's success. For instance, our kit manager had a substantial say in the new kit design, and his pride in the final product was apparent to everyone.

Principle 3: Team Management

As chairman, I know a strong management team is crucial for any successful football club. Harmony isn't required at every moment, but effective collaboration is essential to keep things running smoothly. This requires understanding the nuances of communication – knowing when to listen actively, engage deeply or let others lead.

Finding this balance allows operations to run smoothly while aligning with long-term objectives. I encourage open dialogue where everyone's voice is valued, which fosters mutual respect and trust. Each team member brings unique perspectives to enrich the decision-making process.

Leveraging each individual's strengths and ensuring all understand their roles leads to a dynamic, productive environment. It's not about avoiding disagreements but using them constructively to drive innovation and improvement.

Principle 4: Club Culture

Strong club culture is essential for success and cohesion in a football club. At AFC Bournemouth, we carefully cultivated an environment focused on unity and shared objectives. A unique cultural aspect was our use of two dressing rooms, one for the team downstairs and mine upstairs, connected by a shared spirit. This set-up epitomised our unity, ensuring that, win or lose, we experience each moment together as a club.

Football club operations present unique challenges and rhythms, so fostering a robust culture means maintaining continuous and effective communication. Regular interactions with each department are vital. We consistently engaged with the various club departments on their business performance.

Transparency is crucial to ensure everyone understands how their efforts align with club goals. By aligning actions with the club's needs, they see how their work impacts success on the pitch.

Emphasising a culture where challenges and successes are shared nurtures motivation and feelings of value among team members. By cultivating this environment, we promote ownership of roles, realising everyone plays a part in the club's achievements. This collective spirit fosters belonging and pride in our journey, and strengthened the fabric of AFC Bournemouth. This cultural commitment propels us forward, ensuring resilience and dedication in everything we do.

Principle 5: Leadership

When I talk about leadership at AFC Bournemouth, I often describe how our set-up had two dressing rooms.

Eddie Howe masterfully led the dressing room downstairs with his strategic brilliance and inspiring presence.

Meanwhile, the executive team had the responsibility for navigating the operations. I called this the upstairs dressing room. This ensured that our strategies and vision were in harmony with the club's goals. Synchronising these spheres was essential for fostering a united and effective leadership model, which enabled the club to function cohesively as one entity. In effect 'Two Dressing Rooms, One Common Heartbeat'.

From my experience I have learned that leadership is about being authentic with people, working with and empowering them, rather than just giving orders. It embodies the values you wish to instil within your organisation.

At AFC Bournemouth, every decision and action had to reflect our commitment to unity and a shared purpose. Leading by example wasn't just an approach – it was a necessity. By dedicating myself to our goals and maintaining transparency in processes, I reinforced a sense of togetherness, motivating everyone to strive for collective success.

Effective leadership at AFC Bournemouth was about building trust and respect, forging strong relationships, and ensuring everyone understood and valued their role within the club. This approach fostered a resilient and disciplined team, clearly demonstrating that every effort collectively shaped the club's destiny. By living these leadership values, we cultivated a legacy of unity and achievement.

Principle 6: Effective Partnerships

For me, partnerships are the cornerstone of growth within a football club and the broader community. During my tenure as chairman of AFC Bournemouth, the partnership we established with Bournemouth University embodied this philosophy. Universities are centres of educational excellence, while football clubs serve as influential community hubs.

My relationship with Bournemouth University was extraordinarily enriching. Several key club members, like Rob Mitchell our Commercial Director, a university alumni, naturally formed a strong bond between our institutions. This connection was both professional and personal, as we built on shared experiences and grew together. As Bournemouth University expanded its global reach, collaboration felt inevitable. Rob's connection to the university led to their sponsorship of our women's team, with players proudly donning jerseys adorned with the Bournemouth University name.

Our multifaceted collaboration included interactions through their football teams and our Community Sports Trust. Rob Mitchell and Steve Cuss fostered close ties, launching an educational initiative for Chinese students before the pandemic. Bournemouth University offered prestigious courses, such as FA licences for Stage One coaching qualifications, alongside elite institutions like Loughborough University. Through this partnership, the university provided academic education while we delivered football coaching expertise, creating seamless learning opportunities.

As chairman, I respected Rob's role in direct commercial negotiations while actively supporting initiatives at various levels. Steve Cuss contributed to coaching programmes while I emphasised the symbiotic relationship between our club and the university, highlighting how our combined efforts enhanced Bournemouth's global profile. The city's transformation, driven by development and international interest, was inspirational.

This partnership is encapsulated in my mantra: Bournemouth University is a hub of educational excellence, and our club is a community influence centre. This perfect marriage fostered tremendous growth, teaching me the immense value of partnerships and a collaborative mindset. It also bolstered the visibility of Bournemouth City and its community.

Through collaboration, we reinforced the importance of structure and organisation – qualities embodied by the university and beneficial to our club's commercial and community initiatives. This partnership yielded mutual benefits, including the university's sponsorship, a crucial revenue stream. Additionally, we created educational opportunities for players wishing to further their studies post-career. The university's state-of-the-art facilities, like the mock hospital utilised by the NHS during Covid-19, showcased practical collaboration potential. Our head of medicine, Craig Roberts, contributed insights to enhance these facilities alongside Ian Jones.

Pivotal to our efforts, Ian Jones was an essential part of the leadership trio with the chancellor and vice chancellor. A devoted Nottingham Forest supporter, he appreciated it when I secured him tickets to the Wembley play-off, an exciting moment for any keen fan. Our Partnership included the annual Bournemouth University BIG Match. These BIG Match days were Bournemouth University branded and themed for students at the University. Ian often chose games of personal interest, adding an element of fun and engagement to our partnership. Moreover, many university students enriched the club's commercial and media teams through work placements, fostering an exchange of skills and knowledge.

The club evolved significantly from its early days, with a modest set-up managing accounts and media. Initially, many of us wore multiple hats, but the club grew remarkably, thanks in part to our strong relationship with Bournemouth University. This partnership model benefitted both institutions and the wider community, highlighting the dynamic synergy between education and football.

> **Jeff's influence transcends the realm of football**, emerging as a beacon of ambassadorship for the sport and beyond. His unwavering commitment to fostering connections, including with those from his humble beginnings in Manchester, speaks volumes of his character.
>
> **IAN JONES #THECHAIRMAN**

IN THEIR OWN WORDS ON JEFF

Ian Jones
Head of External Engagement at Bournemouth University

In the annals of my memory, Jeff's introduction into my world occurred during the early days of AFC Bournemouth's collaboration with Bournemouth University, approximately eleven years past. It remains vivid, his arrival marked by a radiant smile and an extended hand, which seamlessly transformed into a warm embrace. His demeanour, far from the stereotypical football club chairman, exuded an aura of familiarity, as if we were old acquaintances meeting anew. His hospitality during that meeting was deliberate and inclusive, leaving an indelible impression of genuine warmth and camaraderie. In retrospect, his presence felt like that of a long-time friend, despite our recent acquaintance – an attribute truly unique to him. His kindness, palpable and genuine, infused every interaction, igniting a sense of excitement for the club's collaborative endeavours with Bournemouth University.

Recollections intertwine as I reminisce about meeting Jeff and Rosie, his partner, in the intimate setting of their boardroom, during a pre-match dinner preceding an AFC Bournemouth versus Nottingham Forest encounter at the Vitality Stadium. Jeff's thoughtful gesture of inviting us, knowing of my allegiance to Forest, showcased his innate generosity. Rosie, equally gracious, ensured our integration into the gathering, introducing us to fellow Forest representatives with effortless charm. As a duo, Jeff and Rosie epitomised hospitality, their synchronicity in hosting reflecting a shared commitment to ensuring every guest felt welcomed and at ease. Their genuine kindness, punctuated by infectious laughter, seemed effortless and was thoroughly admirable.

Jeff's influence transcends the realm of football, emerging as a beacon of ambassadorship for the sport and beyond. His unwavering commitment to fostering connections, including with those from his humble beginnings in Manchester, speaks volumes of his character.

Amid accolades and invitations to exclusive gatherings, Jeff remains grounded, a testament to his humility and enduring values.

His enthusiasm, palpable in every interaction, illuminates the room, forging authentic connections with his audience. His passion resonates deeply, leaving an indelible mark on those fortunate enough to engage with him. If tasked with encapsulating Jeff in a single word, 'humble' would undoubtedly suffice.

One memory, etched in gratitude, epitomises Jeff's benevolence. When tickets for Forest's pivotal play-off final sold out in a heartbeat, Jeff's intervention, securing seats for me and a colleague, left an indelible mark of friendship. His silent yet steadfast generosity, devoid of ostentation, exemplifies the essence of his character.

Jeff's stewardship of AFC Bournemouth has not only transformed the club but also the town of Bournemouth and its global recognition. Both a father figure and an ambassador, his influence extends far beyond the pitch. As the team soared to the Premier League, Jeff's unwavering dedication to community and civic duties redefined the perception of Bournemouth, both locally and internationally. His enduring commitment to the town he loves ensures that his legacy of kindness and impact will endure for generations to come.

Principle 7: Governance

For me, governance is the backbone of a football club's success. It becomes particularly crucial when the pressure mounts – when fans become critical and emotions run high. In those moments, a solid governance framework keeps us grounded, providing a clear plan for operations and decision-making. It's unsustainable to operate beyond budgetary limits and hope things go well; such a path leads to instability.

With strategic governance, we understand that our efforts this year could lead to reduced losses next year if commercial efforts succeed, paving the way for future profitability.

Challenges with investment plans in football often arise from short-term thinking. Proposing a five-year plan is difficult for a club with multiple divisions to navigate within that timeframe. This is where governance becomes vital, particularly in managing the player budget, the most significant cost.

By establishing principles with the chairman, owner and board it is possible to ensure adherence to any strategic plans that have been made. Governance is about having a structured approach that everyone at the club agrees on and follows. Through this discipline, we strive to achieve our goals.

Principle 8: Payment Structures

The importance lies in transparency and communication. By ensuring that everyone understands the structure and expectations, perceptions are managed and misunderstandings are reduced. Each year, a cautious and conservative approach to budgeting allows finances to be managed prudently, with any higher positioning providing additional revenue to reinvest in the club.

One crucial lesson is the importance of honesty and integrity. Giving a star player a secret pay rise and expecting confidentiality is unrealistic – it would quickly become team knowledge. Maintaining a transparent payment structure is essential, fostering an environment where every staff member feels valued and respected. Doing so not only promotes fairness but also encourages the dedication and motivation needed to run a club successfully.

Principle 9: Physical and Mental Well-being

I can't stress enough how fundamental this principle is; it could easily be an entire book. Nevertheless, it's a crucial element when you're at the helm of a football club or working within one.

When I bought the football club in 2006, I was 61 years old, a time when many folks dream of retiring. But I knew I had to stay vigilant about my physical and mental health, and do so even today as I reach 80 years old! Running a club or being part of one stirs up a whirlwind of emotions, pressure and expectations. That's why I made a deliberate effort to maintain my physical fitness and diet. Even Eddie Howe took note of my dietary habits when eating with the team, to ensure my wellbeing.

Taking Eddie's advice to heart, I started taking my nutrition more seriously, despite the chuckles from those who know my affection for a banana sandwich! However, the relentless demands of football caught up with me, resulting in a heart attack – a stark reminder of why I now view physical and mental well-being as non-negotiable.

In the high-stakes world of a football club, where players, coaches and directors are driven, ambitious and often single-minded, the emphasis often falls on results rather than well-being. It's easy for mental health to be sidelined amid long hours, constant travel, media scrutiny and pressure. The nature of football leaves little room for recovery, compelling players to sometimes forgo personal care in the pursuit of peak performance, leading to burnout and mental health challenges. I'm thankful to see mental health gaining the global recognition it deserves, reinforcing how vital it is to our overall well-being.

Meeting performance psychologist Melissa Dhillon at a Women's Football Summit was enlightening. She advocates three principles crucial for mental health in high-performance football:

1. Understanding the impact of mental health on football: Mental health is vital for success, influencing mindset and decision-making. It should be viewed as mental fitness, and crucial for managing stress and avoiding burnout.

2. Understanding burnout: The drive for success in football can lead to neglecting well-being. The culture demands results, often at the cost of personal care, leading to burnout. True success lies in mental resilience.

3. Creating a structured club culture: A supportive environment is essential. Confidentiality encourages openness. Prioritising mental health at all levels fosters a thriving, successful team culture.

In conclusion, integrating mental health into club culture leads to sustainable excellence, supporting both individual well-being and team success.

"

Jeff's self-confidence, particularly in how he speaks to and connects with people, has profoundly influenced my personal development and character.

MELISSA DHILLON #THECHAIRMAN

"

IN THEIR OWN WORDS ON JEFF

Melissa Dhillon
Performance Psychologist

My first real, profound connection with Jeff Mostyn happened under the bright lights of the Athens Women's Football Summit 2024. I was on stage, delivering my talk on the power of performance psychology, and as I moved across that platform, scanning the audience, many avoided holding my gaze except for Jeff and Rosie. Sitting in the front row, directly before me, Jeff's presence anchored me. His eyes locked with mine, and in that shared moment, I felt a surge of connection and energy, an unspoken understanding, as if he was silently saying, 'I'm here with you.' When we exchanged a smile, it felt magical, so pure and fleeting that I didn't even process who I had smiled at.

After my talk, Jeff approached me as he was leaving, and his words left an impression that has stayed with me ever since: 'I loved how you locked eyes with people in the audience. That was powerful.' He spoke about his own experiences as a keynote speaker and the art of truly connecting with an audience, recognising a similar quality in how I had presented myself. I was struck not just by his insight, but by how much he valued something I deeply hold: the importance of character. It was clear to me then that our visions, purpose and values were aligned.

Rosie joined our conversation, and her sparkling eyes and warm smile made me feel immediately at home. As we continued to talk, Jeff's words and feedback left a lasting mark on me, a reminder of the power of connection and the way Jeff embodies his purpose: to leave a trademark on others, not through words alone, but through how he makes them feel. That magical moment led us, quite serendipitously, to share a table at the gala dinner later that evening – an unplanned, yet electrifying continuation of a connection that felt as though it was always meant to be. Some moments in life are orchestrated by more than chance; they're a spark of something greater, and this was one of them.

From my experiences in this world, stepping outside your home often means instinctively carrying a fight-or-flight response consciously or unconsciously just to protect yourself. The world can feel unrelenting, especially when you're young, ambitious and a woman in business striving to make a difference. What struck me most about Jeff and Rosie, however, was how they dissolved that invisible armour. For the first time in a long time, I felt safe. Their warmth, genuine intentions and unshakeable presence created a rare moment of security, one you don't often encounter upon meeting someone for the first time.

It wasn't just their words; it was the unspoken understanding that passed between us. They truly saw me without me needing to say much about myself or my thoughts. That kind of connection is extraordinary. I'm drawn to people of character, and Jeff and Rosie exuded the very qualities I value most: humility, empathy and authenticity. It became clear to me, as they shared stories of football, life and their personal struggles, that they knew pain and the battles life can bring.

Jeff's humility stood out profoundly. As the chairman of Bournemouth FC, he spoke of how he would make it a point to hug, greet and welcome every single person in a room, ensuring they felt seen, valued and special. For him, success wasn't defined by trophies or accolades but by the lasting effect of how he made people feel. That ethos spread through the club, contributing to an extraordinary seventeen years of success. And yet, Jeff also spoke of his struggles and how some people failed to value his worth or felt intimidated by his energy and presence. His confidence and self-assuredness, however, have allowed him to know that those people simply don't belong at his table.

Rosie, too, left an indelible impression on me. A strong, unique and beautiful soul inside and out, she is undeniably the backbone of their success. Her warmth and grace made me feel instantly welcomed, and her presence, like Jeff's, carried an effortless strength that inspired those around her.

What truly resonated with me was the humility both Jeff and Rosie possessed, a humility that many lose when they climb their mountains of success. Their achievements, though remarkable, never overshadowed their characters. I couldn't even see their success at first glance; it quietly radiated in the way they carried themselves, never boastful, always grounded. That left me inspired, walking away with a quiet promise to my future self: I want to live like that. I want to carry success with such grace, humility and love.

Their stories brought a spark to my life and a reassurance that I'm on the right path. Jeff and Rosie reminded me that when you align yourself with people of integrity, character and heart, you get closer to your purpose. Inspiration is magnetic, and their lives are a testament to that. The universe, it seems, brought us together not just by chance, but as a clear sign that I'm exactly where I'm meant to be.

I admire Jeff's humility and the way he truly prioritises making others feel valued and understood. This has been the foundation of his earned respect in the football world. His ability to connect with people, creating a sense of belonging and encouragement, sets him apart and makes him highly respected in the football community.

Jeff's self-confidence, particularly in how he speaks to and connects with people, has profoundly influenced my personal development and character. Watching him command a room with authenticity and assurance gave me the courage to embrace my voice and presence. It wasn't just his words but his genuine connection with others that inspired me to own my story and perspective.

The word I would use to describe Jeff is giving. His unwavering generosity, whether it's his time, energy or wisdom, creates an environment of support and positivity around him. Jeff's giving nature empowers and inspires those he meets, fostering a sense of value and connection that resonates deeply.

Principle 10: Enjoy the Moment and the Journey

Reflecting on my time with the football club, I've learned that one of the most crucial principles is to truly enjoy the journey and savour each moment. It's easy to get caught up in the pressures and expectations, but remembering to appreciate the experiences along the way has been key to my fulfilment.

When I bought the football club in 2006, it marked the beginning of an incredible chapter in my life. I embraced the challenges and joys that came with running a club. Each match, each interaction with players and staff, and every high and low provided unforgettable moments filled with learning and growth.

These experiences taught me the importance of taking a step back to appreciate the present. Whether celebrating a victorious match or navigating a tough season, relishing the journey has enriched my perspective and deepened my passion for the sport. It's a reminder that success isn't just about reaching the end goal; it's about cherishing each step along the way.

Enjoying the moment is about being present and grateful for what is unfolding. This perspective has not only enhanced my leadership but also my personal well-being. By embracing this principle, I've found that each day at the club is a reward in itself, reinforcing why I embarked on this incredible journey to begin with.

* * *

In conclusion, none of the ten principles would be effectively implemented without the support of an incredible executive and management team around you. I am proud to say we had both at AFC Bournemouth and a great deal of the club's success is entirely down to their individual areas of expertise. Whether you're running a club or aspiring to work within one, remember, the executive and management team offer a roadmap for sustainable growth and communal success. Embrace these values with dedication, and you will be well equipped to lead with authenticity, achieving a lasting impact and prosperity in your endeavours.

PART 3. THE JFK DECISION-MAKING METHOD

In my journey, mastering communication was just the beginning; the next vital skill I developed was decision-making. Every day presents us with countless choices, and the effectiveness of these decisions shapes the lives we aim to lead.

Whether I was running Abacus or being the chairman at AFC Bournemouth, making informed, effective decisions was fundamental to my success. I have honed my decision-making skills with a practical approach that brings clarity to choices, enabling well-calculated actions.

This approach is embodied in my trusted JFK checklist, inspired by the strategic decision-making of former American President John F. Kennedy. It is a method that has been crucial in helping me rationalise decisions in both business contexts and as chairman of AFC Bournemouth. I've shared this method not only with my children but also with soldiers during my time in the military and with team members at AFC Bournemouth.

To implement it, I start with an A4 sheet of paper and draw a line down the middle. I label one side 'For' and the other 'Against'. For any situation, personal or professional, I list the reasons on each side. As the list grows, the best decision often becomes clear, allowing me to make choices that are well-informed and considered. It also clears the mind of any conflict or confusion.

While it might seem simplistic at first glance, I've found that simplicity often leads to clarity and ultimately to success. Keeping decisions straightforward has been essential for personal development and achieving results. Using this method, I have gained greater confidence in my choices, ensuring they are aligned with my goals and values.

The JFK Decision-Making Method isn't restricted to major business or leadership decisions; it's equally effective in day-to-day life. This approach offers a straightforward means of addressing daily decisions with clarity and confidence.

Whether deciding on a career move, making a purchase, or contemplating a routine change, the JFK Decision-Making Method provides a clear, effective strategy for navigating life with purpose.

PART 4. THE POWER OF MENTORS IN BUSINESS, FOOTBALL AND LIFE

The power of having a mentor in one's life cannot be overstated. In my own experience, mentorship was the catalyst that transformed me from a run-of-the-mill salesperson, working day in and day out without a clear vision, into someone who could harness and maximise my innate abilities. Early on, I knew that my knack for communication, whether through speaking or using gestures, was a tool I could use to make a living. I discovered this through small ventures, like selling commodities where buying low and selling high was sufficient. However, I had no real vision of what my career could look like beyond these transactions. That's where my mentor came in, providing guidance that illuminated a path I had never considered.

I have often mentioned Noel Audley in this book, as he was my first mentor and without a doubt influenced my development. Noel possessed the incredible ability to see beyond the surface. He analysed my natural talents, such as my capacity to connect with and envelop people in warmth, and positively influenced my perception of what I could achieve. Noel convinced me that my skills far exceeded those required merely to label oneself as a salesperson. I was encouraged to broaden my perspective by studying psychology and body language. This new knowledge enabled me to interpret subtle cues from others, like how someone sits or their facial expressions. It became a silent conversation of sorts, where I could have an unspoken dialogue with someone and adapt my approach to communicate more effectively. This skill was indispensable, transforming my sales strategy from simple persuasion to genuine connection and understanding.

Among the greatest benefits of mentorship is the confidence it instils. Before I had a mentor, I might never have had the courage to dream bigger or aim higher. Their faith in my abilities was contagious, and it spread throughout other areas of my life. This experience has inspired me to help others as well. In my capacity as a financial adviser and in working with our commercial team, I've prioritised mentoring others, encouraging them to discover their strengths and helping build their confidence. Much like how my mentor guided me to realise my potential, I strive to be the catalyst for others' growth.

An illustrative example of this is Amy Marks, who on several occasions expressed admiration for my public speaking. Amy remarked how she was impressed that I could deliver speeches without notes or slides. I assured her that she was just as capable. The lesson I learned from my mentor became invaluable.

Noel advised me that when speaking in front of a large audience, it helps to focus on one familiar face for reassurance. During Amy's first presentation, I took on that supportive role. I was her anchor in the audience, providing silent encouragement. This technique allowed her to overcome nerves and realise that the audience wouldn't know if she deviated from her planned remarks because only she knew what she intended to say. This newfound confidence began to flourish in her, just as it did in me.

A direct benefit of having a mentor is learning how to navigate challenges, particularly those related to selling or negotiating. One profound lesson from my mentor was how to reinterpret a customer's hesitation into an opportunity. For example, when a customer says, 'I want to think about it,' many salespeople see this as a setback. Noel taught me to see it as a step forward. This response typically masks a customer's polite way of saying no, yet it signifies interest. My mentor encouraged me to respond by expressing excitement over their interest and offering to help them think through their decision. This approach validates their feelings and positions me as a partner in their decision-making, rather than an adversary. It's about transforming hesitations into problem-solving discussions.

MY MENTORSHIP IN THE FOOTBALL INDUSTRY

Looking back through my journey in the football industry, I have the found the guidance and wisdom of mentors invaluable. These relationships have not only enriched my understanding of the game but also provided me with the tools to navigate the complexities of leading a football club. Each mentor brought unique perspectives and expertise, contributing significantly to my growth and success as chairman. They offered support, challenged my ideas, and inspired me to strive for excellence. In an industry as dynamic and demanding as football, having trusted mentors has been a key factor in achieving both personal and professional milestones. Their influence has shaped my leadership style and reinforced the importance of community, integrity and resilience.

Throughout my tenure as Chairman at AFC Bournemouth, I have been fortunate to learn from many remarkable professionals in the football industry. However, five individuals have stood out as pivotal mentors who have profoundly influenced my journey.

Cliff Crown, Chairman of Brentford FC

Cliff Crown possesses a remarkable analytical mind, honed through his background as a financier. His experience with Brentford, while he worked as chairman alongside owner Matthew Benham, has been invaluable to me, especially when dealing with compliance matters. Cliff has guided me through the intricacies of the EFL, particularly after our relegation, helping navigate the complexities associated with Premier League clubs, parachute payments and financial fair play changes. His role as an England ambassador during our trip to Seville is just one example of his wide-reaching influence on my time as chairman.

"

If I was asked to describe Jeff in one word it would have to be 'welcoming' because whenever you are visiting Bournemouth or whenever you are in his company he makes you feel welcome.

CLIFF CROWN #THECHAIRMAN

"

IN THEIR OWN WORDS ON JEFF

Cliff Crown
Chairman of Brentford FC

I first met Jeff at the EFL Annual Conference in June 2014 and I was immediately struck by his warmth and friendliness. He had a huge smile and I immediately thought what a lovely man.

We had just been promoted to the Championship and we enjoyed one season together in 2014/15 before Bournemouth were promoted to the Premier League, and so that enabled us to attend EFL and Championship meetings together during the course of that season. And I think it's fair to say that the two of us were always quite vocal at those meetings!

I particularly remember my first visit to AFC Bournemouth and the warm greeting from Jeff and Rosie in the boardroom at that enormously large table where we sat and ate our pre-match meal. In fact, as a result of the close friendship we had struck up, Jeff invited me and my best friend to join him as his guests in the following season when Bournemouth were at home to Arsenal, so that I could watch the team I grew up supporting. At that time, the Premier League seemed a long way off and so I was extremely grateful to be given that opportunity by Jeff.

In the summer of 2016 I was elected on to the Board of the EFL, which gave me the opportunity to represent the EFL at both FA Council and the FA Cup Committee, and this gave me the chance to see Jeff again on a regular basis at meetings which were held at Wembley Stadium as he too was a member of both.

In fact I was asked to be chair of the FA Cup Committee for the 2018/19 season and Jeff was my vice chair that season.

My favourite memory of the times I have spent with Jeff is undoubtedly our trip as representatives of the FA to a Nations League game in Seville when England played Spain in October 2018. It gave us the opportunity to spend the afternoon on a walking tour of Seville and I have this lovely picture of the two of us in Santa Cruz square. We were already close but this really was a most delightful day that we spent together, and England went on to win 3-2!

If there is one outstanding quality which sums up Jeff, it is his warmth and friendliness and his smile. You cannot fail to be charmed by his infectious enthusiasm and devotion to Bournemouth, which was self-evident from the moment you met him. He always made you feel at ease and everyone loves Jeff! In that regard I think Jeff is almost unique but I would say that his warmth and openness is something I admire and have certainly sought to emulate throughout my career in football.

On to season 2020/21 and Bournemouth and Jeff found themselves back in the EFL and so the opportunity to meet up regularly throughout the season was renewed. It was a particularly challenging period off the field, partially as a result of the impact of Covid, and it resulted in the two of us, alongside Zoe Webber from Norwich, collaborating on a detailed note to all of our colleagues in the Championship on the negative impact of potential changes to our regulations which were being considered. During that process we had numerous calls and meetings to consider our best course of action and drafting and re-drafting of what turned out to be a very lengthy letter which was delivered in January 2021. As you would expect, Jeff played a full part in that process, advising and supporting us to enable us to end up with a very comprehensive and detailed summary of all of the issues which we believed needed openly debating.

As it turned out, our two clubs ended up meeting in the play-off semi-final at the end of that season. Bournemouth were naturally hoping to bounce back at the first time of asking, and after a cagey affair down at the Vitality Stadium, Bournemouth took a 1-0 lead into the second leg. It was during Covid and so there was a small crowd allowed in and Jeff looked after us as usual, but without the benefit of the full dining package!

In the return leg, Jeff sat a few rows behind me in a separate area of the Gtech due to Covid restrictions and was naturally delighted when Bournemouth took an early lead. However, it wasn't to be and Brentford ran out 3-1 winners on the day and qualified for the play-off final. Despite the bitter disappointment, Jeff was gracious in defeat and I know, had Covid protocols allowed, he would have given me a massive hug!

If I was asked to describe Jeff in one word it would have to be

> 'welcoming' because whenever you are visiting Bournemouth or whenever you are in his company he makes you feel welcome.
>
> A gentleman and a true friend. And above all else a wonderful man. That's our Jeff!

Steve Parish, Owner Chairman at Crystal Palace FC

Steve Parish is one of the most experienced club owners and chief executives within the Premier League. From the moment we were promoted, Steve embraced me and became a trusted mentor on football-related matters. His dual perspective as both an owner and chairman is unique and incredibly informative. Whenever I needed insights, whether about recruiting or other football operations, Steve was just a phone call away. His flamboyant character and extensive industry knowledge were invaluable to me, and his advice was always candid and supportive.

Alistair Mackintosh, CEO at Fulham FC

Alistair Mackintosh has a unique passion for both Fulham and AFC Bournemouth, the latter due to his father's long-standing support. Our relationship deepened over shared experiences, such as the memorable Championship match when Bournemouth beat Fulham 5-1 in 2015. Even after stepping down, Alistair's invitations to Craven Cottage and his genuine inquiries about Rose have highlighted the strength of our friendship. His respect and care extend beyond business, embodying the true spirit of camaraderie in football.

Paul Barber OBE, Chief Executive and Deputy Chairman at Brighton & Hove Albion FC

My relationship with Paul Barber OBE began while he was the chief executive of Vancouver Whitecaps in 2011, and I was seeking a collaboration with AFC Bournemouth. Although our initial partnership didn't materialise, our bond strengthened when Paul took over as chief executive of Brighton & Hove Albion FC. Paul became not only a professional ally but also a personal friend, assisting my family in Brighton, where my sons live. His extensive knowledge of compliance and football, coupled with his close relationship with Tony Bloom, the Owner of Brighton & Hove Albion, has been inspiring. Paul's approachability and leadership have been a source of inspiration and motivation for me.

* * *

These mentors have provided me with guidance, encouragement and friendship, enriching my journey in the football industry. Their wisdom and support have been invaluable in shaping my leadership and the success of AFC Bournemouth.

"

It's a skill that few have and it can be quite disarming. But to take Jeff's easy humour for a lack of intelligence or substance would be a huge mistake – he has both in abundance.

PAUL BARBER OBE #THECHAIRMAN

IN THEIR OWN WORDS ON JEFF

Paul Barber OBE
Chief Executive and Deputy Chairman
at Brighton & Hove Albion FC

We often talk about 'characters' in football. Most of the best are found on the pitch. Some are in the technical area. Very few are found in the directors' box but Jeff Mostyn is one of them!

Smart but funny, competitive but kind, Jeff's contribution to football – and particularly to AFC Bournemouth – over so many years cannot be underestimated. And, yes, even if he is writing it himself, Jeff's contribution to football is well worth a book!

I got to know Jeff while our respective clubs were battling it out for south coast seaside primacy back in the EFL Championship in the mid-2010s. We connected first through the incredible journey our clubs had been on – both close to extinction in the not-too-distant past, but both determined to follow their dream to the Premier League's promised land – and also through a shared, slightly warped, sense of humour! With Jeff, laughter always comes first. Never shy to break the ice in any room or situation, Jeff's easy charm, quick quips and mischievous teasing turned many a tense debate around the shareholders' table into a more pragmatic and conciliatory discussion.

It's a skill that few have and it can be quite disarming. But to take Jeff's easy humour for a lack of intelligence or substance would be a huge mistake – he has both in abundance.

A hugely successful businessman way before the lifelong Manchester City fan led the charge to save AFC Bournemouth for its fans and community, Jeff helped Eddie Howe make the Cherries one of the country's favourite second teams for a period. It's very difficult, and some achievement, to beat top Premier League clubs with one of the lowest budgets and smallest stadiums, but Jeff and his team at AFC Bournemouth did just that!

Jeff Mostyn

Andy Ambler, Director of Professional Game Relations at the FA

Reflecting on my journey as chairman, Andy Ambler stands out as a mentor for whom I have immense admiration. He was the first chief executive I met after taking over the football club with Steve Sly in March 2007. I vividly recall Andy and his peers visiting our boardroom, which was starkly lacking in hospitality as we could only muster some sandwiches at the time. Despite these humble beginnings, Andy extended a gesture of generosity by contributing to our save the club collection, demonstrating the camaraderie and compassion that would define his relationship with me.

Our bond was cemented at my first EFL conference in Portugal, where Andy warmly embraced both me and Rose. Our friendship blossomed, leading to the honour of speaking at his wedding, a testament to the deep respect and affection I hold for him and his wife Nicola.

Andy's career journey is remarkable. From his role as chief executive at Fulham, where he excelled, to navigating the vastly different environment at Millwall, he showed an unwavering commitment to genuine leadership. At Millwall, often perceived as challenging due to its historical reputation, Andy managed to foster respect and appreciation across the League. Throughout my tenure, Andy was always available to provide me advice and guidance. Andy's integrity ensured that our conversations remained confidential, respecting the sensitivities of every situation. Whether I needed guidance on a complex issue or a connection to a key individual, Andy was always willing to help, never compromising his principles.

His reputation extends beyond his roles at Fulham and Millwall, having served on the boards of both the EFL and Premier League. His current position as Director of Professional Game Relations at the FA is a testament to his exemplary skills and experience. I am truly grateful for Andy's unwavering support and friendship during my time as chairman. His influence was invaluable and his character a model of excellence in the football industry.

As chairman, Jeff prioritised the club above personal gains, navigating through challenging post-game emotions with an admirable sense of composure. Football is an emotional rollercoaster, especially in adversity, but Jeff's approach was exemplary.

ANDY AMBLER #THECHAIRMAN

IN THEIR OWN WORDS ON JEFF

Andy Ambler
Director of Professional Game Relations at the FA

The first time I crossed paths with Jeff Mostyn was during my first full season with Millwall, as we faced off against AFC Bournemouth. The day stands out in my memory, not for the downpour that accompanied our 2-0 defeat, but for the impression left by Jeff. His club, at that time, was battling financial strains, yet he exuded unwavering pride in AFC Bournemouth. Despite the constraints, Jeff ensured we were treated with remarkable hospitality, even if it was with just a simple cup of coffee and a sandwich.

From that initial meeting, Jeff's unique ability to host stood out, setting a benchmark in the football world. His genuine warmth and respect for everyone he met made him not just a great host with his wife Rosie, but an exemplary figure who showcased what it truly meant to be a gracious human being, even when the going got tough.

As chairman, Jeff prioritised the club above personal gains, navigating through challenging post-game emotions with an admirable sense of composure. Football is an emotional rollercoaster, especially in adversity, but Jeff's approach was exemplary. Whether celebrating victories or shouldering defeats, he maintained a composed demeanour and offered unwavering support. This quality distinguished him and made him beloved among the football community, testifying to his capability to foster strong, positive relationships.

Leadership at a football club involves managing intricate relationships, particularly between the chairman, the chief executive, the manager and senior executives. Success hinges on these dynamics; a chairman must cultivate an environment that encourages open dialogue, trust and respect.

The best chairmen, like Jeff, are those who prioritise listening over dictating and who trust in the senior people around them. Mistakes are part of the journey, whether it's partnering with the wrong commercial entities or recruiting the wrong players. But throughout these challenges, a leader's role is to support and empower the team.

> Jeff Mostyn's tenure at AFC Bournemouth exemplified this, as he collaborated effectively with Eddie Howe on the pitch and nurtured a club culture of unity and shared vision. Building a football club culture requires patience, emotional intelligence and a commitment to respecting and inspiring those around you, traits Jeff possessed in abundance.
>
> The journey to the Premier League was not just about the tactics on the pitch, but the solidarity and leadership off it, which was personified by Jeff. His legacy continues to inspire, demonstrating the power of genuine leadership and the impact he had at AFC Bournemouth. Jeff led from the heart.

HOW TO FIND THE RIGHT MENTOR

Mentors do more than impart knowledge, they inspire. The relationship I have with my mentors is built on the cornerstone of genuine care and encouragement. They rejoice in my accomplishments and encourage me to reach new heights, beyond the goals they've set. This genuine support is uncommon. Some mentors, driven by ego, may not wish for their mentees to outshine them, fearing it might reflect on their own capabilities. However, I have been fortunate to have mentors who not only encouraged my success but also excelled alongside me.

Here are five tips in identifying the ideal mentor:

1. Identify your goals and needs: Before seeking out a mentor, it's crucial to understand what you hope to achieve with their guidance. Think about your personal and professional goals and identify areas where you need support or development. This clarity will help you find a mentor whose expertise aligns with your aspirations.

2. Seek someone with relevant experience: Look for mentors who have experience in the fields or skills you wish to develop. Their first-hand knowledge and insights can provide you with valuable guidance and shortcuts to success. Consider their achievements and how they relate to your goals.

3. Look beyond immediate areas: Sometimes the best mentors are those who aren't directly linked to your current industry or field but can provide insight into transferable skills like leadership, negotiation or communication. They can offer diverse perspectives that might be especially valuable.

4. Assess their mentoring style: Everyone has a unique way of teaching and guiding others. It's important to find a mentor whose style resonates with you. Whether they lead by example, offer structured advice, or provide motivational support, ensure it fits your learning preferences.

5. Build a genuine connection: Establish a rapport by genuinely engaging with potential mentors. Show interest in their work and be respectful of their time. A strong personal connection can enhance the mentorship experience, making it more rewarding for both parties.

True mentorship extends beyond teaching certain skills or guiding career decisions. It is about unlocking one's potential and laying a foundation of trust and encouragement. A mentor serves as a mirror, reflecting back the best of who we are and what we can become. With their guidance, self-imposed limits can dissolve, allowing for personal and professional growth. Their belief in our abilities, even when our confidence wavers, is powerful. The mentorship dynamic is about the mentor fostering the mentee's capabilities and inspiring them to achieve greatness they may not have realised possible.

* * *

The wisdom gleaned from the key areas I've discussed – The Art of Communication, My Ten Principles of Running a Successful Football Club, The JFK Decision-Making Method, and The Power of Mentors in Business, Football and Life – have had a profound impact on my journey. With effective communication, guided by the use of our two ears and one mouth, alongside the invaluable mentorship and a phase I use a lot when in adversity by having a 'siege underdog mentality'. How do I know this? You're reading it from my lived experience.

Success, at its core, is built on collaboration, dedication and unwavering enthusiasm. I'm not suggesting you'll be able to purchase a football club tomorrow; believe me, the path is demanding. But what I've shared with you in this chapter is meant not just to inspire you to close the book but to ignite the belief that you hold the reins to your destiny. You have the power to shape a life filled with success and fulfilment. Embrace these insights, and pursue your journey with confidence, knowing that your potential is limitless.

CHAPTER 18
THE FOOTBALL FAMILY

THE PEOPLE WHO MADE A DIFFERENCE

Being chairman of AFC Bournemouth was not a solo endeavour. This incredible story unfolded because of grit, passion and the underdog mentality of a host of vital people. I want to take a moment to express my deepest gratitude to some of those people who worked alongside me on this journey.

STEVE SLY

I want to begin by expressing my gratitude to Steve for the essential role he played in saving AFC Bournemouth. His unwavering commitment during those crucial first six months was vital, paving the way for six years of safeguarding and strengthening the club. I treasure the memory of our first game together as co-owners. Stepping onto the pitch against Millwall was a testament to our shared vision and determination. Securing the Community Mutual Trust Share was particularly important, laying groundwork for investors like Maxim Demin to provide the financial stability needed for our growth on and off the pitch. Steve's dedication and passion made a lasting impact on the club, and I am truly honoured to have embarked on this journey with him.

ADAM MURRY

I owe a debt of gratitude to Adam for his support following the administration, helping to secure the return of the shares from Paul Baker and Alastair

Saverimutto, and forming a consortium with Steve and myself prior to bringing Eddie Mitchell into the club as a partner. Credit is also due to Adam for his vision in recognising Eddie Howe's potential as a manager.

MAXIM DEMIN

Maxim has my heartfelt gratitude for his incredible support for and investment in AFC Bournemouth. His vision and commitment have been instrumental in helping the club thrive both on and off the pitch. His belief in our potential and the resources he provided brought about a transformation that strengthened our foundation and propelled us to new heights. His unwavering dedication to the club's success and his strategic insights had a profound impact on our journey. It has been an honour to work alongside him. I shall be forever indebted to Maxim for having the confidence in me to represent him and the club as chairman, throughout his tenure as owner of the club.

In my humble opinion, without Maxim's financial contribution we would not have reached the dizzy heights of the Premier League. I am immensely grateful for all he did to enrich the legacy of AFC Bournemouth.

MY FELLOW DIRECTORS: IGOR TIKHTUROV, OLEG TIKHTUROV, NICK ROTHWELL AND RICO SEITZ

Thanks are due to my fellow directors for their belief in my leadership during my role as chairman. The contribution they all made to the club's success should never be forgotten. They were part of the inner sanctum that created history.

NEILL BLAKE

Neill Blake has been a constant in our journey. He joined the club post-administration alongside Eddie Mitchell, who became chairman while I stepped down to become vice chairman. It was a significant shift that felt politically right for starting a new chapter. Neill was appointed chief executive by Eddie and has been pivotal in the club's ascent to its current stature.

As CEO, Neill handled the day-to-day operations, while my role as chairman involved strategic decision-making and providing support to Neill, the board and executive team, especially during challenging times. Our shared responsibilities complemented each other well, fostering a strong partnership. Neill thrived in managing operational tasks, particularly after Maxim's takeover, which brought new freedom and responsibilities that he embraced admirably.

While Neill focused on managing the club, my involvement extended to supporting Neill with legal and business matters, earning me the legal nickname 'The Flying Silk' at the club for my hands-on approach, particularly during disciplinary hearings and player tribunals. Complementing Neill, I represented the club in the community, with the media, and at away matches, to show my support to the team and the loyal fans. I also was involved in transfer tribunal cases involving notable players like Harry Arter and Marc Pugh, handling negotiations and ensuring the club's interests were well represented.

RICHARD HUGHES

During my time at AFC Bournemouth as an owner and as chairman, Richard has afforded me the most incredible support. My first engagement with Richard was during the early part of my tenure as owner, during the period when the wages were deferred for a couple of months. Richard was part of the playing staff, and was the first to accept the situation and generously waived some of his entitlement when normal service was resumed. I have never forgotten that gesture of goodwill.

When Maxim Demin took control of the club, Richard was appointed Head of Recruitment and then became the club's first Technical Director with responsibly for first team affairs, supporting Neill Blake our CEO. Richard was very much part of the inner sanctum of Maxim, Neill Blake, Nick Rothwell, Eddie Howe, Jason Tindall and me. His negotiation skill set was as good as any Director of Football in the country. Speaking multiple languages he was able to negotiate transfers in the native language of most European clubs. Richard is now enjoying a similar role at Liverpool FC.

ROB MITCHELL

Rob Mitchell, our Commercial Director, joined the club about a year after I took over. Throughout our journey together, I've had a particularly close working relationship with Rob, largely due to our shared focus on marketing and commercial development. I was delighted to share my insights and experience with him and his talented commercial team.

Rob's dedication has been remarkable. Throughout my time at the football club, his resolve to attract sponsorship, especially when we were just a small club in the lower divisions, truly astounded me. During financially challenging times, his task of securing sponsorships was monumental. Convincing others to invest in a club that, at times, seemed on the brink of closure required incredible perseverance. Yet Rob never stopped, consistently finding ways to engage the community and draw out the best in his team. His role as chair of the Dorset Chamber of Commerce elevated his standing, endearing him to the community, a testament that still holds true today.

ELIZABETH FINNEY, GENERAL MANAGER/OPERATIONS DIRECTOR

Elizabeth was one of a handful of staff members at the club when I arrived in October 2006. Over the next seventeen years we worked as closely together as was possible. Liz's office was next to mine, so you could take that quite literally.

I have often been quoted as saying that Liz was the cement that kept the club going, from an operation and compliance standpoint. In the early years, she filled the role of what is now several separate departments: Equality Diversity and Inclusion Department, Safeguarding Department, Human Recourses Department, Safety Advisory Group and Support Liaison. I am certain I have forgotten numerous other responsibilities, including looking after me! Liz was the font of all knowledge in respect of operations.

As you can imagine, I arrived with significant business skills, but a football club is a completely different animal from what I was used to. My learning curve was like a Saturn V rocket or, for those under the age of 61, a SpaceX rocket.

One of our most satisfying joint ventures at the club was working closely to achieve firstly the Premier League Equality Standard and then the Advanced Equality Standard. We achieved both at the first attempt, supported by an amazing team.

Liz, I am grateful for all your care and support, especially during those early dark days.

ALICE JEANS, MY PERSONAL ASSISTANT

When we were promoted to the Premier League, a moment I shall always remember vividly, Neill Blake came into my office. It was likely to have been a few months after our promotion and he suggested that now that we were in the prestigious Premier League we needed a PA. Up to that point, we had managed everything ourselves, but with the added complexities of compliance and travel in the Premier League, it became clear we needed someone dedicated to those tasks.

The idea of hiring a PA sounded wonderful, and I asked Neill to share his thoughts as to how we would proceed. He had already thought it through, emphasising the importance of loyalty, commitment, and especially confidentiality in this new role, citing the need to maintain privacy with Maxim's ownership and other sensitive meetings. Neill proposed Alice Jeans for the position. Alice had been with the club since she was 15, working diligently in the ticket office and as part of the commercial team, where she proved herself to be invaluable.

We could teach her the requisite PA skills, but her inherent sense of confidentiality and loyalty was irreplaceable, particularly given our multicultural directorate. I wholeheartedly agreed with Neill's suggestion, and Alice became our joint PA. Her presence was so integral that my dear wife Rose humorously remarked that there were now three people in our marriage! Alice meticulously managed my diary, ensuring everything was perfectly organised. I relied on her for everything, from keeping me on schedule to handling countless tasks seamlessly.

Alice later became club secretary before deciding to move on to another local business with which we had a trading relationship. Her departure was a significant loss for me personally and I extend my deepest gratitude to her for providing me with unwavering support and dedication during my tenure as chairman. Thank you for everything.

NEIL VACHER

When it comes to Neil Vacher, I could speak of his virtues endlessly. He is one of the most generous individuals I've ever met, both with his time and his kindness toward others. His dedication and pride in his work set a standard that few achieve. Neil was an invaluable source of inspiration and information, truly embodying the spirit of AFC Bournemouth. Neil was also invaluable with his iconic biscuit jar in his office, which was much enjoyed by Eddie, Jason, the office staff and me.

Having taken over from one of the longest-serving secretaries in the Football League, Neil became indispensable in his role. Clubs across the EFL spoke highly of his professionalism and conduct. His contribution earned him an EFL award, underscoring his impact on the club. Over the years, Neil has held nearly every position at the club except first-team manager, from selling programmes to becoming the club secretary. He even described his role as his dream job when interviewed in the *Bournemouth Daily Echo*, illustrating his deep connection to the club.

Neil is now the club historian, where his unparalleled knowledge of AFC Bournemouth's history is of vast benefit. He can recall intricate details about past matches, players and events. With the club under new ownership, he continues his invaluable work, and I'm honoured to share matchdays with him. Being in Neil's company is not only educational but also a privilege that I cherish immensely.

ALL THE PLAYERS

I would like to express my heartfelt gratitude to all the football players who have significantly contributed to AFC Bournemouth's success during my seventeen years as chairman. Their dedication, talent and tireless efforts have been the driving force behind our club's triumphs, both on and off the pitch. Each of them has played a crucial role in shaping the team's spirit and identity, and their unwavering commitment to excellence has not only propelled our successes but also inspired countless fans and supporters. Witnessing their ability to rise to challenges and achieve extraordinary feats has been one of the greatest joys of my tenure. Thank you for your steadfast passion and for being an indispensable part of the AFC Bournemouth family.

Below is a meaningful message I received during the week I stepped down as chairman, among many other kind words. This one, from former club captain Tommy Elphick, truly touched my heart:

'Always there for you, Mr Chairman. Nothing changes our thoughts towards you and your family. What you have done and how you have served this football club will never be overlooked. You have been more important than any manager or player in our history, and I mean what I say.'

> **What you have done** and how you have served this football club will never be overlooked. You have been more important than any manager or player in our history, and I mean what I say.
>
> **TOMMY ELPHICK #THECHAIRMAN**

THE FINANCE TEAM

I do not think there was a single day in my entire seventeen years at the club that I failed to visit the finance team.

As you can imagine, in the early years I always departed more depressed than when I arrived. They were all such an important part of my life.

To David Holiday, Mark Luther and all the incredible girls, thank you for all your support, love and care. You were always willing to listen to my stories, thoughts and sometimes prayers, through the dark days and, more recently, you were there to celebrate our success.

THE OPERATIONS TEAM

A special tribute goes to those who were there when I first arrived: Neil Vacher, Mark Luther, Elizabeth Finney, Diane Rackley, Steve Hard, Dr Mufeed Niman, Laurence Jones, Neil Moss, Steve Cuss, and Joe Roach, who was our Academy coach. These individuals were part of the club through challenging times, including my early days when, driven by commitment and integrity, they continued working for months with no guarantee of receiving payment. Their unwavering support gave me hope that saving the football club was possible.

Paul Fudge, who led our hospitality team, also deserves heartfelt thanks. He and his team provided exceptional care and attention to detail on every matchday. Vernon and Ese, our brilliant chefs, became dear friends, creating an unmatched dining experience for our boardroom guests.

THE MEDIA TEAM

I'm incredibly proud of our media team. Kelly Somers, who has become a prominent television personality seen across BBC and Premier League productions, began her career at the club. I was fortunate to share many interviews with her, often being her 'guinea pig' as she honed her craft. It's a testament to our rapport that I'm known as 'One-Take Jeff' in the media!

Max Fitzgerald became our first Head of Media, and is now the Head of Media at Wolverhampton Wanderers. Despite challenges, the experiences and skills he gained at AFC Bournemouth prepared him well.

Anthony Marshall, who took over from Max, had previously worked for nine years at Newcastle United without meeting the chairman, but quickly became a part of our close-knit culture. He has since moved on to be Head of Media at Tottenham Hotspur. It fills me with pride knowing we've nurtured such talent.

I remain grateful to our entire media team Elliot, Zoe, Matt, James, Neil Perrett, Andrew and everyone who felt like family to me. I spent countless hours with them, building one of the strongest bonds within the club.

THE RETAIL AND TICKETING TEAMS

I want to express my heartfelt gratitude to Head of Retail Justin Bailey, our retail team and the extraordinary staff at the club shop, or as it is now known, 'superstore'! It's remarkable to think that we now have such a thriving operation. When I first bought the club back in 2006/07, our club shop was nearly empty due to repossessions, with bailiffs lining up at the door. To have had the honour of opening our new club superstore on the day we faced the mighty Real Madrid at our stadium is a memory I will cherish forever. The store has since flourished and become a beautiful showcase, offering something for everyone, from matchday kit to leisure apparel.

The staff at the club have been and remain phenomenal. I recall a humorous incident involving a newly joined member named Jane. I had visited the store to purchase some merchandise for my grandchildren when she asked, 'Good afternoon, sir. Are you a season ticket holder?' Her fellow staff members looked on in amazement, and Jane realised she might have made a blunder.

In my usual manner I responded with, 'Yes, I suppose I am a season ticket holder. I bought the most expensive one in the club's history!' When it was revealed that I was the chairman, Jane turned as red as our famous shirt. I moved around the counter, gave her a big hug, and we both instantly bonded over the experience, creating a friendship that endures to this day.

Finally, my heart felt gratitude to Jazmine, Nick Osborn (who shares my birthday) and all the ticketing team. It is without doubt the most in demand 24/7 department at the football club.

THE AFC BOURNEMOUTH CLUB STAFF

I have always been a great believer in the saying your business is only as good as the staff you employ. I have modified that by saying you are only as good as the staff you work alongside, including the Academy staff, ground staff, medical staff, ticketing staff, matchday staff and stewards, and the development squads providing the future for the Cherries.

Throughout my tenure, I've made it a priority to visit as many members of staff as possible in their workplace each day. Given our club's size, with most staff on one floor, I would routinely walk through our four or five offices to convey my love, gratitude and admiration for their outstanding dedication and work ethic. I've always believed that these gestures of appreciation had an immense and invaluable impact, proving to be one of the greatest intangibles any leader can offer, and it has been my honour to do this as chairman.

I would like to make a special mention to one of my unsung heroes, Duncan Wells, the club's kit manager. Duncan works tirelessly around the clock, ensuring the team and staff members have every aspect of kit required for their training and matchday needs. Another aspect of his job is the huge logistical task of getting the kit, balls, cones, etc., to away matches and overseas tours. I can verify it's all done with military precision. He epitomises everything that is great about AFC Bournemouth.

From the most senior member of staff to the latest recruit, I valued each individual, along with the contribution each of them made to our club's success. I have previously alluded to the fact we established a two-dressing room culture at the club: one downstairs for the manager and players, and one upstairs for the executive team. Yet, it is the unified heartbeat that connects us all. One club, one culture, showcasing the power of teamwork at its very best.

THE FOOTBALL FAMILY

I would also like to take a moment to express my heartfelt gratitude to the entire football family. Without their unwavering support, I wouldn't be here writing this book.

In 2017, I experienced a heart attack, a profoundly humbling and eye-opening event. I was celebrating another season in the Premier League at the AGM conference in Harrogate with the other chairman and CEOs when, at around 2 a.m., I started to feel nauseous. I spent the next two hours trying to make myself sick, and then found myself in the emergency room at Harrogate Hospital at 5.30 in the morning, with a needle in my stomach. Desperate to leave, I pleaded with the doctors to let me go home, suggesting I just needed something to make me sick.

However, they insisted on treating it as a heart attack due to my critically high enzyme levels. Roz Donnelly, the Premier League coordinator, was with me. She had the difficult task of breaking the news to Rose; I was too emotional to speak to her. My PA, Alice Jeans, was trying desperately to arrange a flight for Rose, but flight after flight was cancelled. Eventually, in the early evening a flight was arranged to Manchester. The Premier League laid on a car to pick her up and take her to the hospital in Harrogate, and also sorted out hotel accommodation for her. After a weekend of tests on the coronary heart ward, I was then transferred to Middlesbrough for the stent procedure.

Steve Gibson, the owner of Middlesbrough, demonstrated incredible kindness, by asking his chief executive, Neil Bausor, to ensure I didn't head home immediately after being discharged and then arranged for me to stay at Rockcliffe Hall, his hotel and Middlesbrough's training complex. Upon leaving the hospital, I experienced an overwhelming sense of anxiety. As I sat on a wall, I felt pins and needles, a classic sign of a heart attack. I told Rose that I wasn't feeling well, describing my symptoms of tingling and breathlessness. Returning to the hospital was an option, but as I had been discharged, it would have meant starting the whole A&E process again.

Neil reassured me that a car was on its way and that the club doctor would meet us at the hotel. When we arrived, the doctor conducted a thorough check-up and confirmed it was just anxiety. The hospitality extended by the club's owner was overwhelming. A lovely restaurant was reserved for us, but the doctor advised us to relax, and we opted for room service and rest. Those two days at the hotel provided much-needed comfort.

The support I received from the entire football family, the Premier League, my club, and beyond, was overwhelming. Everyone sent their good wishes, and it was one of the rare times when I truly felt the love and solidarity of the football community. Moments like these or typically those brief silences before a match at Wembley or during council meetings highlight just how deep and far-reaching that support can be. The kindness and generosity shown to my family and me during this difficult period were beyond words, and for that, I am eternally grateful.

The love and respect I have for the ninety-two clubs goes beyond competition. I have made lifetime friendships with the owners and staff of clubs in every division. These are friendships earned by having a mutual respect for one another and an understanding of the huge commitment clubs have to their incredible supporters and communities up and down the country. To this day I know Rose and I would be welcomed into every boardroom in the land as well-respected guests.

MY LOVED ONES

My One and Only Rose

How do I begin to express my gratitude? I'm already feeling emotional as I write this. I still consider myself the luckiest person alive to have Rose in my life. People often find our twelve-and-a-half-year age difference intriguing. It's interesting how, both in youth and later life, we tend to quantify age so precisely. Children love adding those extra halves and quarters, declaring they're 'nine and a half' as if it adds so much significance. Similarly, as we age, every quarter- or half-year seems to carry weight, highlighting what we've lived through and what lies ahead, especially when reflecting on our age gap. I still act like the world's oldest teenager, despite having just turned 80. Rosie thinks I am Benjamin Button!

Still, my perspective is seasoned with deep appreciation for the shared experiences that have enriched our lives.

To my beloved Rose, with whom I've shared forty-five cherished years, with deep appreciation for the shared experiences that have enriched our lives, you are the love of my life.

Most people attribute our achievements to me, but truly, it has always been about Rose and me, united from the very beginning of owning a football club – a venture that seemed fraught with folly and chaos. Yet, never once did Rose object to my dream, knowing all too well my lifelong passion for football.

In the early days, our interactions with the sport were more about supporting our dear friend Kevin Bond at Manchester City, forming close ties with Kevin and his wife Trina, who became like family. Then came the pivotal call from Kevin, inviting me to meet the chairman at AFC Bournemouth, setting off a chain of events that could easily be summarised with 'the rest is history', but that wouldn't do justice to our shared journey.

We started humbly, with a modest boardroom bearing a single table, the embodiment of old-world charm. Rose and I hosted our guests warmly, always ensuring visitors felt welcomed. We quickly developed a unique identity as Mr and Mrs, personally hosting the boardroom events, which was rare in football circles. While I handled my duties as chairman, Rose grew into her role, infusing the room with her confidence and charm, often surprising guests with her strong handshake and assertive presence.

Rose's transformation was inspiring. She evolved from a reserved lady into a pivotal part of the club's fabric, no longer just the chairman's wife, but

Rose Mostyn, a name that stood on its own. Her unwavering support was my anchor, through countless functions and directors' dinners organised by Rob Mitchell. No matter what the occasion, Rose was always by my side, even when it might not have been her first choice of activity. Her presence at away games, where we often stood as the sole representatives, especially during critical matches like the one at Everton in 2020, proved her unwavering support.

One defining moment was a home victory over Manchester United during our early Premier League days. Ed Woodward, then chief executive at Old Trafford, congratulated us, saying that our hospitality surpassed even six-star expectations, and likening our boardroom to a home. This acknowledgement encapsulated our journey, highlighting the magnetic atmosphere Rose and I nurtured.

Rose has been my unwavering support, both at the club and in life. Her presence fortified me through this incredible journey at AFC Bournemouth, and her love remains the cornerstone of all that we've achieved together. If not for Rose, none of this would have been possible. She is my partner, my anchor, my inspiration, and the love of my life.

I once heard a small group of supporters shouting, 'Mostyn out'. All I ever hear now is, 'Jeff, can I have a selfie? Jeff, can I have an autograph?' **His love and loyalty to his beloved AFC Bournemouth** has won over hearts and minds wherever he goes.

ROSIE MOSTYN #THECHAIRMAN

IN THEIR OWN WORDS ON JEFF

Rosie Mostyn
The Chairman's Wife

My husband Jeff is a wonderful, loyal person, with strong principles and both family and business core values.

He is impulsive and a crazy fun person to be around. Following a highly successful career in financial services, he loved expensive cars, and even bought a boat when he went for a casual visit to the Southampton Boat Show.

What surprised most people about that purchase was that he had only ever been on a friend's boat a couple of times, and still can't swim. So, when he came home one day and said he was interested in buying a football club, I must admit, at the time, I thought he needed sectioning. History now tells you he did just that. He followed his dream and bought AFC Bournemouth in March 2007.

When the purchase finally went through and he became chairman, he was as excited and thrilled as a boy with a new toy, albeit a very expensive one. However, once the excitement turned into reality with the discovery of additional debt, the challenge ahead to save this famous south coast club looked almost insurmountable.

I truly believe most people would have given up at that stage, but Jeff is by no means a normal person – I say that in the nicest possible way of course. Alongside his long-time friend Steve Sly, his vice chairman, they were determined to save the club from further financial pain, trying to bring in additional investment to stabilise the club.

Jeff continued to fund the club, paying the staff and player wages, until a solution could be found. I remain so proud of his commitment to the club at that stage, pouring in hundreds of thousands of pounds to keep the club alive. I don't think anyone will ever realise the sacrifices he was making, mentally and physically, to help save AFC Bournemouth at its most vulnerable time.

Ultimately, he had to put the club into administration. He could have walked away at that point, but his love of the club and the supporters, and his loyalty to the staff would not allow him to do that. He continued to fund the club until a new buyer could be found.

There is so much spoken about the famous nod to the administrator Gerald Krasner at the press conference. Having agreed a sale to a group of individuals, Jeff and I went away to Spain to find some time and space for each other. It was the first time for many months that we felt free of the burden placed upon Jeff in funding the club.

The call from Krasner came out of the blue. 'Jeff, get back to Bournemouth, the sale has fallen through. I am holding a press conference next week. You are still the chairman. You need to attend.' We returned home.

On the flight home we agreed Jeff would no longer fund the club going forward. Fast forward to the press conference. Gerald spoke to Jeff and Steve prior to the press conference and told Jeff he needed a cheque for £100,000 or he would wind the club up at the conference. Before Jeff left home for the meeting, I reminded him of our agreement: enough was enough.

Jeff stood at the back of the room. Gerald asked him to shake his head if he was not going to provide the funds and nod if he was. While I was not present, I knew in my heart, after everything he had done to save the club since the day he walked through the front door in October 2006, he would nod agreement.

That simple nod to Gerald saved the club on that never to be forgotten day. That will aways be Jeff's legacy to AFC Bournemouth.

Except for a couple of years as vice chairman following the administration, Jeff enjoyed sixteen years at the club as chairman. During that period the club went from minus seventeen points in League Division Two, through to the Premier League. He remains one of the most loved characters at the club and of equal importance among the football family. Wherever we go to watch football, he is treated with the greatest respect; I know he would be welcomed at any of the ninety-two clubs in the Premier League and EFL.

There was no better demonstration of the love people have for Jeff than when he suffered a heart attack in 2017, ironically at the Premier League Conference in Harrogate. The Premier League went to great lengths to ensure I got to Jeff's bedside in the shortest possible time. I will always be grateful to Richard Scudamore and the Premier League executive and staff for their kindness to me.

On the CV of life, to say that you have been chairman of a Premier League club is something to be so proud of; having saved a football club from going out of business is another level.

Who would have thought all those years ago that Jeff's famous nod to Gerald Krasner would bring so much joy, passion, pride and fulfilment to all those in the community and Cherries supporters worldwide. All these years later I am thrilled that for the first time ever, he ignored my advice and our agreement.

I once heard a small group of supporters shouting, 'Mostyn out'. All I ever hear now is, 'Jeff, can I have a selfie? Jeff, can I have an autograph?' His love and loyalty to his beloved AFC Bournemouth has won over hearts and minds wherever he goes. How times have changed. We as an entire family, including Jeff's brother Mike and his family, have supported the Cherries throughout the journey, and have enjoyed and endured all the trials and tribulations that football can bring. I know Jeff's parents Sadie and Ralph will be looking down with so much pride at what their son has achieved.

'Together, We Have Made Everything Possible.'

My Four Inspiring Children

Serving as chairman of AFC Bournemouth was truly a family endeavour, a collective journey through the highs and lows. I am deeply grateful to my four incredible children: Darren, Janine, Blake and Alexandra, or Alex as she is affectionately known. Their love and commitment have been a constant source of strength and pride.

Darren has an impressive career in the world of TV, film and media, and has worked on some of the most prestigious projects, including four World Cup competitions as an editor, and multiple award-winning documentaries and films as a colourist. Darren's talent has earned him numerous accolades. His recent work for Netflix has soared to number one on their charts, showcasing his exceptional skills.

As technology has evolved and more and more organisations have in-house media and editing facilities, Darren has remained an entrepreneur, keeping one step ahead of the crowd. He has now established his own YouTube teaching channel with over 200,000 subscribers, sharing his immense knowledge and expertise with individuals and businesses alike. His success always fills me with pride, and he certainly shares my work ethic.

Janine has made a remarkable name for herself with her exceptional networking skills in the fields of sport and media recruitment. Her success is widely recognised, and she embodies the true spirit of entrepreneurship. Janine shines brilliantly in her career, earning recognition from some of the most influential figures in the industry. She fills me with immense pride. A vivid memory comes from the final game of the 2006/07 season against Carlisle United, coincidentally the same day as her wedding. Our local radio station, Radio Solent, buzzed with discussions all week about whether I would choose to attend my daughter's wedding or the critical match at Carlisle.

For anyone who knows me, the choice was clear – family comes first. I attended the wedding, equipped with an earpiece provided by Radio Solent to take a live feed from Carlisle so I could keep track of the match's progress. As I escorted Janine down the aisle, we learned the outcome was a draw, leading to our relegation to League Division Two. The mix of emotions hit me hard and I burst into tears. Most guests at the wedding assumed I was emotional at giving my daughter away, not realising the tears were the result of our relegation. It is always difficult to separate football and family when you're personally involved. There was no finer example of that than Janine's wedding day. Janine, you are a shining star, and we are so proud of everything you have achieved.

Blake has pursued his passion as a drummer with incredible energy, performing across the globe with his band Delta Sleep. His ability to share his musical talents coast to coast in America, Japan, Australasia and beyond speaks volumes to his dedication, commitment and expertise. Blake's journey is like that of a professional athlete living out their childhood dreams; few musicians achieve what he has. To me, he's an A-lister because of the vital impact he makes through his music. I vividly recall visiting Blake's school at a parents' evening to be told by his teacher, 'Blake is so talented. If only he could use drumsticks instead of a pen for his exams, he would be a child prodigy.' With my overflowing enthusiasm, I said thank you and took it as a compliment. Blake has proved him right. He is a child prodigy with his drumsticks. In addition to touring with the band, Blake now teaches privately at a school in Lingfield. I would love his teacher to see him now.

Blake's music has lit a path for thousands of aspiring musicians across the globe, with passion, unwavering dedication, and an expressive soul echoing in every beat.

Alex, our youngest, embarked on a similar path towards the arts, with a love of all things dance, ballet and musical theatre. We spent most evenings driving her to one dance class after another to pursue her dream of a stage career. This culminated with her going to the esteemed Tring School of Performing Arts and then on to Loughborough University. While her initial dream was the stage, she realised that rather than standing in audition queues all her life, she would rather follow a passion for event management.

This, by coincidence, took her to Southampton Football Club, joining as part of the events team. After six months she was asked by her manager if she owned a Fiesta that was parked in the club's car park. The manager then asked if she was related to the Mostyn at AFC Bournemouth. When she asked why, the manager said, 'Alex, you have a Follow the Cherries sticker on the back of your car seat.' Nobody had realised the connection. I was so proud of the fact she did not use my name at any time to benefit her. Her remarkable four-year stint at Southampton Football Club included coordinating major events, including concerts for the Rolling Stones, Robbie Williams and Take That. Alex most certainly left a significant mark on the club's event history.

Alex has since moved on to enjoy a very successful career as Group Sales Manager at the Four Seasons Hotel Hampshire.

Each of my children has taken their unique path, standing proudly on their own two feet. What fills me with immense joy is that they embody the work ethic and commitment that I value so deeply. They are all immensely successful in their respective endeavours.

Every gesture of love from them, every Christmas and birthday card, moves me to tears. I never set out to be seen as an inspiration; I simply followed my passion and did what I love. The recognition I've received, both as a father and a professional, is something I deeply cherish.

While thanking all my family, it is important to remember the incredible love and support we have enjoyed over the past forty-five years from Rose's family. From her beloved late parents, Joan and Reg, who quite rightly gave me a hard time when we first met! To her sisters, Barbara and Margaret, and my brothers-in-law, Tony and Jon, who sadly passed away a few months ago.

I often used to say in my business dealings that my personal touch was the difference. When you chose to work with me, you got me, and that added value was immeasurable. I carry this same philosophy with my family. My children have not only respected my journey but have been inspired by it, each in their own special way. They are my pride and joy, my loving legacy, and for that I am profoundly grateful. I couldn't be prouder of my children, each of whom stands as a beacon of creativity and determination.

My Grandchildren and Great Granddaughter

We have four gorgeous grandchildren: Thomas, Lauren, Isabel and Lucy. They are all incredibly creative and entrepreneurs in their own right. Rosie and I are so proud of them and the joy they bring their respective parents, Darren and Janine, as well as the joy they bring to me and Rosie. Plus, the latest edition to the Mostyn dynasty is our great granddaughter Daphne.

MY WIDER FAMILY

My family's support has been instrumental in my journey, and here I must mention my brother, Mike. We are the two remaining members of the Mostyn clan, following the passing of our sisters, and I cherish the bond we share. Mike's unwavering support has been invaluable to me, and I love him dearly. My family's understanding and sacrifices, love and support have allowed me to pursue my career. Born into a working-class family from Manchester, I've always carried concern about where the next pound would come from. Despite my current fortunate position, those northern roots will forever be part of my DNA. I still need reassurance that we have enough food on the table.

Nevertheless, my family's strength and independence reassure me that I'm not alone. We've supported each other through thick and thin, helping one another along the way, without ever taking more than necessary.

My nieces, Reba-Lee and Roxanne, together with my sister-in-law Roweena's family have always give me strength and support. My achievements might have surprised many, including the elders in the family, given my perceived reputation as the 'black sheep' when growing up in Manchester. Yet my journey has been about endurance and determination, and striving to overcome challenges. That's why I continue to pursue success through public speaking, motivation and charity work, finding profound joy in giving rather than receiving.

Looking forward, I'm passionate about spending more time with my family and travelling with Rose.

OUR INCREDIBLE AFC BOURNEMOUTH SUPPORTERS

How do I even begin to express my gratitude for the incredible supporters at AFC Bournemouth?

Before my involvement with the club, I learned a valuable lesson about the true essence of support in football from my neighbour and friend, James Beattie. Despite being at opposite ends of the age spectrum, James and I connected as the only northerners on our street. His insight into the transient nature of the football world was profound. He once told me, 'Chairmen, directors and even players will come and go. The only people with true loyalty and longevity are the club's supporters.' His words have resonated with me ever since.

While chairman, I always regarded my role as that of a custodian. The position was temporary; the heartbeat of the club lies in its fans. Whether we were champions or facing challenges, our supporters have remained steadfast. Football is a tribal sport, and with this comes both intense loyalty and, at times, scrutiny. Yet, despite the ups and downs, one constant remains and that is the unwavering dedication of our fan base. They are our heart and soul, the driving force behind everything we achieve. Their passion fuels the spirit of the club.

During my tenure, I learned that success on the pitch is unpredictable but essential for harmony within the club. As a chairman, it's humbling to realise that glory and criticism are often one match away, influenced heavily by what happens on the field. Yet, it is this unpredictability that deepens my appreciation for our supporters. Their resilience, patience and encouragement are nothing short of inspiring.

Eddie Howe once advised me about the resilience needed in our roles, reminding me that sincere support often comes quietly. The vocal minority can't overshadow the majority's silent faith and admiration. This perspective has been invaluable, especially when navigating criticism. It reassures me that our true measure isn't in fleeting successes but in enduring commitment, which we share with our supporters.

Thank you all for your belief in AFC Bournemouth and your constant presence, whether at the stadium or in spirit. It has been and will remain deeply appreciated.

Jeff Mostyn

You inspired me every day, and I am honoured to have witnessed such passionate loyalty first-hand. Thank you for being the cornerstone of our club, for cheering us on through victories and challenges alike. Your passion is the legacy that inspires our club's future.

"

Chairmen, directors and even players will come and go. The only people with true loyalty and longevity are the club's supporters.

JAMES BEATTIE #THECHAIRMAN

"

IN THEIR OWN WORDS ON JEFF

James Beattie
Former Professional Football Player
and Professional Football Coach

When I signed a new contract at Southampton FC and bought a property in Chilworth little did I know our neighbours were Jeff, Rose, Blake and Alex Mostyn.

One day, Jeff came around to welcome us to Chilworth and introduce himself. At the time, Sarah and I had two Shar-Pei dogs named Harry and Molly. Jeff knocked on the door and waved his hand through the letterbox. Harry, the bigger and slightly more aggressive of the two dogs, proceeded to bite the end of Jeff's finger off! I rushed to the door, opened it, only to find Jeff standing there with his hand covered in blood. He could have turned and left, never to be seen again. Instead, he stood there and said, 'Well, that's bloody nice, isn't it. I only came to welcome you to our neighbourhood,' all with a huge smile on his face. Jeff's zest for life was always palpable.

I invited him in, cleaned him up, and our friendship began, growing stronger over time. In the subsequent days, weeks and years, we talked about nearly everything. Jeff has always been a sounding board for any advice I've needed, whether football-related or otherwise.

A pivotal moment in our friendship came when Jeff asked me whether he should save a football club from administration. I advised him to follow his heart. Jeff's integrity ultimately guided him to make the right decision. His wife Rose, with her skill in welcoming and entertaining guests, complements Jeff perfectly. They are a great partnership both on and off the pitch, and I am honoured to call them dear friends.

Jeff's success was inevitable due to his character, personality and values. I am very proud of the impact he has had on football. Surprised? Not at all.

One quality of Jeff's that has significantly influenced my personal development is his integrity and honesty. If I had to describe Jeff in one word, it would be 'majestic'.

One of the most meaningful memories I have of Jeff occurred when he knocked on my door again. This time, Harry was more accommodating. Jeff looked unusually sad and asked me, 'I don't know what to do. What should I do, mate?' He was referring to whether he should bail the club out of administration. The fact that he sought my guidance showed me his respect for me and the sincerity of our friendship. That moment resonated deeply with me.

Jeff's impact on the club and the town has been resounding. He has left a lasting legacy at AFC Bournemouth and transformed it into a Premier League football team that the town can be proud of.

CHAPTER 19
MY FINAL GIFT TO YOU

As we reach the final chapter of this book, I want to express my heartfelt thanks to you for joining me on this journey. Writing this book has been a therapeutic experience, and as I've stepped back from the twenty-four-hour world of football, it's clear that, contrary to the saying, football never sleeps.

* * *

Reflecting on one of my favourite events of the year, the graduation ceremony at Bournemouth University, I'm reminded of the thrill I feel each year supporting the next generation of talent. In 2017 I was honoured with an honorary Doctorate in Business Administration from the University, a proud moment for someone who left school at 15!

At the 2024 Bournemouth University graduation, Ian Jones introduced me to Alison Honour, the new Vice Chancellor, sharing the story of my graduation speech in 2017. Originally given seven minutes, I spoke for twenty, energised by the audience's enthusiasm. It was one of the most memorable speeches Ian had ever heard, as I spoke without notes, sharing the story of 'The First Day Of The Rest Of Your Life'.

In that speech, I emphasised the power of positive thinking, urging graduates to view today as the start of their future. I highlighted that while they hadn't been in direct competition during their studies, they now faced a world where they must compete. But with focus, positivity and hard work, they could achieve incredible heights. As my father taught me, the secrets to success are simple: work hard, work hard and work hard. A strong work ethic can elevate anyone, even above a natural prodigy who lacks drive.

Vice Chancellor Alison Honour shared two inspiring pieces of wisdom at the ceremony that resonated deeply with me. First, the power of saying yes now and figuring out the details later – a principle that was crucial when I decided to save the club. Second, treating every day as if it's your first, filled with enthusiasm and curiosity, drives true education and development. This echoes the relentless pursuit of self-improvement I've admired in figures like Eddie Howe and Sir Gareth Southgate OBE.

Currently, I am preparing a motivational speech for a group of athletes, and there's a story I love to share about winning and competing that I find truly inspiring.

Around forty years ago, at the beginning of my career while working for TSB, I had the honour and privilege to meet Virginia Leng, now known as Virginia Elliott, a remarkable figure in the world of equestrian sports. However, the real lesson came from Virginia's story, which I have carried with me ever since.

Virginia was one of Britain's leading equestrian riders, having begun her journey at just three years old. She achieved the incredible feat of winning the Burghley Horse Trials five times, becoming the first woman to do so. Her accolades include multiple Olympic and European medals; her dedication and team spirit are truly commendable.

But what stands out most is her perspective on winning. When asked in a Q&A session about how disappointed she was not to have won gold at the Olympics, Virginia gave a response that resonates with me deeply, and that is why I share it with you today. She paused thoughtfully and said, 'What an interesting question. It's not the first time I've been asked it, and my response is this: "Winning is important. However, while you should be ready to compete all of the time, you should also be gracious during defeat and let others have their moment of glory."' I love this quote because it demonstrates compassion.

My time as chairman at AFC Bournemouth, supported by many, has been filled with moments of glory I will forever treasure. These experiences, woven into what I consider to be one of football's greatest ever achievements, is a testament to teamwork, resilience and the joy of the journey.

As I close this chapter of my life, I want to impart one final piece of wisdom that has the power to transform your life: make people feel special. For me, this has often been expressed through my iconic hug and a warm smile. There's no need to overcomplicate it. Throughout this book, I've emphasised the importance of running football as a business, but we must never lose sight of what makes football truly magical: the excitement and emotion on matchday.

It's about creating unforgettable memories and ensuring that everyone involved, fans, players, managers, club staff, owners and the chairman all feel special.

When we embrace this approach, Together, Anything is Possible.

ACKNOWLEDEGEMENTS

I could not have brought *The Chairman* to life without the most incredible support behind the scenes. Writing this book has been an educational journey, and believe me, a great deal of thought has gone into making it a compelling read – it's much more than just putting words on paper!

First and foremost, I want to express my gratitude to everyone who provided perspectives that, in my opinion, truly bring the story to life. I am deeply moved by your words and, most importantly, by how you acknowledged Rose during my time as chairman. My deepest gratitude goes to Sir Gareth Southgate OBE, Eddie Howe, Jason Tindall, Andrew Griffith OBE, Jed McInally, Andy Ambler, Steve Sly, Asmir Begović, Callum Wilson, Clare Gallie, Debbie Hewitt OBE, Cliff Crown FCA, David Hinchcliffe, Richard Scudamore CBE, Eve Went, Ian Jones, James Beattie, John Reynolds, Kashif Siddiqi, Kevin Bond, Marc Pugh, Mark McAdam, Melissa Dhillon, Paul Barber OBE, Peter McCormick, Mike Summerbee OBE, Richard Osborne, Rob Mitchell, Tony Richards, Steve Cuss, Tony Richards, Mark Clemmit, Gerald Krasner, Steve Parish, Trevor Birch, Tommy Elphick, Matt Richie, David Baldwin and my wife Rosie Mostyn.

My gratitude to Jim Frevola and AFC Bournemouth, Alex Smith and the *Bournemouth Echo* for permission to use photos. To Professor Alison Honor, Vice Chancellor of Bournemouth University, for supporting the book in such a passionate way, and to all the staff at the University for supporting the book launch that took place there.

I want to thank Whitefox Publishing for supporting me and my book manager, Ed Bowers, in making this book a masterpiece and sharing my story with the world. Thank you for your guidance and support, Sarah Rouse, Julia Koppitz, John Bond, Tom Whiting and all the team members.

A special thank you to Neil Vacher. This story would not have been possible without your incredible passion for AFC Bournemouth and your loyalty to the club. It's been a pleasure working alongside you over the past seventeen years, during our time together at the club. Most of all, I am grateful for your support in writing this book, especially your wisdom in sharing not just my story but one of the greatest football stories ever told. Neil, in my eyes you are Mr Bournemouth.

I am grateful to Vitality for supporting the book, especially Beth Bacchus and Milly Pain. Thank you for your amazing organisation behind the scenes to make the official book launch in London so special.

To the CEO of Vitality, Neville Koopowitz, words can't express how much I appreciate your wisdom, motivation and friendship over all the years we have known each other. Your support from the very start of my project in helping bring *The Chairman* to life has been an inspiration to me. I am grateful beyond words.

Ed Bowers, meeting you in Athens at the Athens Women's Football Summit led to our first meeting about this book on 25 October 2023, at the Ham Yard Hotel in London. Our conversation lasted two hours and thirty minutes but it felt like mere minutes. It was the start of our book journey. Your thoughts on my story, relating to your reading experience of Carlo Ancelotti's book, and your enthusiasm that I have a story to share with the world beyond just football, meant so much, as did your humorous comment that the book won't be in the Mr Men book section!

Ed, every thought in this book was born from our conversations on your recorder. During over forty-five hours of interviewing me, you made me feel so comfortable – as you did on your podcast. With a few tears and hugs, and many laughs throughout this book journey, I could not include an acknowledgement to you without saying that it's been an honour and a privilege to work alongside you. Your energy is boundless; I spent many a night in a dark corner recovering from our interviews. I recall one six-hour interview with the club legend Ted MacDougall at the Hilton hotel. It started with coffee, and finally finished after two bottles of red. Ted, I am also grateful for your friendship and contribution to my book.

Finally, I want to acknowledge my incredible family, starting with Rosie – I wouldn't be here without your love and support over the past forty-five years. My four incredible children, Darren, Janine, Blake and Alexandra, thank you all for your love, support and passion for my project and everything else in my life. I can say with confidence, given that my son Blake is a drummer, you have all been the rhythm beneath every beat of my journey. To my grandchildren, great granddaughter, my brother Mike, my brother- and sisters-in-law, and all our wonderful family and friends, I treasure you all.

I am eternally grateful for all your unwavering support in turning my story into a book. What began as memories carried in my heart has become more than just a collection of chapters; it's a testament to my journey. I could not have done it without you all.

And of course, to my late parents Sadie and Ralph, thank you for making it all possible.

INDEX

JM indicates Jeff Mostyn.

Abacus Financial Management Limited 18–24, 235
Adjutant General's Corp xi, 24
AFC Bournemouth
  Ability Counts teams 136
  Academy 63, 65, 69, 84, 96, 134, 161, 258, 260
  administration xiii, xiv, xv, 40–2, 50–63, 67, 71, 74–5, 78, 83, 147, 150, 166, 168, 179, 251–2, 265–6, 274, 275
  Advanced Equality Standard 187–8, 254
  AFC Bournemouth – 'Together, Anything is Possible' (documentary) 121
  Championship and *see* Championship
  Cherries Community Sports Trust 63, 65, 136, 187–8, 191, 224
  Chinese Super League and 127–8
  club staff 259–60
  Community Football Programme 127
  Community Mutual 38, 251
  community-run football club, Europe's first 37
  competitions *see individual competition name*
  Dean Court xiii, 35, 36, 37, 69, 76, 93, 101, 104, 168, 169, 181
  debts 36, 42, 43, 73–4, 75, 188, 265
  Demin regains full control of 138
  Demin secures full control of 87–91
  Demin sells full stake to Bill Foley of Black Knight Football 176
  Eddie Mitchell becomes chairman 74
  Equality Champion 136–7
  Fans Club 38
  finance team 258
  football family 251–60
  Football League champions (2014/15) 109–10
  Golden Share xiv, xv, 38, 42, 44–6, 50–1, 56
  ground-sharing agreement with Dorchester Town 37
  Hate Hurts Everyone campaign 162
  JM acquires xiv, 33, 35–46, 147, 159, 168, 179, 187, 229, 234, 259, 265
  JM final season as chairman 173–7
  JM 'nod decision' xiii–xv, 46, 52, 56, 57, 59, 121, 169, 266, 267
  JM reinstated as chairman 87, 96
  JM saves 35–44
  JM vice chairman 74, 88
  Ken Dando Stadium Appeal fund 38
  managers *see individual manager name*
  Match of the Day, first appearance on 124
  media team 258–9
  Minus 17 (documentary) 139
  MLS, collaboration with 122–3
  Murry takes over 69, 73–4
  naming rights to stadium 75, 76, 89, 116
  operations team 258
  players *see individual player name*
  Premier League and *see* Premier League
  Real Madrid friendly (2013) 95–6, 97, 259
  relegations 36, 37, 66, 83, 104, 144, 145, 151, 152, 153, 160–1, 166, 238, 268
  retail and ticketing teams 259
  seventeen-point penalty xv, 56, 63, 67–8, 83
  Sport-6 co-owners 67, 69, 73
  ten-point penalty 51, 83
  transfer embargo on 51, 70, 71, 74, 77
  'Together, Anything is Possible' motto xi, 99, 106, 108, 121, 148, 149, 150, 169, 277
  training complex 134
  Vitality Stadium 26, 95, 114, 116–17, 131, 134, 135, 136, 137, 142, 152, 154, 156, 163, 164, 177, 211, 227, 241
  women's team 65, 136, 163–4, 224
Afobe, Benik 125–6
Aké, Nathan 128, 131
Ambler, Andy 246–9
'An Evening with Jeff' (fundraising event) 188

Arsenal 111, 115, 122, 125, 128, 132, 135, 144, 153, 174, 221, 240
Arter, Harry 84, 92, 93, 109, 133, 140, 253
Aston Villa 102, 115, 124–5, 128, 142, 144, 160, 174, 198
Audley, Noel 5, 11, 14, 15–16, 17, 23, 236–7
Auto Windscreens Shield Final 37

Baker, Paul 67, 69, 70, 73, 88, 251–2
Baldwin, David 72–3
Barber OBE, Paul 242–5
Barrett, Adam 89, 90
Beattie, James 88, 271, 273–5
Begović, Asmir 134, 138, 152, 155–8, 160
Benham, Matthew 238
Bennett, Roger 121–2
Best, George 7, 10
Birch, Trevor 82–4
Birmingham City 6, 101, 103, 154, 162
Blackburn Rovers 68, 123, 153, 174
Black Knight Football 176
Blake, Neill 87, 96–7, 111–12, 143, 145, 151, 176, 252–3, 255
Bolton Wanderers 80–1, 103–4, 107, 130, 159, 180
Bond, Kevin 8, 35, 37, 38, 39–41, 49, 66, 147, 150, 262
Boruc, Artur 101, 123, 138, 143, 152
Bournemouth University xii, 184–5, 223–5, 227–8, 276–7
Bradbury, Lee 85, 89, 90
Bradford City FC 73, 76, 166
Brady, Robbie 161, 174
Brentford FC 68, 90, 93, 102, 154, 155, 160, 209, 212, 238, 240–2
Brighton & Hove Albion 85, 89, 92, 103, 134, 138, 141, 142, 242–3, 245
Brooks, David 137, 138, 140, 141, 152, 159, 161, 176
Brooks, Shaun 89, 90, 91
Burnley FC 85, 86, 90, 91, 101, 141, 142, 150, 161
Burton Albion 76, 77, 98

Cahill, Gary 160, 174
Carabao Cup 132, 134, 137, 139, 175, 221
Care South 187
Caribbean Connection 15
Carling Cup 68, 84, 101–2
Carlisle United 53, 93, 268
Carter-Vickers, Cameron 152
Championship 35, 84, 85, 91, 93–9, 107, 100–110, 120, 126, 128, 132, 137, 151–6, 159–64, 174, 180, 207, 240, 241, 242, 245
Charlton Athletic 85, 89, 98, 109, 110
Charlton, Bobby 3
Chelsea FC 115, 122, 125, 126, 128, 132, 135, 137, 138, 139, 141, 142, 160

Chinese Super League 127–8
communication, art of 218–20
Connell, Alan 68, 76, 163–6
Cook, Lewis 128, 137, 154, 161
Cook, Steve 89, 93, 102, 131, 135, 142, 162
Covid-19 83, 140, 142–5, 152, 154, 191, 194, 195, 196, 208, 212, 224, 241
Crown, Cliff 209, 212, 238–42
Crystal Palace 85, 89, 131, 242
Cuss, Steve 63–6, 136, 187, 224, 258

Dando, Ken 38, 42
Daniels, Charlie 89, 93, 98, 131, 133, 138, 143
Danjuma, Arnaut 141, 154–6, 160
Defoe, Jermain 134, 135, 197
Demin, Maxim 56, 87–91, 96–9, 112, 123, 133, 136, 138, 145, 150–1, 153, 176, 181, 187, 251, 252, 253
Dhillon, Melissa 230–4
Division Two 35, 145, 146, 215, 266, 268
Doncaster Rovers 53, 93, 99
Dorchester Town 37, 73–4
Dorset Cancer Care Foundation xii, 188–90

EC Group Cup 89
Edwardia 7, 10
EFL (English Football League) 35–7, 39, 41, 50, 51, 56, 62–3, 69, 70, 73–5, 78, 80, 82–3, 85, 104, 108, 109, 114, 123, 134, 151, 163–4, 166, 169, 170, 173, 203, 206, 207, 212, 238, 240, 241, 245, 246, 256, 266
Elizabeth II, Queen 173, 175
Elphick, Tommy 90, 92, 109–10, 125, 128, 175, 256, 257
England (national team) 68, 88, 90, 128, 130, 135, 137, 138, 153, 154, 160, 207, 238, 240–1
  JM ambassador for 206–8
  managers 208–9, 211
  Under 21 69, 98, 102, 125, 140–1, 162, 164
Equality Independent Football Commission 188
Everton 123, 125, 126, 127, 132, 144, 160, 177, 263

Feeney, Liam 70, 71, 89
Finney, Elizabeth 49, 191, 254
Fitzgerald, Max 258–9
Fletcher, Steve 70, 71, 85–6, 90, 92, 94, 121
Foley, Bill 173, 176
Football Association (FA) xii, 30, 31, 77, 119, 151, 170, 197, 203, 224
  Board 119–21
  Chair, Debbie Hewitt, JM works alongside 211–16
  Council xii, 83, 115, 119–20, 206–7, 208, 212–13, 240
  Disability Committee 186, 207, 213, 216

FA Cup 6, 51, 68, 84, 98, 102, 115, 127, 132, 156, 162, 208, 213, 240
  FA Cup Committee 115, 208, 213, 240
  JM roles at 206–16
  Membership Committee 207, 213
  Professional Game Relations 246–9
  Youth Committee 207, 213
Football for Peace 197–8
Football Foundation 187
Francis, Simon 89, 98, 103, 128, 135, 137, 142, 143, 152
Fraser, Ryan 92, 108, 131, 135, 143
Fulham FC 102, 159, 161, 162, 242, 246

Gallie, Clare 140, 191, 193–6
Garry, Ryan 70, 89
Gillingham FC 49, 67–8
Gosling, Dan 100–101, 102, 131, 141
Grabban, Lewis 90, 92, 93, 98, 100–101, 125
Gradel, Max 51, 123, 125, 126
Griffiths OBE, Brigadier Andrew (Andy) 27, 28, 29–30, 217
Grimsby Town 68, 71, 90–91
Groves, Paul 89, 90, 91, 92

Hate Hurts Everyone campaign 164
Heggie, Simon 6, 7
Hewitt MBE, Debbie 211–16
Hinchcliffe, David 54–6
Hodgson CBE, Roy 208–9
Hollands, Danny 75, 76
Honour, Alison 276–7
Howe, Eddie xv, 12, 40–41, 43, 56, 62, 66, 74–7, 87, 94, 96–100, 102–3, 106, 108, 110, 121, 123–7, 132–5, 137–9, 141, 143, 145–6, 153–4, 160, 169, 173–5, 180, 208, 223, 229, 245, 249, 252–3, 256, 271, 277
  appointed manager of Bournemouth 68–71
  contract extension with Bournemouth, signs 100–101
  departs as Bournemouth manager, joins Burnley 85
  departs as Bournemouth manager, joins Newcastle 147–8
  returns from Burnley to Bournemouth as manager 91–3
  JM on character of 147–8
  on JM xi–xii, 149–51
  League Managers Association manager of the year, Championship manager of the year and manager of the decade 110
  playing career ends 49–50
Huddersfield Town 73, 86, 97, 98, 101, 152, 162
Hughes, Richard 90, 91, 99, 100, 145, 151, 253

Ibrahimović, Zlatan 132–3

Ings, Danny 66, 74, 84, 86
Iraq War (2003–11) 26–7, 31
ITC Travel 15

JAAQ 201
Jaffer, Abdul 35, 37, 38, 40, 41–2, 48
Jeans, Alice 184–5, 255, 261
JFK Decision-Making Method 218, 235–6, 250
John Brown International (JBI) 16
Jones, Graeme 151, 153, 154
Jones, Ian 224, 226–8, 276
Jones, Laurence 49, 258
Julia's House xii, 196–7

Kelly, Lloyd 140–1, 155, 162
Kenwright, Bill 177
Kermorgant, Yann 98–9, 101, 103, 104, 126
Keswick, Sir John Chippendale 'Sir Chips' 111–12, 221
King, Joshua 123, 125, 138, 141, 142, 144
Koopowitz, Neville ix, 117, 280
Krasner, Gerald xiii, 51–2, 55, 57–60, 63, 121, 169, 179, 266, 267, 279
Kuffour, Jo 51, 68

League One 37, 55, 83–6, 87–94, 140, 183, 207
Leeds United xiii, 100, 128, 163, 177
Leicester City 125–6, 127
Lerma, Jefferson 137, 152, 160–1
Lewis-Manning Hospice Care xii, 181, 191–6
Lithuania 3–4, 209
Liverpool FC 98, 102, 122, 125, 126, 128, 131, 133, 141, 142, 143, 154, 162, 174, 176, 253
London Stadium 130–1, 135
Lowe, Jamal 160, 162
Luther, Mark 49, 153, 258
Luton Town 50, 51, 63, 68, 71, 151

MacDougall, Ted 97, 280
Machin, Mel 36, 69
Major League Soccer (MLS) 122–3
Manchester xiii, 3–8, 46, 200, 226, 227, 261, 270
Manchester City 1, 5–11, 15, 85, 123, 125, 174, 204, 245, 262
Manchester United 5–6, 12, 51, 122, 125, 126, 127, 130, 132, 137, 141, 142, 156, 263
Marcondes, Emiliano 155, 160
Marshall, Anthony 258–9
Match of the Day 12, 124
McAdam, Mark 57, 58–9
McCormick OBE, Peter 115–21
McInally, Lt Colonel Jed 25, 26
McQuoid, Josh 84, 90
Men In Blazers 121–2

mentors in business, football and life, power of 218, 236–50
Mepham, Chris 138, 142, 155, 176
Michael Matthews Jewellery 201
Middlesbrough FC 102–3, 131, 154, 174, 261
Millwall FC 45, 48, 51, 90, 98, 132, 163, 246, 248, 251
Mings, Tyrone 123, 125, 132–3, 140, 198
Minus 17 (documentary) 139
mirror technique 218, 219
Mitchell, Eddie 73–4, 252
Mitchell, Rob 49, 182–4, 223, 224, 253–4, 263
Moore, Kieffer 159, 162, 163, 176
Morecambe FC 68, 71, 74
Moss, Neil 51, 258
Mostyn, Alexandra (daughter) v, 4, 130, 185, 267, 269, 274, 280
Mostyn, Blake (son) v, 185, 267, 268–9, 274, 280
Mostyn, Darren (son) v, 12, 185, 267, 268, 270, 280
Mostyn, Janine (daughter) v, 12, 53, 185, 267, 268, 270, 280
Mostyn, Jeff
  Abacus Financial Management Limited and 18–24, 235
  AFC Bournemouth and *see* AFC Bournemouth
  Armada Dish award xii
  antisemitism and 5, 22
  authenticity ix, 58, 182, 184, 204, 220, 223, 228, 233, 234, 235
  British Army, work with 18, 22–32, 85, 197, 218
  bullied at school xv, 5–6
  car crash 13
  Caribbean Connection and 15
  charity work 181, 186–205
  childhood xv, 4–8, 22
  Coin of Excellence award xii
  communication, art of 218–20 *see also* communication, art of
  courage ix, 30, 56, 215, 234, 237
  decency 10
  discipline 30
  England national team and *see* England
  FA and *see* Football Association (FA)
  family dedications 262–71
  family history 3–4
  heart attack xv, 229, 260–1
  Honorary Doctorate in Business Administration, Bournemouth University xii, 184–5
  International mangers who inspire 208–11
  Iraq War and 26–7
  Jewishness 5, 21–2
  JFK Decision-Making Method 218, 235–6, 250
  John Brown International (JBI) and 16, 17–18
  love for football xv, 5–6
  Manchester and *see* Manchester
  Manchester City, love of *see* Manchester City
  marries 15 *see also* Mostyn, Rose
  mentors in business, football and life, power of 218, 236–50 *see also* mentors in business, football and life, power of
  motivational speaking xiv, 7–8, 277
  next generation of business and football professionals, inspiring 217–24
  physical appearance 5
  positivity 6, 183, 234, 276
  Premier League and *see* Premier League
  respect for others 30
  school xv, 3–7, 22, 33, 105, 206, 216, 276
  selfless commitment 31
  selling skills xv, 7, 11, 13–18, 20–4, 27, 41, 114, 218, 219, 236, 237
  ten principles of running a successful football club 218, 220–35 *see also* ten principles of running a successful football club
  TSB Trust Company, works for 11–15, 18, 277
  work ethic 4, 6, 14, 18, 22, 80, 268, 269, 276
Mostyn, Rosalyn (sister) 4
Mostyn, Rose 'Rosie' (wife) v, xi, xii, xiii, xiv, 16, 22, 26, 28, 31, 40, 45, 51–2, 72–3, 79–80, 103, 107, 109, 110, 115, 120, 146, 151, 169, 170, 177, 179–81, 185, 190, 203–4, 213, 215, 227, 232–4, 240, 242, 246, 248, 255
  AFC Bournemouth administration period and 55
  grandchildren and 270
  JM heart attack and 261, 266–7
  JM on 262–3
  marries 15
  meets JM 7–8
  on JM 264–7
Mostyn, Stella (sister) 4, 186, 221
Motson, John 145, 146
Mousset, Lys 128, 140
Murray, Glenn 123, 125
Murry, Adam 69, 73–4, 251–2

Neto 174, 175
Newcastle United xi, 6, 100, 125, 126, 128, 150, 153, 154, 173, 175, 180, 259
Newman, Rob 49, 68, 147
Nottingham Forest 50, 102, 140, 159, 162, 163, 175, 224, 227
Notts County 75–7

O'Driscoll, Sean 37, 53

O'Neil, Gary 154, 160, 175, 176
Osborne, Richard 178–81

Parish, Steve 242
Parkcrest Construction 42
Parker, Scott 160, 161, 175
Peak6 Football Holdings 138
Pérez, Florentino 95
Peterborough United 84–6, 162
Philadelphia Union 123
Pitman, Brett 53, 66, 70, 71, 74, 75, 76, 84, 92, 93, 102, 123
Pollard, Rob 6, 7
Portsmouth FC 40, 43, 69, 83, 85, 86, 89, 91, 147, 156, 160
Premier League ix, xv, 6, 8, 9, 10, 11, 36, 43, 50, 66, 82, 92, 95, 120–7, 130–58, 166, 169, 170, 173–81, 183, 187–8, 203, 204, 207, 220, 228, 238, 245, 246, 249, 252, 254, 255, 258, 263, 266–7, 275
  AFC Bournemouth promotion to (2014/15) xv, 8, 80–1, 83, 100–10, 114–17, 240–2
  AFC Bournemouth promotion to (2021/22) 159–64, 174
  Annual General Meeting (AGM) 111–12, 114–15, 117, 260–1
  mandatory ground improvements 112, 114
  shareholders' meeting 122, 143, 211, 215
Professional Footballers' Association (PFA) 49–50
Pugh, Marc 77–81, 92, 98, 101, 104, 125, 133, 140, 187, 253
Purches, Stephen 84, 97, 151, 160

Rantie, Tokelo 97, 98, 101
Redknapp, Harry 35–6, 91, 94, 190
Reeves, Kevin ('Revo') 8
Reynolds, John 201, 202–4
Richards, Tony 17, 19, 20–2
Ritchie, Matt 92, 98, 102, 103, 104, 109, 125, 128–31, 173, 174
Roach, Joe 89, 258
Robinson, Anton 70, 89
Robinson, Ben 76, 77
Rochdale FC 75, 76, 85
Rofe, Dennis 91–2
Rotherham United 63, 68, 75
Rothwell, Joe 174
Rothwell, Nick 99, 252, 253

Saverimutto, Alastair 67, 88, 252
Scudamore CBE, Richard 111, 112, 113–16, 267
Sheffield Wednesday 102, 103, 109, 152, 153
Sheffield United 137, 144
Siddiqi, Kashif 197, 199–200

Sky Sports 58, 76, 81, 102, 104, 105, 108, 184
Sly, Steve 37–8, 41–52, 56, 67, 69, 73, 74, 76, 96, 246, 251–2, 265, 266
Smith, Adam 84, 98, 109
Solanke, Dominic 138, 144, 152, 155, 161–3
Southampton FC 49, 70, 84, 101, 125, 126, 133, 135–6, 141, 156, 175, 177, 265, 269, 274
Southgate, Sir Gareth 208–11, 277
Sport-6 67, 69, 73
Stanislas, Junior 100–1, 125, 131, 135, 144, 152, 156
Staveley, Amanda 173
Štěch, Marek 74–5
Stoke City 125, 128, 134–5, 162
Summerbee OBE, Mike 6–7, 8, 9, 10–11
Summerbee, Tina 8, 10
Surman, Andrew 97, 101, 132, 134, 143, 152
Surridge, Sam 142, 152, 159

Tavernier, Marcus 174, 187
ten principles of running a successful football club 218, 220–35
Thomas, Wes 89–90
Tindall, Jason xv, 43, 56, 62, 68–70, 74, 84–5, 87, 91, 99, 100, 108, 110, 132–3, 145, 151, 153–4, 253
Tottenham Hotspur 84, 125, 138, 152, 156, 259
Toulon Tournament 208
Tranmere Rovers 84, 93, 94
Travers, Mark 138–9, 162, 175
TSB Trust Company 11–15, 18, 277

United Nations General Assembly, New York 197–8, 200

Vacher, Neil 49, 121, 167–70, 173, 255–6, 258
Vitality ix, 116–17, 280
Vokes, Sam 51, 63

Watford FC 97, 102, 108–9, 142, 144, 153
Watkins, Trevor 36–8
Wells, Duncan 260
Went, Eve 188–90
West Bromwich Albion 98, 101–2, 131
West Ham United 74–5, 89, 91, 97, 98, 125, 130, 135, 142, 144, 153, 174, 194
Wigan Athletic 102, 128, 221
Wiggins, Rhoys 71, 75, 84, 89
William, Prince of Wales 197, 198, 200, 208
Wilshere, Jack 128, 153
Wilson, Callum 76, 100–102, 104, 106–8, 125–6, 128, 131, 132, 135, 137, 140–3, 152, 173, 184
Wilson, Harry 141, 143
Woodgate, Jonathan 154, 160
World Cup 130, 175–6, 267
Wycombe Wanderers 70, 152